ENDURING
REFORM

PITT LATIN AMERICAN SERIES

John Charles Chasteen and Catherine M. Conaghan, Editors

ENDURING
REFORM

PROGRESSIVE ACTIVISM AND PRIVATE SECTOR RESPONSES
IN LATIN AMERICA'S DEMOCRACIES

Edited by

JEFFREY W. RUBIN

VIVIENNE BENNETT

University of Pittsburgh Press

Published by the University of Pittsburgh Press, Pittsburgh, Pa., 15260
Copyright © 2015, University of Pittsburgh Press
All rights reserved
Manufactured in the United States of America
Printed on acid-free paper
10 9 8 7 6 5 4 3 2 1

Cataloging-in-publication data is on file with the Library of Congress

for Shoshana
 —*JWR*

for Adin
 —*VB*

CONTENTS

MAP OF CASE STUDY LOCATIONS

ENDURING REFORM PROJECT

Map by Bill Nelson

ACKNOWLEDGMENTS

THIS BOOK IS the end product of the Enduring Reform Project, a multiyear research initiative in which a team of researchers in four Latin American countries carried out fieldwork on business responses to progressive civil society–based reforms. Enduring Reform was funded by a grant from the Open Society Foundations (OSF). At OSF we thank, in particular, George Vickers, who supported this project from the moment he heard the idea, and David Holiday, for overseeing the grant process and responding to our requests along the way. We hope that the project and this book are at least small steps toward OSF's goals of fostering a more open society globally.

Jeffrey W. Rubin began to interview business elites when, during a research year in Brazil, a businessman who was a fellow parent at the Pan American School in Porto Alegre asked him, "Why aren't you interviewing *me*?" Jeff's subsequent discovery of businesspeople's hostility toward the city's participatory budgeting project led him to wonder about the responses of business toward progressive, civil society–based reform more generally. Through sabbatical support from Boston University (BU), a fellowship from the American Philosophical Society, and a grant from the Open Society Foundations, he began this project. At BU, he would like to thank Peter Berger and Bob Hefner for the intellectual climate they have fostered at the Institute on Culture, Religion, and World Affairs, where Jeff is a research associate. In addition, we thank David Gillerman, who helped in grant-writing, and Dolores Markey, who has been indefatigable in dealing with the details of grant management.

Vivienne Bennett received sabbatical support from her home institution, California State University San Marcos (CSUSM), freeing her for one of the years of work on this project. At CSUSM, she would like to thank Jan Cushman and Melinda Newsome for their insightful help during the grant preparation phase of the work. In addition, Vivienne thanks the Faculty Center Advisory Council for selecting her to give the Spring 2012 campus-wide Faculty Colloquium on this project.

The Enduring Reform Project consisted of six case studies: one in Argentina, two in Brazil, two in Mexico, and one in Bolivia. Each case study was carried out by a team of two researchers, both of whom already had years of experience with the progressive reform that was the subject of their interviews with local business elites. The Argentina, Brazil, and Mexico cases are represented in this book. We deeply thank all of the researchers who engaged with us on this project for their knowledge and insights: Sergio Baierle, Olivia da Cunha, Sonia Dávila Poblete, Carlos A. Forment, Soledad Gutiérrez, Gaspar Morquecho Escamilla, Martin Ossowicki, Fernando Robledo Martínez, Jan Rus, and Heather Williams.

There are others we would like to acknowledge. Sandra Bacalchuk in Porto Alegre offered invaluable support in arranging the details of our project conference there in 2008, and we thank her for her dedication, warmth, and unflappable good cheer. We thank Ann Helwege, Tony Lucero, Marc Edelman, and Ben Junge for reading and providing insightful comments on the introductory chapter of this book. We thank María de los Angeles Pozas Garza for attending the project conference in Porto Alegre and contributing to our understanding of the role of the business sector in Latin America. Sandy Thatcher generously offered advice and guidance in securing a contract for *Enduring Reform*, and Joshua Shanholtzer provided insightful stewardship at the University of Pittsburgh Press. And we can't thank Millie Thayer enough for sharing her wonderful house in New Hampshire for workweeks in the summers of 2010, 2012, and 2013. Our conversations around the dinner table after we each had finished our daily writing and our round-robin Scrabble games provided a warm environment for this work.

Jeff thanks a number of colleagues and friends in Brazil, at BU, and elsewhere for their friendship and support: Ovidio Waldemar and Olga Falceto; Sergio Copstein and Leda Alimena; Roselí, Betinho, and Clarissa Becker; and Sergio Baierle, Claudia Fonseca, Zander Navarro, Leslie Salzinger, Marc Edelman, Ben Junge, Susan Eckstein, Ann Helwege, Gil Joseph, and Jack Womack, along with Social Movement Consortium colleagues Sonia Alvarez, Millie Thayer, Gianpaolo Baiocchi, and Agustin Lao-Montes. Vivienne thanks the following friends in San Diego for their kindness and support during the years she spent working on this project: Jocelyn Ahlers, Kim Knowles-Yánez, Melinda Newsome, and Marie Thomas. She also thanks Dina Bennett and Tessa Wardlaw for their sustained encouragement and interest in her work, albeit long distance.

As is the custom in acknowledgments, the most important individuals are left to the end: our families. Jeff thanks Shoshana Sokoloff as well as Emma, Hannah, and Esther Sokoloff-Rubin for their humor and patience, companionship and encouragement, love and attention. In the final stages of the project, Esther's singing and dancing provided an invigorating backdrop for serious scholarly work. Vivienne thanks her son, Adin Herzog, who went through all of middle school and high school during the Enduring Reform Project. His presence in the house, his companionship at dinner and with reality TV shows, and the music beating from his room all enhanced the work experience.

We would like to thank each other's families for their support during the years of work that this project entailed. We particularly enjoyed spending time with each other's families during workweeks in our respective homes. Vivienne's friendships with Shoshana, Emma, Hannah, and Esther, and Jeff's friendship with Adin are wonderful and unexpected results of our research collaboration on *Enduring Reform*.

ENDURING REFORM

INTRODUCTION

Jeffrey W. Rubin and Vivienne Bennett

THIS BOOK IS about the responses of businesspeople to successful instances of progressive, civil society–based reform in Latin America since the 1990s. To understand whether and how progressive initiatives will endure beyond the first decades of the twenty-first century, we ask, "Can businesspeople endure them?" Latin America is the region of the world with the greatest degree of inequality (Kim 2013). However, the region's transition to democracy—complex, uneven, and incomplete as it might be—includes new spaces for agency by heretofore excluded citizens. Amid recurring violence and crisis, activists in social movements, neighborhoods, workplaces, and government offices have developed innovative and creative responses to exclusion and inequality. Whether such efforts endure is key to the future of democracy in the region.

For most of the twentieth century, businesspeople in Latin America routinely obstructed progressive initiatives.[1] They did this as part of an interlocking group of elites, including landowners, the upper echelons of the military and the Catholic Church, and leaders of right-wing political parties. Through these alliances, businesspeople supported the use of violence and intimidation to repress efforts by excluded groups—such as labor and peasant unions, electoral coalitions, and indigenous organizations—to challenge the status quo.[2] Since the 1990s, however, businesspeople's historical response of hostility and repression toward progressive reform initiatives has become less automatic, mitigated by the economic uncertainties of globalization, the political and legal constraints of democracy, and the shifting cultural understandings of poverty and race. *Enduring Reform* discerns a new twenty-first-century politics of progressive reform, business responses, and the deepening of democracy.

This new politics has begun to emerge for several reasons. First, dissatisfaction with economic performance under authoritarian regimes, as well as the inability of such systems to deliver security and stability over the long term, made businesspeople somewhat open to the transitions to democracy that began in the 1980s. At the same time, the challenges of neoliberal globalization and the uncertainties it generated brought into question long-held assumptions that progressive grassroots initiatives were incompatible with the imperatives of economic policy making. Second, democracy brings with it constraints on how businesspeople can respond to progressive reforms that they would have rejected in the past. Elites can no longer use the police or military to repress those fighting for social change and count on guarantees of impunity. As a result, businesspeople must grapple increasingly with contestation over progressive initiatives in legal, electoral, and institutional arenas.

Third, as globalization and democracy have changed the orientations of businesspeople, the goals and strategies of social movements and progressive activists in Latin America have changed as well, moving away from revolutionary takeover of the state, overthrow of capitalism, and vanguardist organizational structures. Since the 1980s, Latin American activists have engaged in a mixture of strategies to expand their rights and the quality of their everyday lives, ranging from land takeovers and street blockades to participation in government-run popular councils and participatory budgeting initiatives. Internally, these movements deal in new and often more inclusionary ways with diversity, dissent, demands for voice, and internal democracy. These changes in the positions of progressive activists have produced a language and practice of reform that does not challenge the legitimacy of the state or capitalist markets head-on.

This book explores the front lines of twenty-first-century democracy by analyzing five cases of enduring reform from the small towns of Zacatecas, Mexico, to the favelas of Rio de Janeiro, Brazil, to the factories of Buenos Aires, Argentina. Research for these cases was carried out by teams of scholars as part of the Enduring Reform Project, a research initiative funded by the Open Society Foundations from 2007 through 2010. In this volume we demonstrate significant, albeit limited, degrees of openness to these reforms on the part of businesspeople. We claim neither that this openness is widespread nor that it will persist and expand. Rather, by documenting a significant shift in business responses to progressive reform, we offer a tool for political analysis and describe a possibility that might be realized. These responses shape the trajectories of reform initiatives themselves, alternately deepening them or compromising their central objectives. The major causal finding of *Enduring Reform* is that the ways in which businesspeople respond to progressive reforms do not result primarily from economic interest; instead, a range of cultural and interpretive factors shape how businesspeople evaluate their interests and the actions they take.

The innovations of activists and the responses of businesspeople reflect an unspoken and evolving exchange that will be applauded by some and bemoaned by others, businesspeople and reformers alike. In this exchange, progressive activists accept democracy as well as market structures, and businesspeople begin to "recognize" the basic rights and humanity of all citizens. Our research suggests that a strengthening of this exchange may provide a key path to the deepening of democracy in the twenty-first century.

OVERVIEW OF THE CASES

In 1968, in the midst of tumultuous attempts at democratization and reform in Latin America, Albert Hirschman (1970, 343) suggested that those who look for large-scale social change would best be served by a "passion for what is possible." While this appealing phrase left the question of what is possible provocatively unanswered, Hirschman made clear his predilection for combining an optimist's view of progress with a belief that incremental change could deepen and transform the status quo over time, even and perhaps especially when it occurred through unplanned responses to crisis and creative leaps of interpretation. In assessing the prospects for democracy in Latin America two decades later, in 1986, after a dark period of widespread military rule, Hirschman (1986, 42) took up the same position, urging scholars and policy makers not to focus on rules and preconditions for democratic transitions but rather to "be on the lookout for unusual historical developments, rare constellations of favorable events, narrow paths, partial advances that may conceivably be followed by others."

Today, as democratic politics has survived, and in some cases deepened, the contributors to this edited volume have found "unusual historical developments" in successful reforms that demonstrably improve people's lives in tangible ways across the hemisphere. These reforms—including the *fábricas recuperadas* (worker-run factories) in Buenos Aires, participatory budgeting in Porto Alegre, the "three-for-one" migrant remittance program in Zacatecas, the Afro Reggae Cultural Group in Rio de Janeiro, and Maya self-reliance networks in San Cristóbal de Las Casas—were brought about by the commitments and passions of civil society activists and ordinary citizens.[3] They represent unexpected and creative responses to long-term problems and moments of crisis, inspired by the visions of past and current social movements. Often constructed in interaction with politicians and policy makers, and with a keen eye for combining the possible and the improbable, the kinds of reforms that we examine constitute some of the most important focal points for progressive change in Latin America today.

We ask what are some of the most hopeful examples of change—of the sort that recognize, include, and empower poor people—that occur within the world as it now works and perhaps open the way for broader change? We are not talking about the trickle-down effects of improved growth or about national social welfare or economic policies, important as these may be. We are not talking about opposition political movements or revolutionary struggles. Rather, we examine progressive reforms, neither antimarket nor antistate, of the sort hoped for and in many cases expected by theorists and supporters of democratic politics, part and parcel of the "democratic wager" outlined in the early years of democratic transitions in Latin America and the concomitant enthusiasm for civil society (O'Donnell and Schmitter 1986; and Cohen and Arato 1994).

By "progressive reforms," we mean projects that promote democratic deliberation and decision making, increase citizen control over resources, and/ or foster self-reliance and the expansion of cultural resources among previously marginalized groups. Can the rough and tumble of democratic politics and active civil societies yield new arrangements that change power relations, revise economic structures and cultural representations, and improve people's daily lives? How do those with economic power, who in the past often supported coups, repression, and military governments, respond to such reforms when they occur in democratic contexts today?

The cases examined throughout this book involve new bargains over who gets what that significantly alter existing power relations, in terms of material goods, voice, and recognition. By "recognition," we mean a combination of respect for autonomy, esteem for identity, and a distribution of resources necessary for individuals to participate "on a par with one another in social life" (Fraser and Honneth 2003, as quoted in Thompson 2006, 30).[4] Such recognition fosters what Amartya Sen (1999, 18, 8) has characterized as "the 'capabilities' of persons to lead the kind of lives they value," which he argues can best be achieved when development (or reform) provides "an integrated process of the expansion of substantive freedoms." In considering not only the kind of voice that addresses power "at the top" but "horizontal voice," which shapes culture and collective identity, Guillermo O'Donnell has underscored the interconnection of voice and recognition and their centrality to democracy. Democratic political life, O'Donnell (1986, 266) suggests, depends on people having a "sense of personal worth and self-respect, the feeling that one is not an *idiot*, the hope of achieving valued goals by means of collective action."

Because this book focuses on reforms that alter power relations in a democratic context, we have excluded corporate social responsibility programs, which rarely extend beyond education and training, after-school projects, athletic activities, the provision of goods, and community cultural celebrations (Sklair 2001, chapter 6; and Sanborn 2005). These projects, while providing needed material and technical resources, rarely shift the "terms of recognition" (Appadurai 2004, 66) between businesses and communities. In choosing cases, we have stayed local, though not small, focusing on tangible places and groups of people in cities and their peripheries. The reforms we have studied are knowable, in the sense of having been heard of, seen, participated in, and/or talked about not only by those directly involved or affected but by most people living within a major city or state as well as by significant numbers of others farther afield in adjacent states, national capitals, and international institutions.

Participatory budgeting, for example, which originated in Porto Alegre, Brazil, turns over decisions about infrastructure investment for urban services (such as potable water, pavement, day care, and community health) to neighborhood residents themselves, who meet and deliberate in open meetings that function through democratic procedures. Since 1988, participatory budgeting has become well known and discussed not only across its city of origin but throughout Brazil and in activist and policy-making circles internationally— from the World Social Forum to the World Bank (Baierle 1998; Abers 2000; and Baiocchi 2005). Participatory budgeting has also been replicated in such diverse countries as Mexico, India, and the United States.

In another case, the Afro Reggae Cultural Group fights violence and drug trafficking in Rio de Janeiro's favelas by teaching kids to play drums and dance, do street theater, and perform circus routines. In several of the city's most violent shantytowns, Afro Reggae has provided after-school social centers, local jobs, and access to professional work. For many people, the group has inspired a new sense of self-worth as well as offered protection from violence. Afro Reggae also trains police to negotiate favela streets less violently and to avoid racial discrimination. The group performs with national stars in monthly concerts throughout Rio and in concert halls around the world (Gomes da Cunha 1998; Yudice 2004, chapter 5; Arias 2006, chapter 5; and Neate 2006).

In Argentina, during the catastrophic economic collapse of 2001–2, workers facing unemployment took over the factories where they worked, rather than let those factories close. In so doing, they turned economic crisis into an opportunity to create worker-owned and worker-run cooperatives that competed effectively in the market. These actions compelled the attention of Buenos Aires's businesspeople and put the possibility of alternative, nonhierarchical production and management onto the global radar screen (Rebón 2007 and Monteagudo 2008).

In San Cristóbal de Las Casas, Mexico, the rapid expansion of Indian neighborhoods in the periphery of what was once an exclusively ladino city and the challenge to the status quo posed by the statewide Zapatista uprising have resulted in the claiming of new roles and rights by previously marginalized people. In the city's poor *colonias*, Maya community activists have forged transportation, policing, and marketing networks in their neighborhoods and laid claim to elective office and broader roles in politics and policy making. While outside attention focused on the course of the Zapatista movement and its eventual retreat to autonomous villages in the jungle, businesspeople in San Cristóbal have been grappling with how to employ, do business with, and run the city for and indeed with its now–Maya majority—a process that has pressed them explicitly to reconsider past racist beliefs and policies of exclusion (Peres Tzu 2002; Kovic 2005; and Rus and Vigil 2007).

Finally, migrants from the Mexican state of Zacatecas have carved out transnational lives in cities and towns across the United States. Seen for decades as poor, illiterate, and with no prospects for betterment, thousands of these migrants have turned the tables by forming hometown associations in the United States that collect money from their members and send it back across the border to Mexico. Their successes in repairing churches and paving roads, building sports fields and outfitting ambulances, along with innovative efforts to set up productive businesses (all in Mexico), not only changed the way migrants themselves were viewed on both sides of the border but stimulated Mexican local, state, and federal governments to match the migrants' dollars three-for-one, in Zacatecas and adjoining states. More surprising still, the U.S.-based hometown associations and their Mexican counterparts have succeeded in holding Mexican political officials accountable through transparent, noncorrupt procedures for administering the funds (Goldring 2002; Fernández de Castro, Zamora, and Vila 2007; Smith 2006; Fox and Bada 2008; and Williams 2008).

In the scope of their activities and the reach of the attention they attract, these enduring reforms constitute ideal cases in which to test out the willingness of key actors, and of businesspeople in particular, to countenance the sort of creative and participatory innovation—outside-of-the-box yet constructed from familiar elements—that theories of democracy and civil society promise. Here are significant innovations and experiments, forged in moments of political opportunity, economic crisis, or violence, now working on the ground.

HISTORICAL CONTEXT

Today is not the first time progressive activists have attempted to promote reform in Latin America. Starting in the 1930s, Latin America experienced a period of growth and development that included increased electoral openness, successful industrialization, land reform, and the political mobilization of previously excluded groups, many of whom nonetheless continued to face poverty and deprivation. By the 1950s and 1960s, in the context of democratic openings and competition for votes, social movements and mass mobilizations pressed for deeper socioeconomic reforms across the hemisphere, focusing on the rules governing investment, growth, land ownership, income distribution, and social welfare. The push for more extensive reforms, which arose at the height of the Cold War, generated widespread opposition from business and the U.S. government on the one hand and spurred revolutionary ideologies and mobilizations among leftist activists on the other. Over time, by the 1970s, most viable reformist projects were opposed and sabotaged by shifting coalitions of political leaders, political parties, and military, paramilitary, and private sector actors. Successfully labeled communist and subversive, nearly all progressive projects were destroyed through decades of military and authoritarian governments.

At the start of the twenty-first century, however, when vibrant and enduring democratic politics is widely seen as essential for international security and human well-being, Latin America is once again a hotbed of democratic experiences. Since the 1980s transitions to democracy, economic and political changes have occurred in Latin America with an unprecedented degree of openness. In the big three Southern Cone nations, as well as in many of their hemispheric neighbors, democratic elections have brought a shift to the left with no dramatic interventions by the military, the private sector, or the United States. Simultaneously, the region emerged from the 1980s debt crisis by adopting (or being forced by northern governments and international institutions to adopt) the neoliberal free-market model, which has led to economic growth as well as significant integration of the formal economies of most Latin American countries with the global economic order.

The confluence of democratization with neoliberal economic reform has yielded paradoxical results. Inequality, exclusion, deprivation, and violence persist on a grand scale, appearing at times to be constitutive components of the new democratic regimes, rather than holdovers from the past (Arias and Goldstein 2010). The market-based economic model has not solved these problems, and Latin American societies remain the most unequal in the world (Castañeda 2011 and Kim 2013). As wealth has increased for leaders of the formal economy, millions of workers have remained trapped in the informal economy, and the wide gap between rich and poor persists. New opportunities and guarantees for investors have coincided with increasing vulnerability for the majority. In promoting economic growth, governments have eased rules for repossession and foreclosure, facilitated the use of temporary work contracts and the individualization of unemployment savings, and placed de facto limits on the quality of services in public schools and hospitals to reduce fiscal deficits. Under these market-oriented policies, when growth slows, all but the well-to-do are unprotected.

Yet despite the depredations of the free-market system for the majority of Latin Americans, spaces exist (or are carved out) where poor people move beyond merely coping to developing enduring mechanisms to improve their lives—what Mark Goodale and Nancy Postero (2013) have called interruptions to neoliberalism. As the harms of neoliberalism led people to organize, protest, and innovate in this democratic context (Shefner and Stewart 2011), progressive reforms and social changes such as those examined in this book have flourished, aided by several other contextual factors. Trade liberalization and the concomitant increase in direct foreign investment have reshaped the elite by decimating sectors of mid-level businesses. Economic crises—like those in Argentina at the turn of the millennium—have pressed poor and middle-class citizens to take action to survive, at the same time that increased levels of education have provided a platform of knowledge and the ability to connect analysis with action. Changing demographics have enabled formerly excluded groups to have some electoral clout, while cultural globalization has contributed to making racism visible and accorded value to multiculturalism.

The progressive reforms examined here, which have arisen largely independent of legislative processes, are among the most hopeful and innovative solutions to inequality and exclusion in the world today. They demonstrably improve poor people's lives, and the future of democracy in Latin America depends in part on the willingness of powerful social actors, including businesspeople, to tolerate and even promote these reforms. However, despite the existence of incisive scholarly research on the institutional and economic components of democratization (O'Donnell 1993; Ames 2002; and Hagopian and Mainwaring 2005), on social movements (Alvarez, Dagnino, and Escobar 1998a; and Stahler-Sholk, Vanden, and Kuecker 2008), and on innovative policy making (Tendler 1997 and Grindle 2004), there are little scholarly literature and minimal activist knowledge about the nexus between contemporary progressive change and business responses to that change. *Enduring Reform* explores this nexus.

THEORETICAL FRAMEWORKS ON THE SIGNIFICANCE OF REFORM AND BUSINESS RESPONSES

Conceptualizing Civil Society and Reform

The reforms discussed in this book are neither utopian nor abstract: they are pragmatic, working crystallizations of social movement and civil society visions, hammered out in practice. By "crystallization," we mean the outcome of a process whereby disparate forces and social actors coalesce into a coherent project. The activists and ordinary people we study seek to enter into mainstream civil and political society, to claim the citizenship and well-being that democracies and markets ostensibly offer. They are not doing politics elsewhere or completely differently, in contrast to Partha Chatterjee's (2004) findings on India, where he argues that the real "politics of the governed" occurs outside of the frameworks of civil society and electoral democracy. Nor are they seeking "alternatives to modernity"—ways of thinking and living outside of the framework of Western beliefs and practices—of the sort Arturo Escobar (2008) discerns in the knowledge and visions of Afro-Colombian activists on the Pacific Coast of Colombia. Rather, the reforms we examine, and the people who established and engage with them, seek to make the democracies and citizenships, markets and capitalisms that Western modernity offers work on the ground to improve the lives of poor people. In this sense, these reforms are one of the hopes on which the project of an inclusive and egalitarian democratic modernity rests.

In examining to what extent real, working reforms make a difference, along with whether and in what ways businesspeople welcome, tolerate, or oppose them, we follow Barbara Cruikshank (2010) in revising and broadening conventional notions of reform itself, looking beyond the daily workings of reform programs to the cultural and political terrains on which policies are crafted and to the textured knowledges and interpretations that activists and businesspeople bring to and take from reform initiatives. We also identify the differences between the internal dynamics of reform initiatives and the broader systems of which they are a part. Much as J. K. Gibson-Graham (1996) sees multiple capitalisms that establish variety and alternatives within what appears to be a monolithic economic system, we observe that the reform projects studied exist within democracy and neoliberalism, compatible with their practices but differing from them significantly. These reforms function by different internal norms and may, as they endure, challenge and revise political and economic arrangements from within.

In studying the ways in which reform experiences may reshape the institutional relations of which they are a part, this book looks at the interplay between what businesspeople think and what they do. Changes in culture—in the representations through which people make sense of the world—occur slowly and unevenly, in complex interaction with economic and political circumstances. To learn about this process, we asked, among other questions, do businesspeople change their minds? Do those who regulated the presence of Indians in San Cristóbal for centuries—insisting that they move off the sidewalk to allow ladinos by and that they return to highland villages every night, well into the 1980s—ever question their racism and enact a different stance? If so, in what ways and up to what point? Can entrepreneurs in Buenos Aires long accustomed to speaking only in deprecating terms of workers, even to this day, come to recognize the competence and humanity of those workers and do business with them on equal terms, when the workers own and run factories? What makes this sort of rethinking and new actions possible? Conversely, can successful and cosmopolitan business magnates in Porto Alegre decline to see—or in the political theory sense, to recognize—one of the most successful experiences in citizen education and empowerment in the world (participatory budgeting) and replace it, in the 2000s, with a system of corporate social responsibility that they themselves control? What makes it possible to wield false or ignorant claims successfully in the face of widespread evidence to the contrary (Sedgwick 1990, 7–8)? We find that all of these responses indeed occur, pressed forward by rethinking and what Escobar (2008) has called "counterwork"— grassroots efforts to establish new conceptual and practical norms—as well as by ignorance and the rejection of evidence.

At times, this mixture produces ongoing, significant reform, in which the alternative nature of a reform experience not only sets up residence within the world as it is, amid neoliberal practices of economy and citizenship, but revises those practices over time, bringing an alternative society more visibly into being. We evaluate this reform process by looking in a textured, ethnographic, and interdisciplinary way at cases of practical change, providing examples of how different regional societies have forged and grappled with reform. In our analyses, we underscore both the internal ambiguities and contradictions of reform experiences and the limited and partial results they achieve, avoiding romanticization and identifying harms as well as benefits. We are keenly aware that reform initiatives simultaneously accept and challenge the cultural beliefs and political and economic constraints amid which they are enacted. In studying these reforms now, we seek to turn a corner in scholarly inquiry, moving from claims that civil society and democracy necessarily enable reform—or alternately that significant reform is impossible in the context of electoral democracy and neoliberalism today—to the study of working, innovative reforms and the responses of powerful actors to them. In so doing, we identify commonalities regarding the characteristics of successful reform across cases, the factors that shape business responses, and the nature and range of those responses.

Evaluating Civil Society-Based Reform in New Democracies

Scholars from a wide range of political, disciplinary, and methodological positions concur in seeking information about the inner workings of new, emerging bargains and how they compare to "class compromises" or "pacts" in earlier decades (Sandbrook et al. 2006; and O'Donnell and Schmitter 1986). Those who hope that active civil societies will contribute to well-being recognize that for this to be so, civil society actors must come up with and implement solutions that "[solve] particular public policy dilemmas in ways that are just and effective" (Edwards 2004, 39). In order to be a force for well-being and peaceful coexistence, democracy must enable key actors to "create options for promoting new and viable collective projects" that bring about more equitable conditions in critical economic, social, and environmental arenas (UNDP 2004, 7). Even proponents of democracy who assume the value of neoliberal markets and downplay the question of equity have realized that processes of democratic consolidation do not happen through predictable, rational sequences or technocratic expertise. Instead, "they are chaotic processes of change that go backwards and sideways as much as forward, and do not do so in any regular manner," so that evaluating the quality of democracy cannot be achieved through an "institutional checklist" but rather necessitates the close examination of actual reform processes and their ability to address pressing problems (Carothers 2002, 15).

Scholars approaching mobilization and reform in Latin America from the perspective of a Foucauldian critique of neoliberalism (Boas and Gans-Morse 2009; Gledhill 2005; and Lazar 2004) reach a similar conclusion. While deeply suspicious of civil society–based reform as part of a project of neoliberal governmentality, such scholars nevertheless underscore the importance of figuring out what actually happens when reform is attempted. The work of the Consortium on Social Movements based at the University of Massachusetts–Amherst, including research institutes, scholars, and activists throughout the hemisphere, takes up this task explicitly, analyzing the results of civil society participation initiatives while focusing on the mixtures of "civil" and "uncivil" actions that promote reform (Alvarez et al. forthcoming b). S. Robins, A. Cornwall, and Bettina von Lieres (2008, 3–4), while skeptical of claims that citizenship fosters equality or that "participation" brings results people want and need, nonetheless direct our attention to "the actual processes whereby the marginalized are enabled to enter organized political life and effectively take up wide-ranging issues and causes," urging us to study "how they work in practice, how and why they last, how and why they transform, and how different forms of authority get differentiated." And despite his initial mapping of the Pacific Coast of Colombia through an either/or lens of destructive modernity and empowering indigenous knowledge (and a hope for alternatives to modernity), Escobar (2008, 196) goes on to call for detailed study of the on-the-ground results of the reformist development initiatives developed by Afro-Colombian social movements and NGOs in interaction with state and private sector actors.

With the exception of participatory budgeting in Porto Alegre (from its inception) and the Maya activists in the San Cristóbal colonias (later on in their networking initiatives), the reforms and activists we examine steer clear of political parties and direct involvement in electoral politics. The cases we identify as serving to deepen democracy distance themselves, paradoxically perhaps, from the main arenas of democratic politics. In this way, the reforms are not about "democratic learning" in the conventional sense—learning about the practices of party, electoral, and legislative participation. Rather, they demonstrate other kinds of political and cultural learning—regarding recognition, pragmatism, deliberation, and problem solving—that can take place in democracies. And although these reforms originate and act largely outside of the state, the protagonists in the cases studied here interact strategically and forge partnerships with elected officials and policy makers in order to craft and manage policies necessary for their projects to function and expand.

This book looks at progressive, civil society–based reform—rather than at forms of government or market-induced change—because of the success against great odds of these instances of "innovative crystallization," because of the attention they garner, and because of the ongoing role they play in public debate and imaginaries as well as in policy making and, indirectly, electoral politics. We do not claim that these reforms expand, scale up, or stimulate broader progressive change (although they may) or that they are the only or primary pathways for progressive change (they are not). We examine these cases of reform because they represent new relationships among societal actors in democracies, lessen inequality and exclusion, and shift the ground of perception, debate, and policy making.

The Centrality of Culture in Explaining Businesspeople's Responses

Our case studies analyze what businesspeople do to understand, describe, negotiate with, outmaneuver, support, or limit the fruits of civil society–based democratic innovation, a topic on which there is little literature addressing the period since the transitions to democracy began in the mid-1980s.[5] We address this question because of the multiple kinds of power held and exercised by private sector actors and the frequent centrality of business in political and community affairs, including the establishment of what counts as fact and what is judged to have value. In assessing business responses to reform, each of the case study chapters examines, first, whether and in what ways the business sector engages productively or unproductively (or in partial, ambiguous, contradictory ways) with the reform project, including businesspeople's openness to talking and dialogue and the degree of pragmatism in their responses.

Second, the demand for recognition, and correspondingly for new conceptions of citizenship, is a central component of all of our reform cases, and we examine varying degrees and kinds of recognition, including the extent to which the business sector recognizes the humanity, autonomy, rights, and capacities of the previously excluded people who are involved in the progressive changes. Third, the case studies reveal contestation over language in the interaction between businesspeople and reform projects, bringing out the ways in which this contestation develops, shapes responses to reform, and influences the ways in which reform endures and is endured. Finally, the case studies analyze the counterproposals developed by business in order to gain votes and implement policies that simultaneously address, modify, and control the issues made visible by enduring reforms. Counterproposals, we argue, are one of the most visible and consequential responses of businesspeople to reform. Embodying both concessions and constraints, they mark the changing terrain of both electoral politics and enduring reform.

Our research shows that in democratic contexts where forms of outright repression common in the past are not readily available, businesspeople have to "deal": that is, they have to view and confront reformist initiatives using the range of noncoercive mechanisms available to elites in democracies. The line between coercive and noncoercive action is blurred, of course, particularly given the ubiquitous violence and police power in Latin America's cities and rural areas alike and the centrality of policing to Latin America's democratic projects (Huggins 1998; and Arias and Goldstein 2010). In confronting reform that they do not wish to endure, businesspeople can take advantage of violence (such as the repression of Indians after the Zapatista uprising in San Cristóbal [Rus, Hernández, and Mattiace 2003] or the police attacks in Rio's favelas [Arias 2006]) as well as of institutional practices that favor business and elite interests (such as judicial proceedings regarding land ownership in the same locations [see Bobrow-Strain 2007 and Holston 1991]). Despite these continuing forms of repression and influence, however, democracy has changed the rules of power in Latin America. In contrast to long histories of hostility to progressive, civil society–based reform—and to those who fight for and benefit from such reform—businesspeople today respond to reform with notable kinds of openness as well as with marked refusals and effective outmaneuverings. We hope to focus the attention of scholars and activists on this space of uncertainty and possibility, on its harsh imperviousness to recognition and redistribution as well as its moments of surprising shift and openness.

In highlighting this point of tension in businesspeople's responses to reform, where possibilities of new bargains emerge, we find support for our conclusions regarding the centrality of culture in recent scholarly literature that identifies interpretation and negotiation at the center of the establishment of social democracy and elite views of poverty. In analyzing four twentieth-century examples of the establishment of social democracy in the Global South—Costa Rica, Kerala, Mauritius, and Chile—Richard Sandbrook, Marc Edelman, Patrick Heller, and Judith Teichman (2007) found that it was not the presence of strong labor movements closely linked with socialist parties that facilitated the establishment of new forms of recognition and social welfare, as had been (incorrectly) assumed from earlier European cases, but rather pragmatic compromise over progressive goals. Reassessing the European past, Sandbrook and his coauthors argue that critical political conjunctures enabled negotiation between social classes when elites perceived classes as interdependent, viewed the state as potentially reliable, and understood their own interests to include "human capital productivity, social peace, and superior conflict management" (Sandbrook et al. 2006, 7; and Sandbrook et al. 2007). The authors reach similar conclusions in their studies of non-European countries since the 1960s; social democracies in the Global South happen when business is willing to see commonalities between their interests and those of other groups and negotiate pragmatically (Sandbrook et al. 2006, 81).

Similarly, in their seminal works on successful policy reform in areas of health, education, employment, and urban services in Brazil and Mexico, Judith Tendler (1997) and Merilee Grindle (2004) find that the construction of trust, collaborative decision making, effective leadership, and "policy entrepreneurship" predict reform success more effectively than preexisting configurations of political power or economic interest. This work supports our finding that culture shapes the ways in which businesspeople understand reform initiatives and determine their own interests and responses. Tendler describes a process whereby state-level policy makers initiated their programs with a commitment to according considerable trust to public workers. Policy makers publicized this trust and implemented it by granting the workers a notable degree of autonomy. The local communities thus came to respect public workers, who felt a greater responsibility and sense of duty. As a result, they made the most of their relative autonomy in the implementation of their programs, using their discretion to further the communities' interests rather than their own (Tendler 1997). The virtuous circle Tendler describes, much like the successful aspects of Enduring Reform cases, occurs at the intersection of culture, representation, and the politics of leadership and innovation.

The unique survey work of Elisa Reis and Mick Moore (2005) on elite views of poverty reinforces this point about the importance of representation and interpretation to reform.[6] Through survey research, they have found that the ways in which elites perceive, understand, and respond to poverty differs significantly among five countries across the Global South. These differences, they argue, stem from trajectories of belief and the interpretation of experience, rather than from differences in national economies or the wealth or vulnerability of elites themselves. In addition, Reis and Moore (2005, 18) observe that "many of the perceptions of poverty conveyed to us were in some way or another 'unreal'—so highly abstract, idealized or generalized, or so at variance with the facts, that we are tempted to label them 'misperceptions.'" This misperception recalls what Eve Sedgwick (1990) has described as "open secrets" whereby key social facts can be simultaneously known and unacknowledged, by individuals and in the public sphere.[7] In Reis and Moore's (2005, 7–8) analysis, both technocrats and activists interested in reform have ignored the tenacity and significance of these misperceptions: "The former bet on technical skills and the latter on moral determination. Both tend to forget that ongoing perceptions may constitute powerful obstacles to policy effectiveness as well as promising conditions for successful initiatives."

Our comparative analysis underscores the centrality of what might broadly be called cultural factors—of representation and interpretation, of what is seen and how, of the construction of fact and value—in shaping the course of reform projects in Latin America today. In using the term "culture," we borrow from poststructuralist and cultural studies notions of culture as multiple, competing strands of representation and interpretation that may or may not cohere or endure in the form of cultural systems but that emerge out of and influence material and political phenomena, exerting power and shaping events (Dirks, Eley, and Ortner 1994; and Rubin 2004). The major causal finding of *Enduring Reform* is that culture—understood in this way to encompass the images and narratives that shape how people perceive and understand their own and others' experiences—shapes outcomes significantly, together with factors of economic interest and political institutions. How businesspeople react to progressive reform depends on culturally constructed beliefs about politics, poverty, and democracy, including beliefs about the identities and capacities of poor people and the relationships between elites and the reform projects themselves. Our cases demonstrate that these beliefs are shaped by such factors as crisis, surprise, visibility, media representation, experiences of invitation and inclusion, and contestation over language.

Our research highlights a potential exchange, with crucial and open-ended consequences, that comes into view as reform endures: as the left and progressive members of civil society in Latin America accept and work within a framework of democracy and markets, the right and the private sector may *recognize* with greater force and clarity the citizenship, humanity, and competence of people who are poor and marginalized, along with the justice of their claims to material well-being and inclusion.[8] Such an exchange of market acceptance for deep human recognition—the latter rarer and more difficult to achieve even than reform itself, as our case studies demonstrate—would change the terrain on which reformist initiatives are enacted to favor enduring reform. The possibility of this exchange presses us to ask what happens as reforms endure and businesspeople endure reform. Does the act of enduring involve negotiation and conflict that produces cultural change? In a world of global free trade, this exchange of market acceptance for recognition is perhaps the exchange of greatest potential consequence for a future of inclusion, equality, and well-being.

METHODOLOGY

Enduring Reform is the culmination of a multicountry research initiative, the Enduring Reform Project (www.enduringreform.org), funded by the Open Society Foundations from 2007 to 2010. The project was directed by Jeffrey W. Rubin and Vivienne Bennett with a research team of twelve (four from the United States and eight from Latin America) working on six cases, five of which are presented here. Each case was carried out collaboratively by a team of two researchers who had many prior years of direct experience in their research location and a deep familiarity with the evolution of her or his reform case. Researchers conducted interviews for the Enduring Reform Project (ten to twenty interviews in each case location) with progressive activists and local businesspeople using an interview template that was prepared in Spanish and Portuguese (see Appendix A for the interview template in English). The template provided open-ended questions from which researchers could explore activists' and businesspeople's knowledge, opinions, and actions with regard to the reform case itself and the larger context of democratization and economic change in which it occurred. The use of the same template by all the Enduring Reform researchers means that comparable questions were asked of the activists and businesspeople across all cases. Research was conducted from May through September 2008; researchers wrote fieldwork reports in the fall of 2008; and the entire Enduring Reform Project team met in Porto Alegre, Brazil, in November 2008 for a four-day conference to present and discuss the research findings. Two external discussants attended the conference as well, one with expertise on the role of social movements in progressive reform and the other an expert on the history and views of the business sector in Latin America.

All but one of the contributors to this edited volume are original members of the Enduring Reform Project.[9] The coeditors of the book directed the project. The analysis in each case study chapter, based on original research that has not been published elsewhere, derives its strength from the researchers' long-standing experience with their cases as well as the multiyear process of focused collaborative research, discussion, and writing for the Enduring Reform Project.

Our selection of cases was based on finding places where civil society–based progressive reforms had endured within democratic and market systems. We chose cases where the reforms had demonstrably improved daily life for a significant number of local residents in terms of their economic well-being, political voice, and/or cultural identity. Because of the newness of our subject of inquiry and our interest in identifying commonalities of response across cases, we chose examples that focused on different objectives and occurred in a range of national contexts. These cases include different kinds and degrees of challenges to elite economic interests, from music and antiviolence programs in favelas, which do not challenge business interests directly, to factory take-overs in Buenos Aires, which defy private property norms. In proceeding in this fashion, we agree with Judith Tendler (1997) about the value—indeed the necessity—of comparing different cases for which one has potentially incommensurate data. Tendler (1997, 13) has observed, with regard to the cases of government-led reform she studied in the Brazilian state of Ceará, that "each of these four cases represents a sector for which a self-contained literature and a corresponding body of advice exists. . . . No one writes in the same breath about agricultural extension agents, barefoot doctors, small-enterprise assistance agents, and drought relief workers. While this book [Tendler's 1997 book] grounds each case in the debates of each of these sectors, its greater significance lies in the findings that run across the cases."

Our ethnographic methodology facilitates comparison across cases. Our conclusions reflect the combination of extensive on-site experience and multihour, open-ended interviews on which our key informant, small-sample method is based. We sought to understand the views that shaped businesspeople's responses and actions as well as track and analyze those actions. We also wanted to understand the evolution of the progressive reform experiences from the perspective of their leaders and participants. Our interviews enabled us to connect beliefs and experiences—as reported by interviewees and evaluated by researchers familiar with the context—with the trajectories of reform initiatives.[10] Through open-ended conversations with businesspeople, we discerned ideas usually hidden beneath the surface, outside public view and often inaccessible to scholars, and identified connections between businesspeople's ideas and the actions they took toward reform initiatives. In Porto Alegre, for example, it was only far into our interviews that some businesspeople expressed the frank realization that they could effectively be outvoted in the democratic procedures of participatory budgeting (Rubin and Baierle, this volume). From unexpected jumps in our conversations, we learned that the city's businesspeople were willing and able to travel to confront and reevaluate their prejudices about people in other regions of Brazil, but they were unwilling to engage with poor residents in their own city at civic meetings and reevaluate their prejudices at home. Our understanding of this construction of ignorance, and the power relations out of which it occurs, in turn helped us unravel the puzzle of why cosmopolitan businesspeople in a prosperous city so fiercely opposed an internationally renowned reform that served to regularize property rights and provide basic services in poor neighborhoods.

All the activists and participants from the progressive reforms who were interviewed for the Enduring Reform Project were founders of the reform or had participated extensively in its process. Therefore they were knowledgeable about the history, goals, strategies, setbacks, and/or successes of the reform experiences in which they had participated. In selecting the businesspeople to be interviewed in each case location, we looked for a range of characteristics, such that some interviewees were among the entrepreneurial elite in their locations, others had high levels of involvement or influence in business associations or community affairs, and still others had little or no knowledge of or direct involvement in public affairs or the reforms under consideration. Because of the range of case locations—from a major pole for domestic and international investment to a provincial commercial and agricultural city—the characteristics of our business interviewees vary from case to case, from industrial producers for domestic and international markets (Buenos Aires and Porto Alegre) to providers of medical services and merchants of artisanal goods (San Cristóbal de Las Casas). The characteristics of businesspeople varied within cases as well; thus our interviewees in Porto Alegre ranged from the owner of a restaurant in an upscale neighborhood, to the owner of industrial plants in both Brazil and the United States, to a high official in the statewide business association, himself a successful executive. In some cases, we carried out interviews among a somewhat broader category of elites who exercise economic power and influence but whose primary current activity is not business. In all of these cases, our interviewees held positions of relative economic power and political influence in their cities and regions.

ORGANIZATION OF THE BOOK

The first two chapters of *Enduring Reform* present an analysis of Latin America's economic history and development models since the 1940s and provide a discussion of social movements in the region since the 1980s. In chapter 1, Ann Helwege explores reasons for businesspeople's economic fears and for their hostility to progressive reform in the past; she links these to business support for political repression. Helwege turns conventional wisdom on its head, however, when she demonstrates that even the ostensibly pro-business policies that governments pursued from the 1940s to the 1990s, in the context of this repression, did not in many cases effectively promote the economic interests of business. Precisely because of their awareness of these past failures, Helwege argues, the private sector in Latin America has exhibited openness to the economic policies pursued by democratic governments since the 1990s and, correspondingly, a newfound willingness to tolerate progressive initiatives. In chapter 2, Wendy Wolford provides a brief history of the ways in which Latin American social movements have changed over time, outlining their shift from antistate and antimarket projects and visions, including revolutionary movements, to engagement with existing democratic politics and markets. Wolford shows how the variety of social movement tactics, as well as movements' frequent engagement with state actors, mirror the worldviews and approaches of the reforms and reform participants.

Chapters 3 through 7 of *Enduring Reform* present the case studies: indigenous self-reliance networks in San Cristóbal de Las Casas, participatory budgeting in Porto Alegre, worker-run factories in Buenos Aires, the three-for-one remittance program in Zacatecas, and the Afro Reggae Cultural Group in Rio de Janeiro. In these chapters, the contributors make their cases for the innovative and far-reaching character of each of the reforms, explain how and why they occurred, and delineate business responses. In chapter 8, we compare the cases in detail. We set out four conclusions: that cultural factors of language, belief, and perception shape business responses to reform; that economic and political crisis can facilitate reform; that businesspeople are more open to progressive reform goals of economic betterment than political empowerment; and that enduring reforms today involve an exchange of acceptance of democracy and markets by activists for recognition by businesspeople. We apply these conclusions to the reform cases, summarizing the successes and limits of the reforms in each location and tracing the impact of these four factors on the evolution of business responses.

One of the great, unresolved problems of the current world order is how to address inequality, poverty, and exclusion through constructive and affirmative actions. With an understanding of social movements and civil societies as nurturing grounds for progressive change, we hold the conviction that democracy in Latin America will be meaningful and enduring over the long haul only if it enables significant progressive reform to occur and endure. This book focuses on those innovations that foster progressive reformist results in democracies and encourage people to move from the "streets" to the "institutions" to secure basic political rights and economic well-being. By examining the responses of businesspeople, we problematize the notion that active civil societies and democratic political systems foster well-being and inclusion. Whether they do so hinges on the "enduring" of reform in the two senses we have set forth—that reforms continue through time and that businesspeople tolerate or withstand changes that they may neither welcome nor like. Our research shows that to understand the prospects for progressive reform in Latin America, we must look to cultural factors of representation and interpretation, of what is seen and how, and of the construction of fact and value. Representation in the cultural sense, and thus cultural politics and the creation of meaning (Alvarez, Dagnino, and Escobar 1998b), are as central to the politics of reform and the prospects for democracy as representation in the conventional electoral sense.

Groups with opposing interests—economic, political, and cultural—must battle it out, with greater or lesser tempestuousness, for a more socially just world to come into being. Our research shows that such contestations are happening on the ground without the high levels of violence of previous decades and with significant shifts in business worldviews and practices. By identifying the possibilities and limits in business responses to reform and the centrality of culture and meaning in shaping them, we seek to explain the trajectories of a striking set of progressive initiatives and, by delineating the stages and pathways by which they proceed, to make further recognition, negotiation, and enduring reform imaginable.

NOTES

The authors thank Marc Edelman, Ann Helwege, Ben Jurge, and José Antonio Lucero for their close reading of this chapter as well as their feedback.

1. By "businesspeople," we mean individuals who are engaged in the production or sale of goods and services for profit (Bernstein, Berger, and Godsell 1996).

2. While on rare occasions subgroups within business elites took the lead in crafting reform, and some business sectors joined in progressive and populist coalitions during the mid-twentieth century, most reverted quickly to an underlying hostility to progressive change as reformist governments proceeded (Brennan 1998; Hamilton 1982; and Schneider 2004). In his pioneering archival work on Colombian elites in the mid-twentieth century, E. Sáenz (1992) has shown that in defining and lobbying for their economic interests, Colombian industrialists routinely allied with the most reactionary elements of the Conservative Party, opposed progressive reform initiatives as well as Colombia's then fragile democratic institutions, and supported U.S. Cold War policies in Latin America, including attacks on leftist labor groups. B. Weinstein (1996) has presented an important contrasting case of commitment to social welfare training and education programs on the part of an elite subgroup of businesspeople over a relatively long period of time in São Paulo.

3. We refer to "civil society" in the Gramscian sense of actors outside of the state, acting on a terrain of legitimation and contestation where a counter-hegemonic project could but need not emerge (Alvarez et al. forthcoming b). We do not assume that civil society necessarily exhibits characteristics of civility in the Tocquevillean sense but rather that civil society is itself shot through with power relations (Buck-Morss 1995 and Edwards 2004). For a useful account of the political and scholarly development of the concept in recent decades, see Alvarez et al. 2012b. For further elaboration of the concept and connections between civil society and progressive reform, see Edwards 2004.

4. In Charles Taylor's (1995) words, "A number of strands of contemporary politics turn on the need, sometimes the demand, for recognition" (cited in Thompson 2006, 2).

5. There is ample literature on business responses to national and regional progressive initiatives and protest before the democratic transitions. See, for example, O'Donnell 1973, Williams 1986, Winn 1986, Maxfield 1990, and Schlesinger and Kinzer 2005 on national initiatives. On regional cases, see Bennett 1995, Weinstein 1996, and Rubin 1997. Also see note 2 in this chapter. Correspondingly, there is broad literature on business responses to government transitions and reforms at the national level since the 1980s (Payne 1993; Weyland 1996; and Kingstone 1999).

6. Reis and Moore (2005) note that no previous research has been done on this topic.

7. On the phenomenon of the "open secret," Sedgwick draws on D. A. Miller (1989). Sedgwick's discussion of ignorance suggests a way of approaching the "unreal" perceptions of poverty Reis and Moore confront in their interviewees: "perhaps there exists instead a plethora of ignorances, and we may begin to ask questions about the labor, erotics, and economics of their human production and distribution" (Sedgwick 1990, 8).

8. We draw here on the political theory of recognition (Thompson 2006).

9. Ann Helwege joined us during the preparation of the manuscript to write the chapter on business and economic change (see chapter 1).

10. Sherry Turkle (2008) has described this as intimate ethnography, because it seeks to link big social changes to the ways people experience and conceptualize these changes.

REFERENCES

Abers, R. 2000. *Inventing Local Democracy: Grassroots Politics in Brazil.* Boulder: Lynne Rienner.

Alvarez, S., G. Baiocchi, A. Lao, J. Rubin, and M. Thayer, eds. Forthcoming a. "Interrogating the Civil Society Agenda, Reassessing 'Un-Civic' Contention: An Introduction." In *Beyond Civil Society: Social Movements, Civic Participation, and Democratic Contestation.* Durham: Duke University Press.

Alvarez, S., G. Baiocchi, A. Lao, J. Rubin, and M. Thayer, eds. Forthcoming b. *Beyond Civil Society: Social Movements, Civic Participation, and Democratic Contestation.* Durham: Duke University Press.

Alvarez, S. E., E. Dagnino, and A. Escobar, eds. 1998a. *Cultures of Politics/Politics of Cultures: Revisioning Latin American Social Movements.* Boulder: Westview Press.

Alvarez, S. E., E. Dagnino, and A. Escobar, eds. 1998b. "Introduction: The Cultural and the Political in Latin American Social Movements." In *Cultures of Politics/Politics of Cultures: Revisioning Latin American Social Movements,* edited by S. E. Alvarez, E. Dagnino, and A. Escobar, 1–29. Boulder: Westview Press.

Ames, B. 2002. *The Deadlock of Democracy in Brazil.* Ann Arbor: University of Michigan Press.

Appadurai, A. 2004. "The Capacity to Aspire: Culture and the Terms of Recognition." In *Culture and Public Action,* edited by V. Rao and M. Walton, 1–29. Redwood City: Stanford University Press.

Arias, E. D. 2006. *Drugs and Democracy in Rio de Janeiro: Trafficking, Social Networks, and Public Security.* Chapel Hill: University of North Carolina Press.

Arias, E. D., and D. M. Goldstein. 2010. *Violent Democracies in Latin America*. Durham: Duke University Press.

Baierle, S. G. 1998. "The Explosion of Experience: The Emergence of a New Ethical-Political Principle in Popular Movements in Porto Alegre, Brazil." In *Cultures of Politics/Politics of Cultures: Revisioning Latin American Social Movements*, edited by S. Alvarez, E. Dagnino, and A. Escobar, 118–38. Boulder: Westview Press.

Baiocchi, G. 2005. *Militants and Citizens: The Politics of Participatory Democracy in Porto Alegre*. Redwood City: Stanford University Press.

Bennett, V. 1995. *The Politics of Water: Urban Protest, Gender, and Power in Monterrey, Mexico*. Pittsburgh: University of Pittsburgh Press.

Bernstein, A., P. Berger, and Bobby Godsell. 1996. *Business and Democracy: Cohabitation or Contradiction?* Development and Democracy series, edited by A. Bernstein. Johannesburg: Centre for Development and Enterprise.

Boas, T., and J. Gans-Morse. 2009. "Neoliberalism: From New Liberal Philosophy to Anti-Liberal Slogan." *Studies in Comparative International Development* 44 (2): 137–61.

Bobrow-Strain, A. 2007. *Intimate Enemies: Landowners, Power, and Violence in Chiapas*. Durham: Duke University Press.

Brennan, J. 1998. "Industrialists and Bolicheros: Business and the Peronist Populist Alliance, 1943–1976." In *Peronism and Argentina*, edited by J. Brennan, 79–123. Wilmington: Scholarly Resources Books.

Buck-Morss, S. 1995. "Envisioning Capital: Political Economy on Display." *Critical Inquiry* 21: 434–67.

Carothers, T. 2002. "The End of the Transition Paradigm." *Journal of Democracy* 13 (1): 5–21.

Castañeda, J. 2011. "What Latin America Can Teach Us." *New York Times*, December 10.

Chatterjee, P. 2004. *The Politics of the Governed: Reflections on Popular Politics in Most of the World*. New York: Colombia University Press.

Cohen, J. L., and A. Arato. 1994. *Civil Society and Political Theory*. Cambridge: MIT Press.

Cruikshank, B. 2010. "Endless Struggle: Sustaining Political Life." Unpublished manuscript.

Dirks, N. B., G. Eley, and S. B. Ortner. 1994. Introduction. In *Culture/Power/History: A Reader in Contemporary Social Theory*, edited by N. B. Dirks, G. Eley, and S. B. Ortner, 3–45. Princeton: Princeton University Press.

Edwards, M. 2004. *Civil Society*. Cambridge: Polity Press.

Escobar, A. 2008. *Territories of Difference: Place, Movements, Life, Redes*. Durham: Duke University Press.

Fernández de Castro, R., R. García Zamora, and Ana Vila. 2007. *El Programa 3x1 para migrantes ¿Primera política transnacional en México?* Mexico City: Miguel Ángel Porrúa, Universidad Autónoma de Zacatecas, Instituto Tecnológico Autónomo de México.

Fox, J., and X. Bada. 2008. "Migrant Organization and Hometown Impacts in Rural Mexico." *Journal of Agrarian Change* 8 (2 and 3): 435–61.

Fraser, N., and A. Honneth. 2003. *Redistribution or Recognition? A Political-Philosophical Exchange*. London: Verso.

Gibson-Graham, J. K. 1996. *The End of Capitalism (As We Knew It): A Feminist Critique of Political Economy*. Oxford: Blackwell Publishers.

Gledhill, J. 2005. "Citizenship and the Social Geography of Deep Neo-Liberalization." *Anthropologica* 47 (1): 81–100.

Goldring, L. 2002. "The Mexican State and Transmigrant Organizations: Negotiating the Boundaries of Membership and Participation." *Latin American Research Review* 37 (3): 55–99.

Gomes da Cunha, O. M. 1998. "Black Movements and the 'Politics of Identity' in Brazil." In *Cultures of Politics/Politics of Cultures: Revisioning Latin American Social Movements,* edited by S. E. Alvarez, E. Dagnino, and A. Escobar, 220–51. Boulder: Westview Press.

Goodale, M., and N. Postero. 2013. "Revolution and Retrenchment: Illuminating the Present in Latin America." In *Neoliberalism Interrupted: Social Change and Contested Governance in Contemporary Latin America,* edited by M. Goodale and N. Postero, 1–22. Redwood City: Stanford University Press.

Grindle, M. 2004. *Despite the Odds: The Contentious Politics of Education Reform.* Princeton: Princeton University Press.

Hagopian, F., and S. P. Mainwaring. 2005. *The Third Wave of Democratization in Latin America: Advances and Setbacks.* Cambridge: Cambridge University Press.

Hamilton, N. 1982. *The Limits of State Autonomy: Post-Revolutionary Mexico.* Princeton: Princeton University Press.

Hirschman, A. 1970. "The Search for Paradigms as a Hindrance to Understanding." *World Politics* 22 (April): 329–43.

Hirschman, A. 1986. "On Democracy in Latin America." *New York Review of Books* 33 (6): 41–42.

Holston, J. 1991. "The Misrule of Law: Land and Usurpation in Brazil." *Comparative Studies in Society and History* 33: 695–725.

Huggins, M. K. 1998. *Political Policing: The United States and Latin America.* Durham: Duke University Press.

Kim, Jim Yong. 2013. "Latin America's Next Challenges." *Los Angeles Times,* July 1. Online at http://articles.latimes.com/2013/jun/30/opinion/la-oe-kim-latin-america-20130701. Accessed July 1, 2013.

Kingstone, P. R. 1999. *Crafting Coalitions for Reform: Business Preferences, Political Institutions, and Neoliberal Reform in Brazil.* University Park: Pennsylvania State University Press.

Kovic, C. M. 2005. *Mayan Voices for Human Rights: Displaced Catholics in Highland Chiapas.* Austin: University of Texas Press.

Lazar, S. 2004. "Education for Credit: Development as Citizenship Project in Bolivia." *Critique of Anthropology* 24 (3): 301–19.

Maxfield, S. 1990. *Governing Capital: International Finance and Mexican Politics.* Ithaca: Cornell University Press.

Miller, D. A. 1989. *The Novel and the Police.* Berkeley: University of California Press.

Monteagudo, G. 2008. "The Clean Walls of a Recovered Factory: New Subjectivities in Argentina's Recovered Factories." *Urban Anthropology* 37 (2): 175–210.

Neate, P., and D. Platt. 2006. *Culture Is Our Weapon: Afroreggae in the Favelas of Rio.* London: Latin American Bureau.

O'Donnell, G. 1973. *Modernization and Bureaucratic Authoritarianism: Studies in South American Politics.* Berkeley: Institute of International Studies.

O'Donnell, G. 1986. "On the Fruitful Convergences of Hirschman's Exit, Voice, and Loyalty and Shifting Involvements: Reflection from the Recent Argentine Experience." In *Development, Democracy, and the Art of Trespassing: Essays in Honor of Albert O. Hirschman*, edited by A. Foxley, M. S. McPherson, and G. O'Donnell. Notre Dame: University of Notre Dame Press.

O'Donnell, G. 1993. "On the State, Democratization, and Some Conceptual Problems: A Latin American View with Glances at Some Post-Communist Countries." *World Development* 21 (8): 1355–69.

O'Donnell, G. A., and P. Schmitter. 1986. *Tentative Conclusions about Uncertain Democracies*. Baltimore: Johns Hopkins University Press.

Payne, L. 1993. *Brazilian Industrialists and Democratic Change*. Baltimore: Johns Hopkins University Press.

Peres Tzu, M. 2002. "A Tzotzil Chronicle." In *The Mexico Reader*, edited by G. Joseph and T. Henderson, 655–59. Durham: Duke University Press.

Rebón, J. 2007. *La Empresa de la Autonomía: Trabajadores recuperando la producción*. Buenos Aires: Colectivo Ediciones.

Reis, E. P., and M. Moore. 2005. *Elite Perceptions of Poverty and Inequality*. London: Zed Books.

Robins, S., A. Cornwall, and Bettina von Lieres. 2008. "Rethinking 'Citizenship' in the Postcolony." *Third World Quarterly* 29 (6): 1069–86.

Rubin, J. W. 1997. *Decentering the Regime: Ethnicity, Radicalism, and Democracy in Juchitán, Mexico*. Durham: Duke University Press.

Rubin, J. W. 2004. "Meanings and Mobilizations: A Cultural Politics Approach to Social Movements and States." *Latin American Research Review* 39 (3): 106–42.

Rus, J., R. A. Hernández Castillo, and S. Mattiace. 2003. *Mayan Lives, Mayan Utopias: The Indigenous Peoples of Chiapas and the Zapatista Rebellion*. Lanham: Rowman and Littlefield, Publishers.

Rus, J., and J. D. Vigil. 2007. "Rapid Urbanization and Migrant Indigenous Youth in San Cristóbal, Chiapas, Mexico." In *Gangs in the Global City*, edited by J. Hagedorn, 152–84. Urbana: University of Illinois Press.

Sáenz, E. 1992. *La Ofensiva Empresarial: Industriales, políticos y violencia en los años 40 en Colombia*. Bogotá: Tercer Mundo Editores.

Sanborn, C. 2005. "Philanthropy in Latin America: Historical Traditions and Current Trends." In *Philanthropy and Social Change in Latin America*, edited by C. Sanborn and F. Portocarrero, 3–29. Cambridge: David Rockefeller Center on Latin American Studies.

Sandbrook, R., M. Edelman, P. Heller, and J. Teichman. 2006. "Can Social Democracies Survive in the Global South?" *Dissent*, 76–83.

Sandbrook, R., M. Edelman, P. Heller, and J. Teichman. 2007. *Social Democracy in the Global Periphery: Origins, Challenges, Prospects*. Cambridge: Cambridge University Press.

Schlesinger, S., and S. Kinzer. 2005. *Bitter Fruit: The Story of the American Coup in Guatemala*. Cambridge: David Rockefeller Center on Latin American Studies.

Schneider, B. 2004. *Business Politics and the State in Twentieth-Century Latin America*. Cambridge: Cambridge University Press.

Sedgwick, E. K. 1990. *Epistemology of the Closet*. Berkeley: University of California Press.

Sen, A. 1999. *Development as Freedom*. New York: Alfred A. Knopf.

Shefner, J., and J. Stewart. 2011. "Neoliberalism, Grievances and Democratization: An Exploration of the Role of Material Hardships in Shaping Mexico's Democratic Transition." *Journal of World-Systems Research* 17 (2): 353–78.

Sklair, L. 2001. *The Transnational Capitalist Class.* Oxford: Blackwell Publishing.

Smith, R. C. 2006. *Mexican New York: Transnational Lives of New Immigrants.* Berkeley: University of California Press.

Stahler-Sholk, R., H. E. Vanden, and G. D. Kuecker. 2008. *Latin American Social Movements in the Twenty-First Century: Resistance, Power, and Democracy.* Lanham: Rowman and Little-field Publishers.

Taylor, C. 1995. "The Politics of Recognition." In *Philosophical Arguments*, edited by C. Taylor, 225–56. Cambridge: Harvard University Press.

Tendler, J. 1997. *Good Government in the Tropics.* Baltimore: Johns Hopkins University Press.

Thompson, S. 2006. *The Political Theory of Recognition: A Critical Introduction.* Cambridge: Polity Press.

Turkle, S. 2008. *The Inner History of Devices.* Cambridge: MIT Press.

United Nations Development Program (UNDP). 2004. *Democracy in Latin America: Towards a Citizens' Democracy.* New York: UNDP.

Weinstein, B. 1996. *For Social Peace in Brazil: Industrialists and the Remaking of the Working Class in São Paulo, 1920–1964.* Chapel Hill: University of North Carolina Press.

Weyland, K. 1996. *Democracy without Equity: Failures of Reform in Brazil.* Pittsburgh: University of Pittsburgh Press.

Williams, H. 2008. *From Visibility to Voice: The Emerging Power of Migrants in Mexican Politics.* Project on Global Migration and Transnational Politics. Fairfax: George Mason University.

Williams, R. G. 1986. *Export Agriculture and the Crisis in Central America.* Chapel Hill: University of North Carolina Press.

Winn, P. 1986. *Weavers of Revolution: The Yarur Workers and Chile's Road to Socialism.* Oxford: Oxford University Press.

Yudice, G. 2004. *The Expediency of Culture: Uses of Culture in the Global Era.* Durham: Duke University Press.

1

SOCIAL POLARIZATION AND ECONOMIC INSTABILITY

TWIN CHALLENGES FOR ENDURING REFORM

Ann Helwege

RAPID ECONOMIC GROWTH and democratization have transformed Latin America in the past decade. With a few exceptions, repression and revolution have given way to the ballot box and growing faith in the legitimacy of public institutions. Despite the fact that Latin America remains one of the most unequal regions in the world, poverty rates have declined sharply, partly because of more progressive public policies. Modern political discourse is now about how—not whether—to build inclusive societies. A striking aspect of this transition is the apparent accommodation of social reform by traditionally conservative business elites. While contemporary social initiatives are less likely to upend the status quo than leftist movements of the past, the response of the right has also become radically less hostile. Repression and fear of reprisal for small acts of civic agency no longer typify Latin America. As the cases in this book demonstrate, marginalized groups find increasing access to venues for participation and voice in the larger society. What has changed to make business elites less resistant to political change and popular engagement? Are the foundations of this era of conciliation strong enough to support more substantial and enduring reform?

Social conflict in Latin America is often attributed to high levels of inequality and struggle over shares of economic output. Much of the political tension of the twentieth century was tied not only to distributional conflict but also to economic instability. Although businesses opposed the socialist movements of the Cold War that threatened expropriation, they also struggled for survival under far less revolutionary, even conservative, regimes. While elites everywhere seek secure property rights, low taxation, and cheap wages, Latin American businesses have been vulnerable to shock from debt crises, sudden trade liberalization, poorly managed monetary policy, and exchange rate volatility. The region's combustible mix of volatile commodity-driven economies and social polarization has repeatedly undermined sound economic policy.

Rapid growth since the early 2000s has mitigated class struggle and made social reform possible. Between 2004 and 2013, economic growth averaged 4.2 percent, almost double the pace of the prior two decades. An extraordinary commodity boom has created job opportunities, closed fiscal deficits, and enabled democratic regimes to begin to deliver on promises of better schools, housing, and health care without raising tax burdens. Political compromise has been made easier by the fact that many constituencies are getting part of what they seek. While a resilient economy will make ongoing reform easier, changing cultural norms and stronger political institutions can also contribute to the securing of rights. As the region seeks to put political strife behind it, more inclusive economic and social policies can actually ensure stability and growth in the long run.

This chapter identifies the economic policy changes that underlie new business openness to progressive social reform. In contrast to previous repressive, pro-business policy regimes, more moderate contemporary economic policies offer a more secure framework for business growth. I suggest that businesspeople have learned that the economic policies and political regimes they defended in the second half of the twentieth century, in the name of opposing communism and fighting leftist reform, were by and large not good for business, or only unevenly so. The path for business prosperity going forward requires a new approach for resolving distributional conflict. This awareness, while not necessarily leading to business support for progressive change, provides room for reformist initiatives, as businesspeople consider their options in the context of democracy and a rapidly changing global economy.

THE NEW NORMAL: DECLINING POVERTY AND PERSISTENT INEQUALITY

The region's history of instability is intrinsically linked to its cyclical struggle over distribution: inequality prompts demands for higher wages, land reform, and social services, but resistance to bearing the financial cost of such redress, as well as the costs in resource distribution and power that successful demands from below would incur, leads to authoritarian efforts to retain control over the economy.[1] Much of this conflict derives from colonial subjugation, which rigid inherited institutions have failed to mitigate, with the result that inequality is mirrored in racial and ethnic tension, bureaucratic dysfunction, and a striking contrast between those who live in poverty and the affluent who enjoy world-class luxuries.[2]

Without a broad consensus on the distribution of income and appropriate redistributive policies, populist leaders of the twentieth century frequently resorted to inflationary use of the printing press to retain power. Reactionary repression, often through military coups, stopped inflation but exacerbated inequality. This pattern of Latin American political and economic instability persisted throughout the twentieth century, culminating in some of the highest rates of inflation in world history and six major financial crises between 1994 and 2002. This vicious cycle of economic instability and political repression has finally been interrupted in the twenty-first century with faster growth, stronger democratic institutions, and better macroeconomic management. Rising income and lower political risk have fostered a growing middle class, more constructive policies in education and health, and greater opportunities for entrepreneurship. Poverty rates have plummeted, both as a consequence of job growth and new welfare programs (figure 1.1).

Figure 1.1. Poverty headcount ratio at $2 a day (percentage of population).

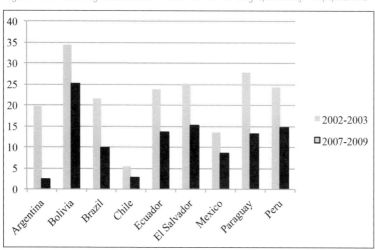

Source: World Bank, World Development Indicators, accessed October 21, 2011.

Recent data suggest that inequality has also begun to decline in several countries. The Gini coefficient in Brazil, long among the world's highest, dropped from .58 in 2002 to .54 in 2011 (World Bank 2014). Argentina, El Salvador, Ecuador, Paraguay, and Peru have also experienced declining inequality in recent years. Yet the distribution of income in nearly every Latin American country remains far more unequal than it is elsewhere, outside of Africa. The average income Gini coefficient in Latin America is 8 points higher than in Asia, 18 points higher than in Eastern Europe and Central Asia, and 20 points higher than in the developed countries (Gasparini and Lustig 2011, 3). The bottom income decile now receives just 1 percent of income and depends on social welfare programs like Bolsa Familia in Brazil, Oportunidades in Mexico, and Juntos in Peru for small income transfers, while the top decile—Latin America's elite—receives 41 percent.[3] Even as some countries work toward greater economic inclusion, the share of income that accrues to the poorest quintile remains small throughout the region (table 1.1.)

Table 1.1. Share of poorest quintile in national consumption

Country	1990 level	2008 level
Latin America	3.2	3.5
Argentina	4.2	3.7
Bolivia	3.2	4.3
Brazil	2.1	2.6
Chile	3.5	4.1
Colombia	2.0	2.9
Costa Rica	4.3	4.4
Dominican Republic	3.2	2.9
Ecuador	4.8	4.4
El Salvador	3.4	3.4
Guatemala	2.7	2.8
Honduras	2.3	1.9
Mexico	3.9	4.0
Nicaragua	2.1	3.5
Panama	3.2	4.6
Paraguay	5.2	5.0
Peru	3.0	4.0
Uruguay	4.8	4.9
Venezuela	4.3	5.2

Source: Economic Commission on Latin America and the Caribbean 2010, 391.

These numbers suggest that while democracy and more inclusive social norms are slowly healing class divisions, much of the progress experienced by the working class hinges on growth. Particularly in South America, where natural resource exports have fueled growth, nearly every class has enjoyed rising incomes. Mineral royalties and profit taxes have filled government coffers with revenue even as tax reform remains low on the political agenda. With a surfeit of job opportunities in the public and private sector, there is little clamor for more substantial redistributive policies. If the current commodity boom can be sustained, more inclusive economic development can accompany Latin America's impressive progress in political and social reform. Without rapid growth, progress will depend on whether privileged groups are willing to cede a still larger share of income and political power— that is, on how they understand and respond to reform initiatives that establish new rules and social mores, at the national level as well as in cities and rural communities.

The closing of this short window of growth is increasingly apparent. Much of the recent boom has been tied to growth in China. China is now the largest or second largest export market for Brazil, Chile, Argentina, Colombia, and Peru, and it is Mexico's third largest market. Trade between China and Latin America grew 31 percent *per year* between 2000 and 2008. Prices of oil, soy, copper, iron, gold, silver, and tin all increased threefold or more. As growth in China eases, and U.S. and European financial crises play out, the investment boom in Latin America will soften and dampen overall growth. As growth slows, does the region risk reversion to the instability, financial crises, and political repression of the past? Or has social conciliation—including new openness to progressive, civil society–based reform on the part of some businesspeople—made possible a consensus about responses to recession? Better macroeconomic management makes the spectacular financial crises of the past unlikely, but the prospect of instability still haunts the region and nurtures a conservative bias against transformative social policies. To understand the resistance of Latin American elites to substantial economic reforms, it is worth looking back at the experiences that color perceptions of progressive economic policies. Encouragingly, it seems unlikely that any class will call for measures that repeat the twentieth century's darkest years.

ECONOMIC DEBACLES OF THE TWENTIETH CENTURY: HARD LESSONS ABOUT THE COST OF SOCIAL POLARIZATION

The economist Javier Santiso (2006, 1) has succinctly described Latin America's postcolonial history until recently as "a long season in hell." Certainly for the average businessperson, challenges to the balance of power recall experiences with hyperinflation, erratic real exchange rates, banking collapses, and property expropriation. Within his or her lifetime, a fifty-year-old businessperson in Latin America has seen:

- complex tariffs and licenses that require close alliances with corrupt politicians;
- five radical socialist experiments (Cuba, Chile, Nicaragua, Venezuela, and Bolivia) involving property expropriations;
- authoritarian conservative regimes whose repression created dysfunctional levels of terror;
- several cases of hyperinflation that rank among the highest in world history;
- heterodox stabilization plans that treated inflation as a social disorder rather than as a consequence of monetary expansion;
- neoliberal trade liberalization that invited a flood of imports without adjustments to ensure the viability of local firms;
- privatization of state-owned water and energy utilities that led to monopolistic rate increases;
- exchange rate anchors intended to secure credibility that ended in currency collapse and a loss of bank deposits;
- the demise of manufacturing and migration of workers into the informal sector, where few pay taxes, shifting the burden to the formal sector;
- popular support for regimes that promise to correct for a half millennium of inequity in a sexennial.

These experiences have left the business community profoundly distrustful of active state intervention in the economy, leery of any effort intended to improve the lives of economically disadvantaged groups.

The early Import Substitution Industrialization (ISI) era between 1940 and 1970 is often referred to as a period of consensus and social reform. Populist leaders—Juan Perón, Getúlio Vargas, José María Velasco Ibarra, and Rómulo

Betancourt—all aimed to consolidate their support through generous welfare programs for urban workers. Formal sector workers gained social security pensions, health care, education, housing, minimum wages, and perhaps most important, the right to unionize. Even if only a minority of workers benefited from these policies, the social achievements of ISI left a profound impact on Latin American constitutions.[4] The *sense,* if not the reality, of social justice marks considerable progress compared with the beginning of the era, when workers were denigrated as shirtless ("descamisados") and greasy-handed ("las grasas").

For business elites, the ISI era was a mixed experience. Protectionism and state support created entrepreneurial opportunities in industry, but the model also generated countless frustrations and inefficiencies. Bureaucratic control over access to import licenses, credit, and foreign exchange meant corruption could work in favor of or against an entrepreneur, predictably or capriciously. Even those proficient at manipulating the system saw corruption's corrosive effect in the form of tax evasion, poorly enforced contracts, and a culture of delivering substandard products.[5] Nor was stability a hallmark of the era. ISI's anti-export bias and fixed exchange rates meant that trade gaps had to be closed in one way or another. To prevent capital flight, episodic devaluations occurred suddenly, eroding assets and raising costs. Even crawling pegs involved massive realignments. The Argentine peso, for example, lost about 70 percent of its value from early 1948 to early 1950. For businesses using imported inputs but facing price controls in retail markets, the consequences could be devastating.

Although ISI predates the hyperinflation of the 1980s, the era was beset with price instability. Fiscal deficits, caused by underfinancing of industrial subsidies and welfare programs, were paid for with the printing press. The resulting inflation, often above 50 percent, undermined savings.[6] Political accommodation of worker protests led to mandated wage increases on the order of 20 percent to 70 percent. Even if warranted by higher costs of living, real wage adjustments became unpredictably erratic while inflexible labor laws made layoffs difficult. Union strikes routinely disabled firms. Because of fiscal imbalances, trade gaps, and bureaucratic efficiency, in one way or another many of the benefits associated with ISI came at the expense of growth and genuinely inclusive economic equity. The ISI era was, as John Sheahan (1987, 84) has noted, "not so much a one-dimensional triumph of industrial interest as a general shift of power to the urban sector, especially to organized groups, at the expense of previously dominant primary export interests. And, to a great extent, at the expense of the urban poor." As memories of the mid-twentieth century fade, it is worth noting that common reference to "multiclass alliances" under ISI casts a misleadingly benign light on the era. The ISI era was dominated by military regimes. Figure 1.2 indicates the prevalence of military regimes in the mid-twentieth century.

Figure 1.2. Total number of military dictatorships in Latin America, annually.

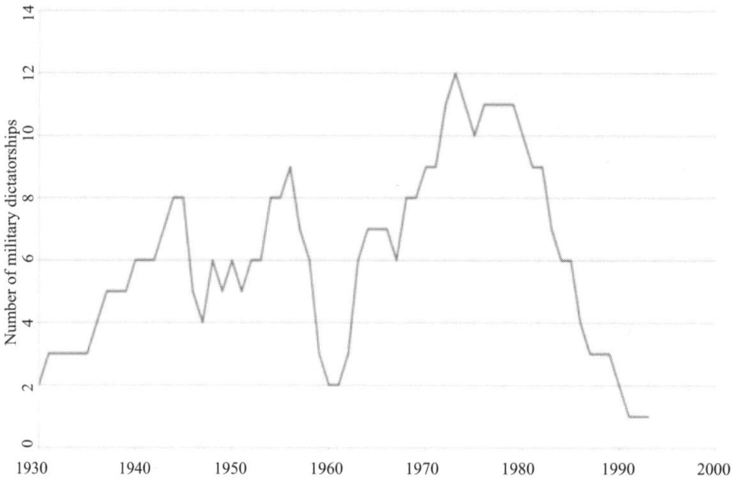

Source: Based on Dix 1994; and Loveman and Davies 1997.

Nor were these benign dictatorships. Rafael Trujillo of the Dominican Republic was said to have fed his opponents' bodies to the sharks; Nicaragua's Anastasio Somoza sold donated blood intended for victims of an earthquake; Peru's Manuel Odría, a self-proclaimed "champion of the poor," lived sumptuously while stifling electoral opposition; Juan Perón himself engaged in repeated violations of constitutional liberties, imprisoning and torturing his opponents and silencing intellectuals with slogans like "Build the Fatherland. Kill a Student." Such repression stifled progressive elements during the ISI era but it also undermined confidence in political stability. Business support for such political repression did not necessarily accompany or produce policies that were uniformly good for business itself.

The rise of socialism in Cuba, Chile, and much later Nicaragua further polarized the region. In Cuba, the adoption of central planning simply eradicated the private sector. In Chile, a combination of expropriation, social legislation, and inflation led to political upheaval under Salvador Allende. Explicit U.S. interference in Nicaragua vanquished hopes for reviving an already moribund economy. Outside of these socialist regimes, perspectives on private property rights became extremely polarized, so that even modest reform met with stiff private sector resistance. Most countries undertook some form of agrarian reform, whether aggressively (as Juan Velasco did in Peru in the late 1960s) or more commonly, with much fanfare but token effort.

The range of state interventions from this era that conservatives saw—and continue to see—as "sovereign theft" is broad. In addition to the inflation tax and banking freezes, it includes coerced sales of property, the withdrawal of concessions in irrigation and mining, the imposition of requirements to exploit unused land (to prove productivity) or to refrain from use (for natural resource protection), and demands for higher "voluntary" royalty payments on mineral concessions (Tomz and Wright 2010). Tension over such policies reflects divisive cultural norms about private property and social entitlement to resources. This tension is still evident in conflicts over mining concessions, dams, and forest protection; policies accepted elsewhere as reasonable regulatory oversight are resisted as infringements on property rights.

As political trends to the left threatened revolution in the 1970s, military regimes turned to hardline neoconservative policies, dramatically clamping down on workers and peasants. In the Southern Cone countries, silencing vocal activists meant torture, death, and disappearances by the tens of thousands. Some thirty thousand Chileans were tortured and perhaps as many Argentines killed in the dirty wars of the 1970s. Uruguay and Brazil followed form with military repression, while political deaths in Colombia and Guatemala were attributed to civil wars that also involved class division.[7] The conservative narrative of this era is that social demands had exceeded the economy's resources, igniting inflation and making repression "necessary" for economic stability. From the perspective of business elites, did the embrace of free market neoconservatism succeed in the 1970s? In fact, this was an era of deep instability that imposed heavy costs on ordinary businesspeople. As in the preceding period, business support for repressive regimes and hostility to progressive reform in the 1970s did not yield policies that were clearly good for business.

In the case of Argentina, the policies under the military dictatorship (1976–83) won early support by reducing inflation to "just" 100 percent, but these policies also led to severe currency overvaluation, rising national debt, and capital flight. The failure of exchange rates to adjust to rising prices meant that real manufacturing costs relative to trade partners doubled between 1977 and 1981 (Dornbusch and de Pablo 1987, 5). Few firms could compete in this situation, particularly as trade liberalization brought in cheap imports. Because of private speculation and public deficits, Argentina's external debt doubled between 1975 and 1979, and then doubled again before the regional debt crisis struck in 1982. The collapse of Argentina's dictatorship in 1983 is often remembered as a consequence of the Malvinas War, but economic chaos had as much to do with the situation. An estimated four hundred thousand firms went bankrupt; most but not all were small and medium-sized firms. Paul Lewis (1992, 461) has recounted the long-established firms that shut down, including La Cantábrica Steel, Austral Airlines, CAMEA Aluminum and Lead Milling, SNIAFA Chemicals, Celulosa Pulp and Paper, General Motors, Chrysler, Citroën, Deutz, John Deere, Singer Sewing Machine, and countless firms in the financial sector. An economy that had grown by 1.7 percent per capita from 1945 to 1975 declined by 1.7 percent per year between 1975 and 1985 (Dornbusch and de Pablo 1987, 3).

Similarly, when Augusto Pinochet's regime took power in Chile in late 1973, it sharply devalued the currency, eliminated price controls, demobilized labor, and forced a dramatic decline in wages. Monetary contraction and financial deregulation increased real interest rates to 178 percent. With sudden trade liberalization, firms faced stiff competition from a surge of imports. As in Argentina, bankruptcies soared. Chile's GDP fell 14 percent in 1975 and again fell 14 percent in 1982 during Latin America's debt crisis (Cardoso and Helwege 1992, 183, 187). Despite a dramatic decline in real wages, businesses unambiguously suffered. Only when the state stepped in with more moderate policies, including temporarily higher tariffs, easier credit, and support of key sectors such as agricultural exports, did sustained growth take off.

Whether the shock treatment menu of economic policies facilitated Chile's later growth in the long run remains a matter of debate. No scholar today argues that authoritarianism is essential to economic growth, but this position long dominated the region's political discourse. As Karen Remmer (1990, 317) noted at the end of the 1980s: "Either because economic austerity is seen as posing different kinds of risks for democratic and authoritarian governments or because the capacity to impose unpopular adjustment programs is assumed to vary with regime type, authoritarianism has been repeatedly linked with the successful management of economic crises, and democracy with failure." Remmer's work challenged this assumption. She found that "the experience of Latin American countries since the outbreak of the debt crisis establishes no basis for asserting that authoritarian regimes outperform democracies in the management of economic crisis" (Remmer 1990, 333).

Bit by bit, as elites came to terms with the economic effects of military rule and the first years of democratic governance, their perspectives regarding both economic policy and politics shifted. To different degrees across the region, elites came to question repression as a default strategy for resolving economic crises. To the extent that "enduring reform" reflects a deep shift in cultural values, this transition—particularly the rejection of torture to intimidate advocates for the poor—is significant.

Even if authoritarianism lost credibility, the neoconservative era of the 1970s reveals an ongoing and paradoxical use of recession as a tool of conservatives. It seems implausible that business elites would benefit from an environment in which sales are plummeting and bankruptcies are widespread. Yet the region has repeatedly resorted to shock treatment instead of more measured adjustments to imbalances. One explanation for support of this strategy is that recessions serve a social function, as unemployment and declining incomes reduce the bargaining power of labor. From a political economy perspective, recessions reset the balance of power between workers and employers. While many firms went bankrupt at the end of the 1970s, unable to adjust to higher interest rates and trade liberalization, others gained from the silencing of wage demands, the opportunity to discipline labor with the threat of layoffs, and the evisceration of unions. Weighed against the longer-term loss of labor's voice, the cost of recession can be seen as small.

The profound recession caused by the debt crisis of the 1980s provided no such advantage to elites. The shock of high global interest rates after a decade of easy borrowing to cover fiscal and trade imbalances set regional output per capita back by 6 percent during the 1980s (Singh et al. 2005).[8] Economic retrenchment was felt by every class. Fiscal deficits and private investment could no longer be financed with foreign loans. But austerity and economic collapse also reduced tax revenues, plunging the region into a contractionary spiral. Unable to impose the cost of debt repayment on any class, governments turned to the printing press; a pandemic of hyperinflation ensued. Inflation peaked in Argentina at 3,079 percent, Brazil at 2,948 percent, Bolivia at 11,750 percent, and Peru at 7,482 percent per annum (IMF 2012).

Business suffered miserably in this lost decade as the burden of debt repayment led to continuous distributional struggles. Governments sought to stop hyperinflation without economic contraction—and without resolving the issue of who should bear the burden of recession—on the theory that inflation was mainly "inertial." Heterodox policies in Argentina, Brazil, and Peru entailed the introduction of new currencies and quixotic efforts to enforce price controls. The costs were immense: the start of each counterinflation phase involved sharp increases in real wages, which then declined rapidly before readjustment. Workers and firms scrambled to circumvent the erosion of income and the distortion of relative prices. The repeated failure of heterodox plans entailed banking crises, freezes on withdrawals, and losses of deposit value. Particularly in Peru, economic dysfunction fueled social dysfunction: violence and guerrilla activities increased as Sendero Luminoso took control of much of the Central Highlands.

In the face of failed efforts to navigate crises without imposing a burden on any class, Latin America lurched to the right again in the 1990s, adopting neoliberal polices associated with the so-called Washington Consensus. These included trade liberalization, privatization of state-owned enterprises, incentives for foreign investment, and the evisceration of labor laws.[9] Although this market-based approach is similar to traditional IMF and World Bank prescriptions, Sebastian Edwards (2008) has argued that its adoption in Latin America was "home grown." Certainly it reflects a resurgence of elites' power to drive policy in favor of business interests despite popular protest. Using exchange rate anchors to establish monetary credibility, inflation was brought well under 10 percent in all but two countries in the 1990s. At first, it seemed a corner had been turned. Mexico's engagement in NAFTA drew foreign investment in pursuit of fresh export opportunities; Argentina's currency board stabilized inflation for the first time in a century by guaranteeing peso convertibility to the U.S. dollar; and Brazil's adoption of the real under the popular Fernando Henrique Cardoso helped the country regain its confidence.

Yet all three of these cases led to spectacular collapse. Mexico's 1994 peso crisis cut imports by a crippling 25 percent and set poverty rates back by a decade. Four years later, the Brazilian real, theoretically anchored to the dollar, lost a third of its value. Argentina's currency board collapse entailed a 30 percent loss in the value of the peso and a stunning 11 percent drop in GDP in 2002. Colombia, Ecuador, and Uruguay also suffered shocks at the turn of the millennium.

What might have given way to authoritarianism in an earlier era met popular anger in democratic elections. Dissatisfaction with neoliberalism brought a wave of leftist leaders to power in the early 2000s. This "ola rosada" revived fears of expropriations, higher taxes, and antibusiness attitudes. In the case of Venezuela's Hugo Chávez and Bolivia's Evo Morales, these fears were realized as policies turned sharply leftward. Elsewhere, even under Nicaragua's Ortega, the rhetoric was not matched in deed. In fact, Michelle Bachelet, Luiz Inácio Lula da Silva, Rafael Correa, Alejandro Toledo, Mauricio Funes, Tabaré Vazquez, and Néstor Kirchner turned out to be far more moderate than anticipated, and their relatively centrist economic policies paved the way for successors like Rousseff, Humala, and Fernández de Kirchner. In the context of an extraordinary commodity boom, these left-leaning regimes have maintained broad popularity and are credited with making substantial headway in reducing the hardship endured by the region's poor. At the same time, they have embraced free-market policies that encourage entrepreneurship among local business elites. A decade that began with financial crises in Argentina, Brazil, and Ecuador and polarized elections of leftist leaders closed as one of the region's most economically dynamic and politically conciliatory periods in its history.

THE TWENTY-FIRST-CENTURY COMMODITY BOOM: THE END OF RECURRENT CRISES?

It is no surprise that Latin Americans are by nature forward-looking. The joke that "Brazil is a country of the future and always will be" can also be interpreted as a comment on its fervent resolve to avoid repeating mistakes of the past. The twentieth century made it abundantly clear to Latin Americans that neither the right nor the left can ignore the hard realities of market imbalances. Price controls, fixed or quasi-fixed exchange rates, and debt finance create the illusion of stability, but without accompanying adjustment, they eventually lead to trouble. Once a crisis begins, neither inflationary finance nor the embrace of harsh market discipline solves the problem. Recognition that these policy extremes fail has been an important reason for declining social tension in the region. The left has hewn closer to economic polices acceptable to business, and businesspeople have not called for a return to the repression of the past, tied as they were to economic policies now seen to have been misguided and even harmful. The test of progress will be in how the region adjusts to new economic crises. The cases examined in this book show the ways in which businesspeople have adjusted to progressive initiatives, beginning before the current boom and continuing through it. Although it is not yet clear that the region has embraced the idea of a shared burden in the face of recession, subsequent chapters suggest the possibility of innovative thinking and new political room for maneuver.

Latin America has enjoyed almost a decade of prosperity. Even despite the U.S. financial crisis, regional growth averaged 4 percent between 2004 and 2013. In the four years before the global financial crisis, every country in the region except El Salvador grew as fast or faster than it had in the previous eleven years, and most recovered quickly.[10] Despite a "left turn" in many countries, business confidence rose to its highest point in decades. Stock markets boomed—Brazil's stock market returned an average of 18.5 percent between 2005 and 2010, compared with a loss of 0.5 percent per year in the United States's S&P 500—and the rush of foreign investment prompted controls to stop *inward* capital flows from distorting exchange rates (Bloomberg 2011 and Gallagher 2010).

Much of this boom has been driven by rapid export growth. Prices of metals, soy, and oil have risen sharply, even as the United States and Europe have struggled with recession (see table 1.2). China's sustained growth, speculative demand for gold, and low interest rates in developed economies explain much of the commodity boom. Its impact is far more broadly felt as optimism

Table 1.2. Percentage of change in prices, 2000–2011

Commodity	Percent change
Tin	514%
Soybeans	293%
Silver	873%
Iron ore	1,367%
Gold	650%
Silver	619%
Crude oil	424%
Copper	533%

Sources: IMF 2011a (Primary Commodities database) and World Bank 2011b (GEM Commodities database), both accessed November 1, 2011.

pervades finance, real estate, and retail markets, and governments spend generously on infrastructure and economic development.

Whether this boom is sustainable is open to debate, but it has made it possible to avoid some of the worst policy mistakes of the twentieth century. A recent World Bank report extols the region's sound macroeconomic policies, reduced external debt, and trade diversification as the source and promise of Latin America's success (World Bank 2010). Gone are concerns about inflation, fiscal deficits financed by foreign borrowing, trade gaps, and veiled references to repression. Is the "bias for hope"—political as well as economic—that Albert Hirschman (1971) saw during the heyday of ISI finally warranted? Although financial analysts in the region remain optimistic, contrarians question whether faith in a "super-cycle" fueled by Chinese demand is merely a speculative bubble. If so, the notion that Latin America has moved beyond its difficult past may be, as Edwards (2010, 225) puts it, "wishful thinking at its worst." Much of the debate about Latin America's future hinges on the extent of its dependence on China. China's growing imports have fueled demand and confidence. Between 2000 and

2010, annual trade with China increased fivefold and Chinese direct investment into Latin America rose from $2.7 billion to $59 billion (Leahy 2011b).

China is not the only factor at work driving up commodity prices—droughts, wars in the Middle East, low interest rates in the United States, and currency speculation also play a role. Local business elites are now part of this boom, investing in agricultural land, mining concessions, and oil. Even as foreign money floods into the region, domestic financing accounts for a larger share of investment than it has in the past. If managed right, the boom can provide the foundation for modernization and enduring reform. But a development model based on the assumption of an ongoing commodity windfall is susceptible to the same cyclical disappointments that characterize much of Latin American history. Chinese demand will remain strong—the empty rice bowls of the Cultural Revolution are history—but current supply bottlenecks and speculative forces will inevitably ease, leading to lower prices and slower growth.[11] The development of massive mineral reserves in Africa and the restoration of confidence in global currencies have already brought down metal prices. Similarly, new strategies for soy cultivation in the tropics are being implemented in Africa, and the elimination of biofuel subsidies in developed countries are easing pressure on food prices.

Governments are currently able to finance budgets with help from revenues derived from commodity exports. Absent a commodity boom, they will struggle. Latin American countries continue to avoid the task of raising tax rates on wealthy individuals, relying heavily on commodity taxes and royalties. Peru, for example, depended on minerals for 11 percent of its revenue in 2009, compared with 4 percent in 2002 (Baca, Ávila, and Muñoz 2010). Tax structures ought to be reformed to capture a wider sectoral base, with windfall revenues set aside for a downturn in commodity prices, as Chile has, but democratic regimes find little electoral support for such an approach. Fortunately, and in a testament to lessons learned from the past, few Latin American countries are now deeply indebted in foreign currency. There is also little political pressure to borrow against future commodity earnings to appease current class tensions, as happened in the 1970s. External debt as a share of GDP has fallen by more than half since the early 2000s in Argentina, Brazil, Ecuador, Honduras, and Peru.

Nevertheless, no regime is immune to speculative attack. As Dani Rodrik (2011) puts it: "At the slightest hint of things going awry, investors and depositors pull up stakes and move capital out of the country, thereby precipitating the collapse of the currency." Indirectly, dependence on volatile commodity prices can trigger financial insolvency, capital flight, and exchange rate instability. The good news is that there are more mechanisms in place to cushion a fiscal crisis: central bank independence, generous reserves of foreign currency, and flexible exchange rates enable policy makers to make gradual adjustments rather than postponing matters until a collapse is inevitable. With growth, however, has come an increasingly complex private financial sector that can also trigger instability. Newly affluent consumers are spending on credit, creating a bubble not unlike the subprime mortgage crisis in the United States: as long as growth continues, the loans seem entirely justified (Pearson 2011). As the region becomes a major new market for everything from washing machines to yachts, excessive leveraging puts the economy as a whole at risk. The resulting vulnerability of local banks, to say nothing of overindebted families, depends on how well financial institutions are regulated. Although banking regulation in Latin America is stronger than ever, regulators find it difficult to appraise assets in a boom because all evidence points to strong balance sheets until the bubble bursts. In becoming more like the developed world, the region has taken on some of the same risks.

The region's response to slower growth will almost certainly avoid a reversion to hyperinflation or brutal authoritarianism. Modern social movements and conservative business lobbyists both offer far more sophisticated macroeconomic agendas than those of the twentieth century, and democratic elections now seem to yield less extreme leaders. But as in developed countries, recession will force hard choices between fiscal austerity and higher taxes. Neither extreme will advance political and social reconciliation.

THE CHALLENGE OF CREATING ECONOMIC INCLUSION

What has this commodity-driven boom meant for working-class Latin Americans, and in turn, for political stability? For all of its success in generating foreign exchange, neither agro-exports nor mining nor oil extraction has directly created many jobs. Just 8 percent of Guatemala's Marlin Mine revenues are estimated to go toward local wages (Zarsky and Stanley 2011). Similarly, employment in soy, the region's fastest growing agricultural commodity, has fallen in absolute terms in the past decade (Pérez, Schlesinger, and Wise 2008). Rural poverty rates remain stubbornly high throughout the region. Yet there are jobs, many jobs. As wealth trickles down through finance, construction, retail, and government spending, unemployment rates have fallen. Indirectly, the fortunes of labor are increasingly tied to commodities as other sectors lag. Commodity exports and investment in pursuit of natural resources have caused significant exchange rate appreciation.[12] The resulting loss of competitiveness in industrial exports is most evident in low-skilled, labor-intensive manufacturing, particularly textiles and assembly work.[13] Strong currencies, combined with fierce competition from China and other low-cost suppliers (such as Bangladesh, Cambodia, and Vietnam) have stunted manufacturing growth (Gallagher and Porzecanski 2010). Instead, the service sector is growing.

Economic restructuring in recent years has left workers unwittingly vulnerable to recession: for now, their wages easily buy goods and their children face prosperous futures. But as in the United States and Europe, savings rates are low and poorer residents have few assets to fall back on as commodity prices and capital flows decline. What can governments do to protect social progress in the face of weaker growth? Most countries need more fiscal capacity to counter a downturn, safety nets that provide genuine security to vulnerable workers, and policies that improve competitiveness in globalized economies. In addition, they need reformist initiatives of the sort described in the *Enduring Reform* cases, new policies and institutional arrangements that reshape both development and distribution in progressive directions. By creating more opportunities for entrepreneurship, creative agency, and civic participation, ordinary people who have been marginalized in the past can contribute to building a more resilient economy.

Latin America's industrial challenge is to raise productivity, given its high wages relative to other developing regions. It must move up the skill ladder faster than Asia, a huge challenge given the quality of its education systems. School enrollment is radically higher than it was twenty years ago, but the same is true throughout the developing world. Latin American students score poorly on international exams in reading, math, and science compared against their Asian counterparts (OECD 2010). In these exams, even Chile falls far short of the developed countries, and poorer countries like Peru and Brazil are disturbingly weak across disciplines. Latin American students also suffer more as a consequence of their parents' poor education: adults ages twenty-five to sixty-five have an average of only 8.4 years of schooling (World Bank 2011, 24). The most marginalized and poorest groups are those of indigenous and African descent. Although it is no longer illegal to educate indigenous people—as it was in Bolivia in the mid-twentieth century—indigenous people fall significantly behind their nonindigenous counterparts in education (table 1.3). In the early 2000s, Harry Patrinos, Emmanuel Skoufias, and Trine Lunde (2007, 2) found that "indigenous peoples' poverty has not diminished over time. . . . [E]ven when they are able to accumulate human capital this does not translate into significantly greater earnings or a closing of the poverty gap with the nonindigenous population."

Social reform aimed at ending discrimination, including affirmative action

Table 1.3. Years of schooling, latest year available

Country	Indigenous	Nonindigenous
Peru[a]	6.4	8.7
Mexico[d]	6.3	8.6
Bolivia[b]	5.9	9.6
Brazil[b]	4.6	6.6
Ecuador[c]	4.3	6.9
Guatemala[c]	2.5	5.7

Source: Hall and Patrinos 2012.
Notes: [a] 2001, [b] 2002, [c] 2006, [d] 2008

programs in universities, is just beginning to take hold in the region. For now, indigenous and Afro-Latino people remain too socially segregated to make their way out of poverty. As Patrinos, Skoufias, and Lunde (2007) have argued, marginalized ethnicities rely heavily on members of their own communities ("bonding capital") but often lack enough "bridging capital"—social contacts, mannerisms, common experiences—to gain access to promising career opportunities. All of the enduring reforms described in this book provide mechanisms for addressing these exclusions through political participation, economic initiatives, and cultural recognition of marginalized ethnic groups as and the urban poor.

Inclusion requires more than better schools in poor areas: it entails integrating communities so that interactions occur across a wide spectrum of occupations and incomes. The policies to promote such a transformation are frustratingly difficult to identify. Policies that grant more agency to marginalized groups—participatory budgeting, rights to prior consultation about new extractive industries, broader representation of ethnic groups in legislatures—also involve a loss of control by elites. Small steps such as integrated public housing, affordable public transportation, job clearinghouses, and more effective policing to reduce violence can begin to provide some of the social benefits that Ananya Roy (2005) claims are now denied in an invisible process of exclusion in slums.[14] So far, though, electoral politics have given indigenous and Afro-Latinos only limited "rights to the city."

Even among dominant ethnicities, many workers remain trapped in the informal sector. Estimates of this "tertiatization" of labor range from 40 percent to 60 percent of the labor force. The erosion of formal sector jobs and particularly of union power means that workers gain little from minimum wage increases, labor laws to protect job security, or better pensions. Instead, the precariousness of their situation hinges on macroeconomic conditions and the generosity of redistributive programs. In fact, ninety-three million Latin Americans depend on conditional cash transfer programs (CCTs) like Brazil's Bolsa Familia, Chile's Solidario, Colombia's Familias en Acción, and Mexico's Oportunidades to supplement meager incomes (United Nations 2010). These programs offer critical help to the poor, provided their children attend school and get regular health checkups. Despite the tiny size of these transfers—typically less than fifty dollars per month and less than 1 percent of GDP—they are extremely popular.

In the long run, the focus of CCTs on education will increase worker productivity and raise wages. For now, their main success is in generating political support for incumbent regimes. Despite the efforts of progressive policy makers to broaden eligibility and add dimensions to antipoverty programs, the share of national income accruing to the poor remains small. Regionally, the poorest quintile receives 3.5 percent of national income, only slightly more than the 3.2 percent it received in 1990. In some countries, including Brazil and Colombia, the bottom fifth of the population does not receive even 3 percent of national income (Economic Commission on Latin America and the Caribbean 2010, 391). According to Leonardo Gasparini and Nora Lustig (2011, 8), "it is likely that levels of income inequality in Latin America at the beginning of the second decade of this millennium are not very different from those prevailing in the 1970s."

Beyond narrow design criticisms that are now being addressed—a lack of toddler care, unaffordable school fees, unrealistic expectations for working women—CCTs and related programs are arguably too small to effectively protect the poor and working class from the vagaries of a market economy. Their harshest critics refer to CCTs as compensatory policies that "operate as a buffer in the face of neoliberal reforms" (Domingues 2008, 19) rather than building a genuinely inclusive economy. Even some early proponents now stress the need to incorporate more workers into systems that provide unemployment insurance, pensions, and health care.[15] Yet this is only feasible if workers participate in the formal sector's benefit structure—and for that, workers need regular secure jobs in which they pay taxes.[16]

The task, then, is to create diversified economies that incorporate Latin America's large, informal labor force. In a highly competitive global market, Latin American firms must do so in ways that exploit their locational advantages and natural resource endowments. Mexico has successfully leveraged its proximity to the United States in automobile parts, electronics, and beverages. Brazil has established itself as a leading exporter of steel, airplanes, and oil services, and it has moved "up the value chain" in processing orange juice, poultry, and animal feed. But a closer look at these sectors also reveals foreign names like Honda, Tyson, Cargill, Huawei, and Walmart. Alongside business elites who have thrived in homegrown firms like Vale, Cutrale, Cemex, and Bimbo are others who have faltered in this newly competitive investment environment. "Moving up the value chain" is no easy panacea against global competition. To succeed, workers and entrepreneurs alike must have cutting-edge technical skills, and they must create innovative products with a distinctive Latin American identity that is not easily replicated in regions with cheaper wages.

The virtuous cycle that can promote inclusive, stable growth in the twenty-first century requires unleashing the creativity and capability of Latin America's relatively youthful populations. Here—not in the stilted clubs of the old elite—lies the region's potential. To realize this potential, young adults need better training, more exposure to global markets and trends, and the social support that enables young workers with families to succeed. Nowhere is this more obvious than in the student protests for affordable college in Chile: young people know that their future depends on access to skills that enable them to compete globally. With higher productivity, these workers can generate the incomes that make broader safety nets affordable.

Much is already being done to create inclusive, competitive economies, but in the short run, this is expensive. Absent booming commodity revenues, the wealthy will need to relinquish privilege and pay more taxes. At present, the region not only has a low tax rate as a share of GDP, relying heavily on nontax revenues from commodities, but it also eschews direct taxes that can improve tax progressivity (see figure 1.3 for regional comparisons). As a result, fiscal burdens fall heavily on the working class. According to Nora Lustig (2011), the redistributive effect of taxes—even including transfers—is small: where they reduce the Gini coefficient by 12 percentage points in Europe, the effect in the five largest Latin American economies is only about a 1 percentage point reduction. In Bolivia and Brazil, Lustig (2011) finds that many of the poor are actually net contributors to the fiscal system, despite the fact that they receive transfer payments. The alternative to repression and austerity must combine policies that raise productivity with measures to redistribute income.

Will business elites agree to new taxes? Tax reform rarely sits well politically, particularly when it involves shifting from indirect to direct taxes. Nonetheless, better enforcement of existing laws and a gradual change in tax structures can yield more progressivity. With stricter targeting of social programs, now viewed as political patronage, and more spending on programs that raise productivity, such as technical training, governments can become more effec-

Figure 1.3. International comparison of fiscal burden, 2005.

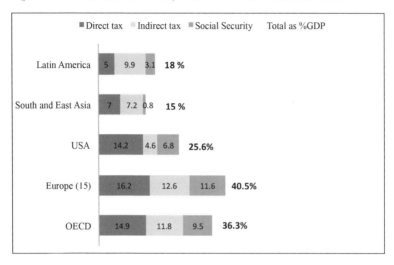

Source: Gómez-Sabaini and Martner 2007.

tive agents of economic inclusion. Combined with efforts to end corruption and reduce financial risk through sound macroeconomic management, such reforms can serve the interests of both business and workers.

BUILDING AN INCLUSIVE FUTURE

If there is an outstanding lesson from Latin America's economic experiences in the twentieth century, it is that conflict over the distribution of income hurts everyone. While business elites share a common interest in secure property rights, low taxes, cheap wages, and reduced vulnerability to shocks, they also benefit from the political stability that comes from finding common ground with their fellow citizens. With democratization and the end of the Cold War, repression is no longer an option in response to popular anger over austerity, and in any case, it hardly proved helpful to long-run growth in the past. The conquering of old nemeses—external debt, inflation, rigid exchange rates—has yielded new confidence in the region's economic prospects. Growth has made it possible for governments to finance business-friendly trade promotion and infrastructure as well as modest increases in social spending. For the first time in years, political debate focuses on how to distribute the fruits of growth rather than the burden of recession. The challenge is now to improve the competitiveness of Latin American firms and reduce the vulnerability of all—business elites and workers—to the vagaries of a primary commodity boom, while at the same time fostering progressive initiatives that construct more equitable and democratic forms of development.

The current boom creates enormous opportunities for reform, and indeed changes are already impressive. A glance back to the twentieth century shows how far the region has come. However, much remains to be done, and some of what is enjoyed today is vulnerable to a collapse in commodity prices. Disappointment risks political instability and a return to economic turmoil. If business elites want less responsibility for those at the bottom of the income scale, certainly the poor want more opportunity to develop their own lives. Is there another strategy that works for both? Policies long opposed as entitlements such as good education and integrated safe cities can raise productivity *and* build a stronger social fabric. Ultimately, Latin America's distributional tug of war must yield to a shared vision for the future. Enduring political and economic stability will come with investments in inclusive social policies.

NOTES

1. See Sachs 1989 as well as Dornbusch and Edwards 1991 for several variations on this theme.

2. As John H. Coatsworth (2008) has pointed out, this history is more complex than mere reference to colonialism suggests. Inequality was roughly as high in New England in the mid-1800s (with Gini coefficients on the order of .70) but fell much faster there in the succeeding century and a half. *Why* this difference occurred is the subject of much speculation. See Vargas Llosa 2005, and the so-called LLSV literature (La Porta, Lopez-de-Silanes, and Shleifer 2008).

3. See World Bank 2011. Notwithstanding this publication's title, *A Break with History: Fifteen Years of Declining Inequality*, it notes that the share of income received by the bottom decile has not changed, "remaining between 0.9–1.0 in fifteen years" (4).

4. Many constitutions guarantee such rights as "education, health, work, leisure, security, social security, protection of motherhood and childhood, and assistance to the destitute" (O'Grady 2001). See Segura-Ubiergo 2007 for a detailed description of the evolution of the welfare state.

5. See Bailey 2006, Seligson 2002, and Svensson 2005 for discussion of the economic consequences of corruption.

6. Several countries experienced high average annual inflation between 1960 and 1969: Brazil (46 percent), Chile (25 percent), and Argentina (23 percent). Sporadic episodes of inflation also occurred in the 1950s—for example, Chile's price index rose 83 percent in 1955; Argentina's rose 50 percent in 1951.

7. Political violence was also evident in Bolivia, with the Massacre of Tolata in 1974, and in Mexico, with the Night of Tlatelolco in 1968.

8. By contrast, Asian economies grew by 60 percent in the 1980s.

9. In fact, inflation had almost entirely eroded minimum wages in the 1980s, accomplishing a de facto collapse of labor protection before the neoliberal era.

10. There are exceptions to this generalization about prosperity: Central American countries beset by drug violence have struggled, as has Venezuela after 2008.

11. A decline in gold and copper prices to half of the current level—a return to 2005 prices—would reduce Peru's exports by nearly a third.

12. The Brazilian *real* rose 47 percent against other currencies between 2005 and 2010 (IMF 2011b).

13. Commodities grew from 40 percent of regional exports in 2000 to 52 percent in 2008 (IMF 2011b).

14. See Roy 2005 and Perlman 2010 for discussion of marginalization and public policy in urban spaces.

15. See Levy 2008.

16. Several countries are experimenting with voluntary payments into state pension plans. For social programs to act as effective insurance, compulsory participation is important to prevent adverse selection and timing of participation to game the system.

REFERENCES

Baca, E., G. Ávila, and A. Muñoz. 2010. *Vigilancia de las industrias extractivas: Reporte Nacional No 11.* Lima, Peru: Grupo Propuesta Ciudadana.

Bailey, J. 2006. "Corruption and Democratic Governability in Latin America: Issues of Types, Arenas, Perceptions, and Linkages." Paper delivered at the meeting of the Latin American Studies Association, San Juan, Puerto Rico, March 15–18, 2006.

Bloomberg.com. 2010. Market data. Accessed November 17, 2011.

Cardoso, E., and A. Helwege. 1991. "Populism, Profligacy, and Redistribution." In *The Macroeconomics of Populism in Latin America,* edited by R. Dornbusch and S. Edwards, 45–70. Chicago: Chicago University Press.

Cardoso, E., and A. Helwege. 1992. *Latin America's Economy: Diversity, Trends, and Conflicts.* Cambridge: MIT Press.

Coatsworth, J. H. 2008. "Inequality, Institutions, and Economic Growth in Latin America." *Journal of Latin American Studies* 40: 545–69.

Da Silva, J. G., E. S. Gomez, and C. S. Rodrigo. 2010. *Latin America's Agricultural Boom and Persistence of Rural Poverty: Some Reflections.* Santiago: Food and Agriculture Organization (FAO).

Dayton-Johnson, J. 2008. "Taxes and Spending in Latin America: First Stability, Now Development." *Policy Insight: OECD Development Centre* 77: 1–2.

Dix, R. H. 1994. "Military Coups and Military Rule in Latin America." *Armed Forces and Society* 20 (3): 439–56.

Domingues, J. M. 2008. *Latin America and Contemporary Modernity: A Sociological Interpretation.* New York: Routledge.

Dornbusch, R., and J. C. de Pablo. 1987. "Argentina: Debt and Macroeconomic Instability." Working Paper 2378. Cambridge, MA: National Bureau of Economic Research (NBER).

Dornbusch, R., and S. Edwards. 1991. *The Macroeconomics of Populism in Latin America.* Chicago: University of Chicago Press.

Economic Commission on Latin America and the Caribbean. 2010. *Achieving the Millennium Development Goals with Equality in Latin America and the Caribbean.* Santiago: United Nations.

Edwards, S. 2008. "Globalization, Growth, and Crises: The View from Latin America." Working Paper 14034. Cambridge, MA: NBER.

Edwards, S. 2010. *Left Behind: Latin America and the False Promise of Populism.* Chicago: University of Chicago Press.

Fiszbein, A., and N. Schady. 2009. *Conditional Cash Transfers: Reducing Present and Future Poverty.* Washington, D.C.: World Bank.

Gallagher, K. 2010. "Control That Capital." *FP.com.* March 29. Online at http://www.foreign policy.com/articles/2010/03/29/control_that_capital. Accessed April 4, 2013.

Gallagher, K., and R. Porzecanski. 2010. *The Dragon in the Room: China and the Future of Latin American Industrialization.* Redwood City, CA: Stanford University Press.

Gasparini, L., G. Cruces, and L. Tornarolli. 2009. "Recent Trends in Income Inequality in Latin America." Working Paper 132. Society for the Study of Economic Inequality (ECINEQ).

Gasparini, L., and N. Lustig. 2011. "The Rise and Fall of Income Inequality in Latin America." In *Oxford Handbook of Latin American Economics,* edited by J. A. Ocampo and J. Ros, 691–714. Oxford: Oxford University Press.

Gómez-Sabaini, J. C., and R. Martner. 2007. "Taxation Structure and Main Tax Policy Issues in Latin America." In *Tax Systems and Tax Reforms in Latin America,* edited by L. Bernardi, A. Barreix, A. Marenzi, and P. Profeta, 19–40. New York: Routledge.

Hall, G., and H. Patrinos. 2006. *Indigenous Peoples, Poverty, and Human Development in Latin America.* London: Palgrave.

Hall, G., and H. Patrinos. 2012. *Indigenous Peoples, Poverty, and Development: A Seven-Country Study of Indigenous People.* New York: Cambridge University Press.

Hirschman, A. O. 1968. "The Political Economy of Import-Substituting Industrialization in Latin America." *Quarterly Journal of Economics* 82 (1): 1–32.

Hirschman, A. O. 1971. *A Bias for Hope: Essays on Development in Latin America.* New Haven: Yale University Press.

Hirschman, A. O. 1987. "The Political Economy of Latin American Development: Seven Exercises in Retrospection." *Latin American Research Review* 22 (3): 7–36.

InterAmerican Development Bank (IADB). 2010. *Ten Years after the Take-Off: Taking Stock of China–Latin America and the Caribbean Economic Relations.* Washington, D.C.: IADB, Integration and Trade Sector.

International Monetary Foundation (IMF). 2011a. Primary Commodities Database. Online at http://www.imf.org/external/np/res/commod/index.aspx. Accessed November 1, 2011.

International Monetary Foundation (IMF). 2011b. *Regional Economic Outlook 2011.* Washington, D.C.: IMF.

International Monetary Foundation (IMF). 2011c. *World Economic Outlook 2011*. Washington, D.C.: IMF.

International Monetary Foundation (IMF). 2012. World Economic Outlook Database. October 2012. Online at http://www.imf.org/external/pubs/ft/weo/2012/02/weodata/weorept .aspx?pr.x=51&pr.y=9&sy=1980&ey=2003&ssd=1&sort=country&ds=.&br=1&c=213%2C21 8%2C223%2C293&s=PCPIPCH%2CPCPIEPCH&grp=0&a. Accessed April 4, 2013.

La Porta, R., F. Lopez-de-Silanes, and A. Shleifer. 2008. "The Economic Consequences of Legal Origins." *Journal of Economic Literature* 46 (2): 285–332.

Leahy, J. 2011a. "Brazil Credit Bubble Fear as Defaults Rise." *Financial Times.* June 19.

Leahy, J. 2011b. "Brazil Ponders the Role of the Renminbi." *Financial Times.* June 6.

Levy, S. 2008. *Good Intentions, Bad Outcomes: Social Policy, Informality, and Economic Growth in Mexico*. Washington, D.C.: Brookings Institution Press.

Lewis, P. 1992. *The Crisis of Argentine Capitalism*. Chapel Hill: University of North Carolina Press.

Loveman, B., and T. M. Davies. 1997. *The Politics of Antipolitics: The Military in Latin America*. Lanham: Rowman and Littlefield.

Lustig, N., coordinator. 2011. "Fiscal Policy and Income Redistribution in Latin America." Tulane Economics Working Paper 1124. New Orleans: Tulane University.

Ocampo, J. A., and J. Ros. 2011. *Oxford Handbook of Latin American Economics*. Oxford: Oxford University Press.

O'Grady, A. 2001. "Too Many Promises: How Latin American Constitutions Weaken the Rule of Law." *Wall Street Journal.* November 16, 2001.

Organisation for Economic Cooperation and Development (OECD). 2010. *PISA 2009 Results: Executive Summary*. Paris: OECD.

Organization of American States (OAS). "Observatorio Interamericano de Seguridad." Online at http://www.oas.org/dsp/espanol/cpo_observatorio.asp. Accessed June 28, 2011.

Patrinos, H., E. Skoufias, and T. Lunde. 2007. "Indigenous Peoples in Latin America: Economic Opportunities and Social Networks." World Bank Policy Research Working Paper 4227, May.

Pearson, S. 2011. "It's Official: Brazilians Are the World's Best Shoppers." *Financial Times.* June 7.

Pérez, M., S. Schlesinger, and T. A. Wise. 2008. *The Promise and the Perils of Agricultural Trade Liberalization: Lessons from Latin America*. Washington, D.C.: Washington Office on Latin America and Global Development and Environment Institute.

Perlman, J. 2010. *Favela: Four Decades of Living on the Edge in Rio de Janeiro*. Oxford: Oxford University Press.

Petras, J. 2006. "'Centre-Left' Regimes in Latin America." *Countercurrents.org.* April 8. Online at http://www.countercurrents.org/petras080406.htm. Accessed July 11, 2011.

Remmer, K. L. 1990. "Democracy and Economic Crisis: The Latin American Experience." *World Politics* 42 (3): 315–35.

Rodrik, D. 2011. "Economists and Democracy." Project Syndicate. Online at http://www.project-syndicate.org/commentary/rodrik56/English. Accessed June 27, 2011.

Roy, A. 2005. "Urban Informality: Toward an Epistemology of Planning." *Journal of the American Planning Association* 71 (2): 147–58.

Sachs, J. 1989. "Social Conflict and Populist Policies in Latin America." Working Paper No. 2897. NBER.

Santiso, J. 2006. *Latin America's Political Economy of the Possible*. Cambridge: MIT Press.

Segura-Ubiergo, A. 2007. *The Political Economy of the Welfare State in Latin America: Globalization, Democracy, and Development*. Cambridge: Cambridge University Press.

Seligson, M. 2002. "The Impact of Corruption on Regime Legitimacy: A Comparative Study of Four Latin America Countries." *Journal of Politics* 64 (2): 408–33.

Sheahan, J. 1987. *Patterns of Development in Latin America: Poverty, Repression, and Economic Strategy*. Princeton: Princeton University Press.

Singh, A., A. Belaisch, C. Collyns, P. De Masi, R. Krieger, G. Meredith, and R. Rennhack. 2005. *Stabilization and Reform in Latin America: A Macroeconomic Perspective on the Experience since the Early 1990s*. Washington, D.C.: International Monetary Fund.

Soares, F., R. Ribas, and R. Osorio. 2010. "Bolsa Familia: Cash Transfer Programs in Comparative Perspective." *Latin American Research Review* 45 (2): 173–90.

Svensson, J. 2005. "Eight Questions about Corruption." *Journal of Economic Perspectives* 19 (3): 19–42.

Tomz, M., and M. L. J. Wright. 2010. "Sovereign Theft: Theory and Evidence about Sovereign Default and Expropriation." In *The Natural Resource Trap*, edited by W. Hogan and F. Sturzenegger, 69–110. Cambridge: MIT Press.

United Nations. 2010. *In Latin America, Cash Transfers Provide Family Safety Net*. Online at http://www.un-foodsecurity.org/node/441. Accessed July 11, 2011.

Vargas Llosa, A. 2005. *Liberty for Latin America: How to Undo Five Hundred Years of State Oppression*. New York: Farrar, Straus, and Giroux.

World Bank. 2010. *Globalized, Resilient, Dynamic: The New Face of Latin America and the Caribbean*. Washington, D.C.: World Bank.

World Bank. 2011a. *A Break with History: Fifteen Years of Declining Inequality*. Washington, D.C.: World Bank.

World Bank. 2011b. Global Economic Monitor (GEM) Commodities Database. Online at http://data.worldbank.org/data-catalog/commodity-price-data. Accessed November 1, 2011.

World Bank. World Development Indicators (WDI). Online at http://databank.worldbank.org/ddp/home.do. Accessed November 1, 2010, and June 1, 2014.

Zarsky, L., and L. Stanley. 2011. "Searching for Gold in the Highlands of Guatemala: Assessing Benefits, Costs and Sustainability of the Marlin Mine." Working paper. Global Development and Environment Institute.

2

RETHINKING THE REVOLUTION

LATIN AMERICAN SOCIAL MOVEMENTS AND THE STATE IN
THE TWENTY-FIRST CENTURY

Wendy Wolford

IT IS HARD TO KNOW when to start this chapter on social movements in Latin America today. A newcomer to the topic could be forgiven for believing that social mobilization in the region began in the 1990s in response to the package of neoliberal economic policies established by northern governments and imposed by "multilateral" financial institutions during the late 1980s and 1990s. This impression is reinforced by the explosion of academic writing on Latin American social movements in the last decade of the twentieth century.[1] Inspired by the Zapatista uprising in southern Mexico on January 1, 1994, grassroots mobilization swept onto the global scene—and conscience—with the first World Social Forum (WSF) held in the otherwise fusty southern city of Porto Alegre, Brazil, in January 2001.[2] This transnational "movement of movements," as the broad alter-globalization landscape has come to be called, gained purpose and momentum organizing against neoliberal economic and political initiatives that lowered trade barriers (particularly in the Global South), privatized natural and capital resources, and reorganized state involvement in the economy, rolling out new regulations to promote an unregulated market.

But this is too recent a moment to begin a history of social mobilization in Latin America. Protests against neoliberalism in the 1990s were honed during the so-called lost decade of the 1980s, when people marched in the streets to demand an end to harsh austerity measures imposed in the name of fiscal balance by the International Monetary Fund (IMF). Public demonstrations against high food prices and subsidy cuts imposed by the technically named Structural Adjustment Programs (SAPs) broke out in many countries, including Bolivia in 1985, Ecuador in 1987, Venezuela in 1989, and Honduras in 1991 (Touissaint 1999 and Danaher 2001). That these measures were regressive and hurt the poor disproportionately was not a matter of debate; where the protestors and the technocrats disagreed was on whether the pain of the poorest was either necessary or acceptable (Karl 2003, 133–37; see also Oxhorn 2003, 50–52).

Even then, Latin American social movements did not have their beginning in the anti-SAP mobilizations of the 1980s. These "rice and bean" demonstrations (or "riots" as they are somewhat dismissively called) were themselves both a cry of disillusionment over the poverty of a much anticipated return to democracy after years of military rule (Eckstein and Wickham-Crowley 2003, 13; and Scherer-Warren and Krischke 1987) and also products of a new repertoire of resistance that grew out of protests against those same military dictatorships (Perrault 2008 and Stahler-Sholk 2008).[3] From the student movement in Mexico to feminism in Brazil to the Sandinistas in Nicaragua and the mothers and grandmothers of the Plaza de Mayo in Argentina, resistance in the shadow of authoritarian rule generated perhaps the first broad and sustained civil society in Latin American history (Alvarez 1990 and Martins 2000).

But the resistance movements of the military period were organized by many of the same leaders and what social movement scholars call "institutional hosts" (Houtzager and Kurtz 2000) that led or facilitated popular mobilizations from the late 1940s through the 1960s (Medeiros 1989).[4] During this period, a fervor of Communist Party organizing, liberation theology–inspired activism, and trade unionism came together with peasant movements, student groups, and more. These organizers were inspired by international discourses of socialism and liberation theology but faithfully national in their attempt to redirect place-specific histories of colonization and exploitation (Lehmann 1990). These mobilizations were initially tolerated by domestic and foreign governments until democratic socialism in sugar-rich Guatemala and party Communism in Cuba threatened to dramatically rework relationships between citizen, state, and property. After 1961, claims for distributive justice (such as then Brazilian President João Goulart's nervous approximation to communist and peasant activists in Brazil) provoked anxiety in government halls to the north and led to military repression in the south.

Even the ill-fated protests of the 1940s and 1960s drew on a long historical legacy of localized and transnational anticolonial, anti-imperial, and antirepublic mobilizations that ran throughout the eighteenth, nineteenth, and twentieth centuries. Contemporary claims for pluriethnic and even plurinational states (in Ecuador and Bolivia, particularly) draw on memories and oral traditions from Latin America's original peoples (Perrault 2008), while race-based and peasant organizing calls upon the strength of fugitive slave communities that developed in conscious repudiation of the Manichean world into which they had been imported or born (Dixon 2008, 182; and French 2009). Many of the so-called new social movements of the 1990s draw their inspiration from the precolonial period; manifested, invoked, and embodied in the organizing for the doomed quincentennial of 1992.[5] They draw on more than five hundred years of exploitation and forced labor (Deere and Royce 2009, 2; also see Escobar 2010).[6]

If social mobilization in Latin America is not by itself new (one thinks of the escalator moving back in time invoked by Raymond Williams in his 1973 book *City and Country*), then what exactly distinguishes and defines the current moment? Arturo Escobar (2010) has suggested that we are at a "crossroads" for social mobilization as movement activists, politicians, and even business elites negotiate new political ontologies—innovative ways of being political. Debates over how best to be and think politically are riddled with a variety of "posts" (postliberal, post-neoliberal, post–Washington Consensus, postrevolutionary, postmodern, postdevelopment), and social movements are actively constructing a political landscape through the "posts," each one of which signifies the failure of yet another grand narrative. The initiatives analyzed in this book provide some examples of actors throughout Latin America who have negotiated the ruptures of "crisis" (environmental crisis, economic crisis, ethnic crisis, and political crisis) to reimagine productive engagements with state, civil society, and market actors.

Although mainstream observers generally see the relationship between social movements and the state in terms of which political candidates social movement leaders will support in formal elections, there is a much broader— and much more important—set of political relationships being created. These relationships do not allow for a neat delineation between social movement and state (different ways of being political) but rather reflect a partial embedding of the two (both strategic and unintentional). Social movements—as organizations, as groups of people, and as sets of ideologies—from Mexico to Argentina are increasingly active partners and even leaders in state politics and practices; they oversee the distribution of resources, demand the construction of new political rules, and protest for a broader set of definitions as to what and who constitutes citizenship. But more than that, as many observers have pointed out, social movement activists are now working within the state such that the supposed division between state and social movement (a division upon which the definition of the latter rested for many years; see Tarrow 1998) is being broken down: guerrilla leaders have become party politicians; coca farmers, indigenous leaders, and trade union activists are presidents; and members of active movements continue to move between technical branches of the government, trade unions, nongovernmental organizations, and political parties, retaining their activist sensibilities and being given new platforms on and with which to work. It is within this specific moment of social movement activity that the reforms discussed throughout this book—related to but distinct from movements—have emerged, often with the imaginaries, support, and activists of social movements behind them.

At the same time, innovative practices have been organized within the state that look more like social movement practices, such as open constituent assemblies, coordinating councils, and participatory budgeting (see chapter 4, "Democracy by Invitation," by Jeffrey W. Rubin and Sergio Baierle in this book). In turn, social movements and other civil society initiatives that strive for autonomy have fought for the space to enact practices of governance in their own fashion: Zapatista communities govern sovereign communities through Juntas de Buen Gobierno; Mayan migrants in San Cristóbal de Las Casas organize transportation and policing networks in newly settled *colonias* (see chapter 3, "The Urban Indigenous Movement and Elite Accommodation in San Cristóbal, Chiapas, Mexico, 1975–2008," by Jan Rus and Gaspar Morquecho Escamilla in this book); workers in the Recuperated Factories of the greater Buenos Aires region organize alternative economies based on collective production and cooperation (see chapter 5, "Recuperated Factories in Contemporary Buenos Aires from the Perspective of Workers and Businessmen," by Carlos A. Forment in this book); and indigenous communities in the Amazon River basin region claim a measure of territorial autonomy linked to ethnic and environmental authority (Allegretti and Schmink 2009).

So even though social mobilization is not by itself novel, it is clearly operating in—and constructing—a new and different context, which has repercussions for a broad range of activism, policy making, and reform that go beyond the work of social movements themselves. This chapter outlines some of the most important aspects of the current conjuncture—the early years of the twenty-first century—to show how the current moment reflects the sedimented power hierarchies of the past while offering new opportunities and challenges for social movement activists. As volume editors Jeffrey W. Rubin and Vivienne Bennett point out in their introduction, these opportunities and challenges are linked to the changing dynamics of global capital accumulation and geopolitics even as they are firmly embedded in localized histories and meanings. I then discuss the rich variety of strategies that social movements have used in moving beyond the dichotomy between revolution and reform to a broader, pluralistic conception of political change. These strategies are important for deepening democracy in the region and making possible a reimagining of what it means to be political, economic, and social in today's world.

Any typology or theory about the relevance of particular social movement strategies must be grounded in particular localized sites: household, community, state, and region. As Rubin and Bennett stress, strategies that work for one group do not necessarily work for others because differences in localized moral economies, histories, and sociophysical environments shape the way in which people are able to deploy different techniques as well as the effects that those techniques will have. Certain claims—to land, identity, municipal services, political autonomy—resonate clearly among particular people at particular times while they may fall flat or short for other people or at other times. This explains the strength of rural and indigenous movements today; these actors are demanding a progressive re-territorialization of livelihood and identity (Escobar 2010) after twenty years of a hegemonic economic and political ideology (neoliberalism) predicated on alienating producers from the means of production (land, raw materials, territory) through various acts of accumulation by dispossession (see also Zibechi 2003, 186).

In the language of social movement theorists, then, we might say that political context—opportunities and challenges—influences the ability to mobilize resources and "frame" a struggle effectively. But these are only proximate causes. Protest happens and strategies will be used when the structural conditions of exploitation align with perceived conditions of exploitation and expectation of redress. In other words, people protest when they feel they are being exploited and think they can do something about it (Auyero 2004 and Kurzman 1996). They may not feel hopeful about accomplishing their goals or redressing their wrongs, but they come to feel that acting publicly and collectively is better than not doing so. Whether or when these two elements—the perception of exploitation and expectation of redress—will align depends on normative evaluations of social justice that are in turn shaped by histories of resource access and what Rubin and Bennett (in their introduction) refer to as the cultural aspects of community identification.

All of this brings me back to where I began: it is hard to know how to start when talking about Latin American social movements. I offer my analysis as someone who has been interested in and inspired by such mobilizations for many years. The theoretical and practical energy has come from the work of the movements and movement activists themselves. Since the early 1990s, I have worked with and studied the Landless Movement of Brazil, so this overview is also admittedly partial: I am more familiar with rural and agrarian movements than with urban ones, and I understand the Brazilian context better than others in the region.

SOCIAL MOBILIZATION IN THE TWENTY-FIRST CENTURY

There are at least four aspects to the current context that draw one's attention as novel. They are political, economic, ideological, and strategic. The first aspect—politics with a capital "P"—includes electoral politics and the deepening of democracy. Most of the countries in the region—with a few exceptions, such as Cuba—are undergoing a consolidation of what others have called the third wave of democratization. The third wave characterizes the period beginning in the 1980s, when military governments broke down or backed out of office, ushering in formal democracies (elections, parties, administrative bureaucracies). Consolidation of the third wave began with the rewriting of constitutions in the 1980s and 1990s that expanded citizenship rights for formerly marginal subjects such as indigenous peoples, Afro-descendants, gays, women, and others (Mainwaring and Viola 1984).[7] More recently, there is a concerted focus on deepening—or improving the quality of—this third wave of democracy (Avritzer 2008), and relationships between the political and personal have come increasingly under scrutiny (Yashar 1999). Improving the quality of democracy may prove more challenging even than facing down military governments; Kurt Weyland (2004) has argued that neoliberal reforms enacted during the 1990s in Latin America may have strengthened the durability of democracy (removing fears of a return to military rule, with the recent exception of Honduras), but overall they have weakened the quality.

There are, however, political experiments in "deepening democracy" that suggest the potential for new and increasingly radicalized modes of regulation, governance, and organization (Oxhorn 2003). Much of the old academic work that analyzes the political activities of social movements assumes a relatively neat delineation between the three spheres of state, market, and civil society. Collective action may blur the lines, but the lines themselves are rarely called into question. This has everything to do with the history and theory of social mobilization. As I have suggested, social movements are seen as "products of the modern age," when sustained contention against a centralized state became both thinkable and possible (Tarrow 1998, 2). Social movements are generally thought to be opposing the state, whether to demand resources or a revolution. Today, however, the line itself between state, market, and civil society is being challenged (Yashar 1999, 77). From autonomous communities organized through the Zapatistas to the solidarity economies of the Recuperated Factories in Argentina and the associations of Mexican migrants in the United States, national leaders from Lula to Correa to Chávez have looked to formerly remote subjects and places for advice on how to connect people more intimately to government. This political shift has been belittled in much academic and journalistic writing as a "pink tide" or the "Left Lite"—and certainly many administrations have failed to live up to campaign promises.[8] However, there is a widespread feeling of political possibility and a search for alternatives.[9] And this isn't just a feeling—as the cases featured throughout this book illustrate, there is real potential for alternatives to "crystallize" and endure.

As many have pointed out, including Evelina Dagnino (2002), this opening may be due at least in part to the values and practices of earlier, more neoliberal administrations. Neoliberal policies geared toward decentralization and civil society participation have increased the everyday interaction and overall articulation between state and social movement actors and institutions. Social movement leaders throughout the region now have a greater presence within formal government spaces as they negotiate for their demands and provide their support (Abers and Keck 2009). At the same time, social movement leaders are now distributing more of the state's resources within their own communities (Wolford 2010a).

A second aspect of the current conjuncture is economic with a capital "E." Latin America as a whole has been the testing (or battle-) ground for a series of economic orthodoxies beginning with free trade in the early colonial period (through colonial mercantilism that laid the basis for the easy acceptance of trade as the "sweet civilizer" of the long nineteenth century), the development of the factory production system (through the technologies of agro-industrial plantation production that began with sugar in the colonies and were adopted in British factories during the Industrial Revolution), and even neoliberalism (as sensible free-market policies were tried out first in Chile and soon imposed or adopted around the world as the only alternative). In the 1990s, protests against neoliberalism spread, becoming regular features of the local, national, and transnational landscape. Popular mobilization against neoliberalism arguably toppled governments (Ecuador, Bolivia, perhaps even Brazil), pushed politicians to the left (Argentina, Chile, definitely Brazil), and opened up space for alternative political coalitions (Mexico, Venezuela).

But neoliberal economic policies have left Latin America in poor condition.[10] In the last two decades of the twentieth century, inequality increased: the GINI index for Latin America as a whole increased from .50 in 1982 to .56 in 1995 and .595 in 2000 (Roberts 2002, 7); and poverty increased: one-third of all Latin Americans lived below the poverty line in 1995 as compared with one-fourth in 1982 (Roberts 2002, 7).[11] Wages fell: the average real minimum wage for the region fell by 30 percent from 1980 to 1997 (Roberts 2002, 7). Landownership became more concentrated, and the total number of rural poor increased in every country with the exception of Brazil, Chile, and Mexico (De Janvry and Sadoulet 2002, 2), and growth rates in agriculture were lower regionwide in 1990 than in 1970 (Deere and Royce 2009, 5). At the same time, informal urban settlements and economies expanded rapidly; for most countries, the informal economy constitutes 30 to 40 percent of gross domestic product at the present (Vuletin 2008, 27), and urban violence is at an all-time high as drug dealers and slum lords from Ciudad Juárez to Rio de Janeiro become the new revolutionary paramilitaries. Protests against these conditions have forced governments to enact new policies. Although far short of anti-neoliberalism, governments distributed land to the rural poor (Bolivia, Ecuador, Venezuela, and in some ways Brazil), increased indigenous autonomy (in some ways Ecuador and Mexico), and provided some immediate support for the poorest (ProCampo in Mexico, Bolsa Família in Brazil, and others). Whether this is productive (and it is certainly not revolutionary or necessarily enough), these efforts at economic policy shape the terrain in which social movements and civil society activists— as well as business elites and government officials—operate today. Social movements, like the reform initiatives described throughout this volume, address the harms of neoliberalism in the context of new forms of grassroots protest and state response.

The third aspect of the current conjuncture is ideological and related to the production of knowledge. The fall of the Berlin Wall in 1989 changed the ideological dynamic in revolutionary corners, streets, halls, and fields around the world. The reform cases throughout this book illustrate that radical thinking today is less Manichean in its design or execution. Social movement activists draw on an eclectic range of philosophers, economists, historical figures, and local ways of knowing to build new traditions. Indigenous practices combine with the idealistic words of José Mariátegui and analyses of Karl Marx to generate fresh theories about the movement of history and possibilities for radical change. This ideological opening and eclecticism is an important aspect of the new social and political landscape; it offers a wide variety of platforms around which to organize but also challenges activists to find unity or common ground among the diversity. The vibrancy—and chaos—of the annual World Social Forums are a reflection of this opportunity and challenge.

A fourth defining aspect of the current conjuncture is tactical. Drawing from examples and cultures of resistance that span the past five hundred years, political activists in Latin America have developed a contemporary repertoire that includes now-conventional elements such as blockades, hunger strikes, demonstrations, and marches as well as new elements such as transnational mobilizations and meetings targeting global economic and political actors, Internet campaigns, well-organized and coordinated land occupations, occupations of strategic sites such as government buildings or squares with attendant settlements established for two or three day "conferences," popular national referenda (plebiscites), and more. Novel technologies of communication and transportation facilitate the spread of these tactics. They are repeated, refined, and disseminated through localized initiatives, transnational mobilization, and media coverage. These technologies shed light on the everyday ways in which once-utopian visions for social change are being realized and made concrete, in social movement mobilizations and other civil society initiatives.

The current moment brings political, economic, ideological, and tactical factors together to provide space and urgency to what was already a regional culture of mobilization, awareness, and resistance. Movements and parties and nongovernmental organizations draw lessons from previous decades but apply them to new ends. There is no one single movement or idea or strategy that unifies or typifies the region. Rather, there is a general movement of movements that is producing innovative ideas about the intersection of politics, economics, cultures, and lives. In turn, this sea change in the nature of social movement activism has also provided some of the ingredients and support for progressive, civil society reform projects.

It is fair to say that in Latin America, few people question the relevance of social mobilization or organization even as they bemoan the difficulty of producing real political change (whereas in the United States, where I sit, few see the need to organize even though most assume that they are empowered to make real political change through formal mechanisms, if they choose to do so). This does not mean, of course, that social movements will necessarily generate significant political change in the region as a whole. But that is not the only question to ask. Seen from the other end—the bottom up—social movements are making enormous changes in people's lives.

STRATEGIES FOR ENGAGING WITH THE STATE IN THE NEW CONTEXT

As I have argued, the relationship with the state is central to the development and evolution of social movements, in terms of both ideology and praxis. While there are challenges inherent in collaborating with the state as well as in rejecting such engagement, collaboration is no longer necessarily seen as co-optation (Dagnino 2002 and Hellman 1992). Contemporary social activism engages with the state in such a variety of ways that it may be less productive to analyze their strategies in terms of state and movement than in terms of the work the different groups do. In other words, we may gain more by analyzing strategies as being geared toward either organization and protest or governance and administration (Wolford forthcoming; and Alvarez et al. 2012). Doing so would allow us to see that government agents often engage in active protest while social movement members participate in the mundane activities of everyday rule, establishing new schools, providing sustenance for their poorest members, and so on. The case studies presented in this book provide examples of movement-state relations along such a continuum.

Some of the strategies employed by social movements, like the search for sovereign community rule, are very clearly intended to repudiate the official system of political governance. Most strategies, however, engage the state in a variety of rhetorical and/or material ways. Even popular notions of autonomy have a complicated relationship to the dominant political system; some grassroots actors define autonomy as complete separation from the state, while others argue that autonomy means independence from state rule, and control over one's position relative to the state, but not separation. Many of these strategies are age-old in Latin America, and all of them are directly and indirectly the result of tactical and strategic decisions carried out by social movement activists and movement members since the mid-1980s (drawing on the longer history and theory of activism). Most social movements or grassroots actors bring together a variety of these strategies, and in so doing they challenge the idea that civil society has a singular and preordained relationship to the state.

Pursuing Independence: Different Visions of Autonomy

Many contemporary movements in Latin America are fighting for some measure of independence or separation from the state. Raúl Zibechi (2003, 186) has argued that the most important contemporary movements in Latin

America share a common rejection of the state and search for autonomy. Rejection and its correlate—autonomy—mean different things for different actors, however. For movements such as the Zapatistas (the Zapatista Army of National Liberation, or EZLN, as distinct from what Xóchitl Leyva Solano [1999] calls "neo-Zapatismo"; also see Swords 2008) in the southernmost Mexican state of Chiapas (Ramírez 2008; Harvey 1998; and Bobrow-Strain 2007), autonomy means complete separation from the state.[12] The EZLN brought together tens of thousands of members, predominantly indigenous peoples who had migrated to the western agricultural frontier of the Lacandón jungle, as well as urban supporters, and organizations of the Mexican Left, such as the National Liberation Forces (Fuerzas de Liberación Nacional), some of whom make up the more visible leadership elite (such as Subcommandante Marcos; see Peeler 2003, 274).

The EZLN rose up and declared itself on January 1, 1994, to protest the implementation of the North American Free Trade Agreement (Harvey 1998). The movement was particularly noteworthy because while members at first invoked Article 39 of Mexico's 1917 Constitution, which "invests national sovereignty and the right to modify government in the people of Mexico" (Collier with Quaratiello 1994, 2), they subsequently repudiated formal politics altogether. After a bloody clash with Mexican military forces, the EZLN put down its arms and demanded that indigenous communities be given the autonomy to govern according to traditional *usos y costumbres* rather than according to the Mexican administrative framework. This grassroots horizontalism was seen as the only alternative to the corruption and clientelism that dominated the formal political system.[13] In 1996, the Mexican government signed the San Andrés Accords, which provided affiliated Zapatista communities with political autonomy as well as certain rights due to indigenous peoples (ratified by the Mexican Congress only in a diluted and contested form in 2000).

In successfully claiming and maintaining political sovereignty or autonomy, the Zapatistas drew on a long history of anarchism in Mexico as well as on traditional Mayan beliefs and practices blended with libertarian socialism (Stahler-Sholk 2008). The quest for autonomy was facilitated and shaped by a moral economy in which colonial practices of labor exploitation utilized preconquest indigenous communities and production relationships (Stahler-Sholk 2008). John Womack Jr. (1999) has argued that the local environment played an important role in shaping the "art of *not* being governed" (see Scott 2009): as migrants gathered in the relative obscurity of the Lacandón jungle, they developed democratic forms of self-organization that were crucial to the widespread adoption of Zapatismo.

Although many other movements list autonomy as one of their goals, most have stopped short of seeking such a complete separation from the state. Many movements struggle for autonomy but define this as accepting state resources while maintaining their distance from the state through antistate rhetoric, withdrawal from elections or party politics, regular mobilization, and refusal to negotiate or meet. What could be called "dependent independence" of this sort is exemplified by certain groups within the broader piquetero movement in Argentina, particularly the more centrist groups not associated with the Communist Party (Alcañiz and Scheier 2008, 271–72). The *piqueteros* (picketers) first mobilized in southern Argentina when the state-owned oil company Yacimientos Petrolíferos Fiscales (YPF) was privatized in 1992, resulting in widespread layoffs (Alcañiz and Scheier 2008, 273). The oil company reduced its workforce from forty-two hundred to six hundred in the first year after privatization (Auyero 2004, 319).

Three years later, popular protest erupted when plans to build a fertilizer plant in the area were cancelled. Protestors took to the streets, first attempting to access the entrance of the YPF oil refining plant in Cutral Có, and then moving to the interstate, where the protests quickly garnered national attention (Sitrin 2006). A year later, people again took to the streets around Cutral Có to demand that the regional governor make good on promises given during the 1996 protests. Coauthors Maristela Svampa and Sebastian Pereyra (2003) have argued that the piqueteros organized around a new identity (revaluing unemployed workers as piqueteros), a new method (the *piquete*, or roadblock), and a new demand (for *the right* to government assistance). Although not completely successful, as suggested by ongoing accusations of co-optation and factionalism within the various piquetero organizations, the active involvement of unemployed workers from both the interior of Argentina and the capital city helped to transform the language of "handouts" and clientelism into a language of rights. This language is also used by members of the socialized work system in the Recuperated Factories who demand access to the traditional rights won by wage laborers. As other case studies in this book demonstrate, language matters. Changing the language is not just a rhetorical or semantic issue; it has direct implications for strategy and tactics used by movements and activists.

Another example of dependent independence, or negotiated autonomy, is the Landless Movement (or Movimento Sem Terra, MST) in Brazil and its official position of separation from the Catholic Church, trade unions, and political parties (Wright and Wolford 2003). When the MST was first organized as a national movement in 1985, some suggested that the movement act as a radical wing of the Catholic Church but others—including representatives of the Catholic Church—argued against such close identification with established and (for the most part) mainstream groups. Since that time, the MST has officially retained its organizational independence, only rarely supporting movement candidates for political office. Activists mobilize regular protests for access to government credit and argue that infrastructure and resources won through pressure are provided by the movement rather than the state. This reframing of agency is central to the cases examined in this volume, such as the three-for-one remittances program in Mexico, in which previously "invisible" migrants become the key actors in a program that spread nationwide. Throughout the 1990s, the MST's strategy of discursive autonomy was extremely effective. For most of the eight years that Fernando Henrique Cardoso was in office (1995–2003), he was associated with neoliberal economic policies and with criminalization of the movement. It was easy to argue that Cardoso would not have delivered resources—land, credit, roads, and water—if the landless had not been mobilized by the MST. The same was still true of Lula (though perhaps for different reasons; see Wolford 2010b), but it was harder to convince people both within the movement and without that such was the case.

Network Autonomy: "Jumping the State" through Regional and Transnational Organizing

If the current context is defined by the four aspects described previously, it is perhaps best exemplified by the rise of new networks that bring groups together at various scales—local, regional, national, and transnational. Networks of indigenous peoples at all of these scales have been particularly effective in pushing for new political representation and valorization of indigenous forms of governance (Yashar 2005). Outside of the state, however, the most active organizing has been by umbrella organizations such as Via Campesina (VC) that serve as a network of movements dedicated to agrarian rights (Baletti, Johnson, and Wolford 2008; and Desmarais 2009). Since 1992, when it began, VC has developed into one of the most active and visible supporters of individual movements and has promoted particular campaigns such as those for land rights and food sovereignty. In 2007, the International Coordinating Committee had 149 representatives from almost every country in the world (Desmarais 2009, 36).[14]

Activists affiliated directly with the network travel throughout the region offering tactical advice and solidarity. As an umbrella organization, VC does not usually engage directly with national states, and its own activities are largely autonomous from any official political regime; most of the network's statements are oriented toward the international community, particularly multilateral institutions. The success of peasant organizing (in terms of visibility, sustained mobilization, and ideological coherence) has to do with four key factors: the economic aspect of the current conjuncture—the severity of the neoliberal assault on peasant livelihoods (Deere and Royce 2009, 5); the existence of well-established solidarity networks dating back to the military era when peasant activists fled their respective countries and met in exile in Mexico and Cuba; the appeal of a peasant-based message to a significant population across ethnic, gender, national, and religious lines; and the easy identification of a common enemy in large-scale industrial agriculture and the unfair practices of the World Trade Organization. Furthermore, most countries in the region have a history of offering handouts to peasants (through land reform or subsidies) that are incomplete and serve to keep the embers of protest alive (De Janvry and Sadoulet 2002).

Although VC is not itself involved in national politics, the network has influenced movement-state relations in different places. One such example is the establishment of the Bolivian Movimento Sin Tierra (or MST-Bolivia; see Crabtree 2005 and Saisari 2009).[15] Organized primarily in Ñuflo de Cháves, Ichilo, Sara, and Cordillera provinces, the movement was assisted by activists from the Brazilian MST who agreed to teach Bolivian landless activists from the Brazilian experience. The Bolivian movement never obtained the visibility of the Brazilian movement, but it is a critical partner in the Bolivian government's contemporary initiatives to undertake a widespread agrarian reform in the country (Saisari 2009). Whether Bolivian President Evo Morales will be able to implement the changes that he proposed and that were ratified in November 2006 will depend in part on the continuing ability of landless activists to pressure stakeholders.

Revolution through Reform: Taking on the State

Although these social movement strategies have received significant attention because of their demands for autonomy and engagement with alternative publics, political strategies that confront the state through disruption and press for redress are still the most common form of protest. Most of these strategies are explicitly spatial or territorial, such as blockades that attempt to suspend or impede the flow of goods, people, resources, or information, usually by making key transportation or communication arteries—from highways to airports to television channels and logging roads—impassable. From the *empates* of Chico Mendes in the Brazilian Amazon to the roadblocks of the piqueteros in Argentina, passageways are blockaded to both symbolic and material effect: symbolically, blockades disrupt the flow of goods or resources that movement activists feel should not be permitted to leave without greater regulation or democratization; materially, blockades can cause significant economic damage, particularly in complicating the smooth flow of exports and suggesting "political instability." Blockades cut off access to transportation nodes (ports, shipping lanes, trucking junctures, airports, interstate highways) and access to key sites within the international economy (banking and financial headquarters) that made visible the often hidden presence of global capitalism.

Blockades were used by the piquetero (picketers) movement in Argentina in the late 1990s (Svampa and Pereyra 2003), and placing obstacles in "heavily trafficked roads (typically vital commercial arteries in the countryside and around the city)" (Alcañiz and Scheier 2008, 275) became critical pieces of the contentious repertoire that defined the piquetero movement. Javier Auyero (2004, 313) has quoted the governor of Salta as saying, "the roadblock is a political practice that has spread throughout the country." It has been argued that this tactic dates back to the French Revolution (Tilly 1978), but it was perhaps particularly useful and effective in southern Argentina as a way of allowing localized protests to "jump scale" (Smith 1993) and challenge national politics and global capitalism.

Another explicitly spatial tactic used to engage the state is the organized takeover of a particular property—usually land or buildings—for the purposes of pressuring the state and/or private landowners to renegotiate ownership and use rights. Of the two occupations—land and building—the former are more common, although the Recuperated Factories (see chapter 5 in this volume) represent structural occupation and homeless movements in various cities as buildings are occupied as a way of highlighting the contradictions between homelessness and building vacancy. Probably the most well-cited example is the Sem Teto (homeless) movement in Brazil, where urban activists met with their rural counterparts (the Sem Terra, or landless) to learn how to most effectively execute occupations. Land occupations are not themselves a new phenomenon, but they are increasingly deliberate, well-planned, and often coordinated with other land occupations in various regions of a country. Although the Brazilian MST is the most visible movement carrying out sustained land occupations, there are others (such as the Bolivian MST and the development of indigenous colonias surrounding San Cristóbal de Las Casas, Chiapas, as described in chapter 3 in this book).

When the Brazilian MST carries out land occupations, they do so according to a new well-defined methodology. Recruits meet for weeks or months beforehand to prepare. They read critical analyses of Brazilian land ownership and private property more generally in order to develop a better understanding of their rights to land. Once activists have selected a rural property that either violates the "social productivity clause" in the federal constitution or can be proven to have been purchased illegally, the recruits occupy the property, usually late at night to avoid immediate retaliation. Land occupations have been extremely effective in the Brazilian context because the country has a spatial imaginary (of itself) as having plenty of land such that landlessness should not exist (Wolford 2007); the prevalence of title forgery is so common that private ownership is not *necessarily* or a priori seen as legitimate. Land occupations have successfully been presented as largely peaceful initiatives, particularly in relation to the armed retaliation of landlords and the military police. Land occupations provide symbolic markers of the struggle for land as well as its territorialization (Fernandes 2005): each occupation has the potential to lead to a new land reform settlement, and while people live in the occupation camps, they develop norms of solidarity, social justice, and loyalty that stay with them well into the settlement process.

Since the mid-1980s, marching, taking to the streets, and holding large-scale protests have become common features of political life. How such mobilizations build and take effect, though, depends on a variety of factors, particularly the nature of the grievance and the extent to which the grievance resonates with both the affected group and a larger, related population. Examples of the different political effects that mass mobilization can have include the two recent resource wars in Bolivia: the 2000 water wars of Cochabamba and the 2003 gas wars. Analyses by Thomas Perrault (2006) and coauthors Susan Spronk and Jeffrey Webber (2008) suggest that while both sets of mobilizations were organized to protest privatization of key natural resources, mobilization to secure access to water remained more localized and focused on water as a human right, whereas mobilization around access to natural gas became a national fight because gas was seen as an inviolable piece of national patrimony—the future of the country. Participants in both the gas and water wars demanded procedural and distributive justice and resisted the privatization of what were seen as collective resources (Perrault 2006, 154). However, the mobilizations differed in extent and scope because of the historical conditions of access to the resources as well as their socionatural properties. The water wars of Cochabamba brought thousands of protestors into the streets in April 2000, when the newly privatized water authority increased the tariffs for water and sewage services by over 30 percent without any attendant investments or improvements in services. Protests shut down the city of Cochabamba—the third largest city in Bolivia—for weeks. They were organized in part by water user groups—irrigators' organizations and community-based drinking water associations—that had grown out of earlier protests against state distribution but also quickly garnered the support of thousands of urban and rural residents (Perrault 2006, 157). The protests did not extend beyond Cochabamba, though, because the issue did not incite public resistance in other parts of Bolivia where access to water and water tariffs, whether privately managed or not, were deemed acceptable. In fact, the themes of the water war resonated more at the transnational level, where activists have come together to fight water privatization schemes in countries across the world (Shiva 2004).

The gas war of 2003, in contrast, swept across Bolivia, bringing people out throughout the country and resulting in the self-imposed exile of then-president Gonzalez Sánchez de Lozada (Goni), who resigned in October of that year. Bolivia has rich natural gas resources, access to which had been controlled by a majority-Bolivian company until the company was sold in 1996 (Spronk and Webber 2008, 80). The subsequent plan to build a pipeline that would send natural gas to Mexico and the United States via the Chilean coast met with increasing resistance as people across the country argued that exporting raw natural gas and building processing plants abroad continued a long history of giving Bolivia's natural resources away (Postero 2007). In 2003, the National Coordination for the Defense of Gas led neighborhood organizations, trade unions, and indigenous groups into the streets. Severe government repression resulted in more than eighty deaths, only coming to an end with the promise of a national hydrocarbons law in 2005 and the election of President Evo Morales in 2006. While both water and gas are important natural resources, and water is arguably more necessary for social reproduction, the historical conditions of access to natural gas make it a valuable commodity for exchange and, as such, for national patrimony—a patrimony seen as important for development, social justice, and identity.[16]

In addition to mobilizing public demonstrations, social movements continually lobby the state in an attempt to change policy or politics through contact with state officials, media campaigns, public awareness, and electoral organizing. Perhaps the best known and most effective example of this is the group that became known as the Mothers of the Plaza de Mayo (Navarro 1989)—a movement that began in Buenos Aires in 1977 with fourteen women and grew to more than twenty-five hundred. The Mothers of the Plaza de Mayo campaigned to have the whereabouts of the disappeared (*desaparecidos*) made known. They conducted (and continue to conduct) weekly marches and disseminated petitions (obtaining as many as twenty-four thousand signatures) while networking with international human rights organizations to gain publicity and protection. The women forced the military to acknowledge the presence of torture by insisting that the number of disappeared victims far exceeded the official count. Parallel to this group, the Grandmothers (Abuelas) of the Plaza de Mayo also organized (Arditti 1999), demanding that the children who had been seized with their parents or born in captivity be returned to their rightful families. The grandmothers saw this as restitution: "The grandmothers see this reunion as an act of truth, a *vuelta a la vida* [return to life] that will restore to them their proper identity, allowing them to grow up without secrets or lies" (Arditti 1999, 103). After the return to democracy, the Abuelas launched a public campaign for information about the missing children, and by 1997 they had gathered thousands of tips from anonymous sources. To date, they have identified over fifty missing children. As Philip Oxhorn (2001, 169) has suggested, the Abuelas have navigated the postauthoritarian landscape well, avoiding internal conflicts, and focusing on finding and reclaiming lost children.[17]

Sometimes grassroots actors go beyond lobbying to create partnerships with state actors, co-organizing or collaboratively implementing government-funded projects (often created through movement pressure). Sometimes referred to optimistically as "participatory democracy," these experiments generally entail some measure of state-society collaboration in the production of new policies, evaluation of government projects, or delivery of services. One of the most talked-about innovations in participatory democracy is the participatory budget (*orçamento participativo*, OP) developed by the Brazilian Workers' Party (Partido dos Trabalhadores, the PT). There is extensive literature on innovations such as the participatory budgeting process, and the most relevant lesson for civil society actors is that some measure of distance or autonomy must be maintained such that pressure can be mobilized in the event that governments do not deliver on the promises they make (Abers and Keck 2009; Dagnino 2002; Fung and Wright 2003; Keck and Abers 2006; Wampler 2007; and Wolford 2010a). Thus it seems clear that even as governments become more participatory and inclusive, the need for an independent and potentially uncivil civil society remains (Avritzer 2002).

"Patria o Muerte, Venceremos!" Taking over the State

The two key strategies used as attempts to take over the state are plebiscites and electoral participation. Plebiscites are defined as direct electoral action whereby particular questions (often only one at a time) are submitted to national popular vote. Plebiscites are not new in Latin American history. Two plebiscites held in Chile famously resulted in Pinochet remaining in power (the results have been questioned), but when held for a third time in 1988 and organized as an electoral campaign by the opposition (Dezalay and Garth 2002, 151), a majority of people voted against continuing military rule and open elections were held in 1990. Another interesting example was the anti-FTAA (Free Trade of the Americas Agreement) and anti-neoliberal plebiscite in Brazil in 2002 in which social movement activists went door to door taking votes on three questions: Should the Brazilian government sign the FTAA accord? Should the Brazilian government continue participating in the FTAA negotiations? And should the Brazilian government turn over part of Brazilian territory for U.S. military control? An overwhelming majority of the one million respondents voted no to all three questions. Although the methods of the plebiscite were questioned, the results led to the feeling that a wave of social movement activity was consolidating and organizing to change the government. Other examples of plebiscites include the 2007 plebiscite in Costa Rica, when respondents voted to accept the Central American Free Trade Agreement (DR-CAFTA), marking the first time a popular vote had been used to ratify a trade treaty. And in the Venezuelan recall referendum of 2004, voters opted not to remove President Hugo Chávez from office.

Beyond plebiscites, social movement actors participate in elections or become a party themselves and/or attempt to reform the state from within. There are examples of guerrilla leaders becoming politicians in many countries in the region (for example, in Colombia, El Salvador, Nicaragua, and Uruguay). But the example of Bolivia stands out. In 2006, Evo Morales, the leader of the Movement toward Socialism (MAS) and executive secretary of a regional coca trade union federation, was elected to the presidency. This was the first time since the presidency of Benito Juárez in nineteenth-century Mexico that an indigenous person had been elected to the executive anywhere in Latin America, let alone one who had been a coca farmer, had opposed the intervention of both the military and the United States into local livelihood matters, and had been elected head of an important social movement. Evo Morales's rise to the presidency can perhaps best be explained as a product of several factors: his individual skill and charisma, solidarity among indigenous communities (for example, Katarismo, a "banner denoting the political and cultural assertion of Aymara identity"; see Peeler 2003, 264) that together make up over 60 percent of the country's population (Postero 2007, 3), his strong identification with coca as part of national and indigenous tradition, and the perception of the link between neoliberal economic policies, unemployment, and persecution of coca farmers (Salazar Ortuño 2003).

The MAS began as a movement of *cocaleros* (coca farmers) and indigenous peoples in central and eastern Bolivia. Many of the coca farmers were miners who had been laid off in the early 1980s and gone into coca farming because of a lack of marketable agricultural alternatives in the tropical lowlands. Organized into trade union federations by 1991, leaders distributed land and services among dues-paying members. In 1995, Morales was elected to Congress as a MAS delegate; he was elected as a member of the Asemblea de la Soberania de los Pueblos (ASP), but the party was not officially recognized and so the then-defunct MAS party became the new vehicle for indigenous leaders and coca farmers. MAS members opposed governmental (U.S.-led) campaigns to eradicate coca growing and defended coca as both economically vital and crucial to national and indigenous identity. In power since 2006 and elected in 2010 for a second term with a significant majority, Morales has worked to create a plurinational state, nationalize strategic natural resources, and distribute land to the indigenous. His government has also overseen a Constituent Assembly to rewrite the national constitution.

HOW DO SOCIAL MOVEMENTS MOBILIZE?

There is no question that since the mid-1980s, social movements have helped to defeat authoritarian rule and reshaped the future of a political-economic ideology that seemed so hegemonic that there could be no alternative. Across the region, social movement activists have met to discuss how to change particular pieces of the everyday world: how to win land or get more female staff in police stations or create a nondiscriminatory advertising campaign against HIV-AIDs. The reforms described in this book—all of them stimulated in part by social movement activism and influenced by the patterns of social movement–state interaction—provide some of the best examples of everyday changes that have the potential to make a real difference in the way that lives are lived throughout Latin America today. In working to change everyday forms of discrimination or exploitation, these changes, actions, and activists have fed into, constructed, and benefited from a sea change in political thinking and leadership throughout the region. Scholars and the lay public tend to focus on sensational moments and extraordinary movements such as the World Social Forums or the gas war and the piquetero protests of 1996, but most of these would not have happened without the much more banal work of everyday organizing.

If people organize when they feel they are exploited and believe they can do something about it, then the visible presence of movements and reforms in political life today may create a virtuous cycle that counteracts the more familiar vicious cycle of poverty, inequality, and violence (Karl 2003). Mobilization is becoming an increasingly common political strategy, and the rich variety of strategies being used by social movements today speaks to their sophistication and flexibility. Most social movement activists in the region, like the enduring reforms described here, use a combination of strategies. Some movements began using one set of strategies when they first organized and shifted when external circumstances or their own internal dynamics changed. The choice of what strategy to use in what situation is not an easy one. Choosing to remain autonomous or work within the state are highly ideological, normative, and theoretical decisions with significant implications for overall movement trajectories. The variety of choices—and the freedom to choose—is a positive development, however. The political landscape is no longer black and white, and social movements are not an automatic threat to democracy.

NOTES

1. In 2010, the library at the University of North Carolina–Chapel Hill had 2,539 books with the subject heading "social movements," 2,036 of which were published after 1990. Perhaps even more telling, the library had 94 books with the subject heading "social movements in Latin America," 83 of which were published after 1990.

2. The WSF was originally located in Porto Alegre, one of the southernmost cities of Brazil, and was heavily attended by Brazilian activists (particularly those in the Workers' Party and in the Landless Workers Movement, or MST) and by transnational activists based in the Global North who had access to the resources and time necessary for attendance. After 2003, meetings began to be held in other parts of the world, notably in Mumbai and Nairobi. At the same time, regional forums have been held in many countries. While such meetings provide energy and opportunities for building solidarity and exchanging information, participants have been frustrated by the difficulty of producing concrete change and the seeming ease with which more conservative organizations, such as nongovernmental aid organizations, have infiltrated the activities.

3. The fact that these uprisings were called riots illustrates the incipient nature of transnational organizing before the 1990s. Today, protests over food prices are "mobilizations" or "demonstrations" and linked to the alter-globalization movement. The disillusionment was not contained to Latin America—the disappointing experiences of the African National Congress (ANC) in South Africa reverberated globally in the second half of the 1990s.

4. Tom Perrault (2008, 1368) has pointed out that some of the military governments—though not the harshest and most notorious—were themselves products of collaboration between the military and such popular groups as the Velasco administration in Peru and the military-campesino pact in Bolivia (see also Peeler 2003, 259–60).

5. This is also the year that Rigoberta Menchú was awarded the Nobel Peace Prize, which

"indigenous communities saw . . . as signaling an opportunity that might restore to them some measure of economic dignity" (Seed 2001, 129).

6. "New social movements" in this context refers to movements recently organized rather than to the label given to movements that came together in the 1960s and 1970s in the United States and Europe. These latter movements were considered "new" because of the diversity of claims and attention to identity-based issues (Melucci 1989).

7. Here I am referring to so-called new People's Constitutions or "multicultural constitutionalism" (Van Cott 2000).

8. Here many people would cite the case of Lula in Brazil, although his defection from earlier radical roots is not nearly as clear-cut as it seems—both because he may not have been as radical as he has been depicted and because his administrations have not been as conservative as they have been depicted (see French 2009).

9. Whether or not social movements in Latin America today are working with or against the state is a subject of discussion and disagreement. Sonia Alvarez has argued, for example, that the women's movement in Latin America has become stronger (if more amorphous) by building movement webs that extend into state offices and onto the streets (see Alvarez's 2009 article softening her earlier arguments against "NGO-ization").

10. See the edited volumes on social movements by Susan Eckstein and Timothy Wickham-Crowley (2003); Carmen Diana Deere and Frederick S. Royce (2009); and Richard Stalher-Sholk, Harry E. Vanden, and Glen David Kuecker (2008).

11. These numbers are disputed; a 2004 paper by Michael Walton points out the variability that is hidden within the regional averages.

12. There are smaller and less comprehensive examples in various indigenous communities in the Amazon rain forest.

13. Hellman 2008 argues that Mexico was the least "democratizing" country in Latin America in the late 1980s and 1990s.

14. Of these, the Latin American Coordinator of Rural Organizations (Coordinadora Latinoamericana de Organizaciones del Campo, CLOC) is the most vibrant (Tiney 2009).

15. MST-Bolivia grew out of the failed agrarian reform of 1953 (Saisari 2009, 124). This agrarian reform was notable in that it "was not part of a prophylactic policy against the spread of communism as occurred in other Latin American countries after the Cuban revolution. Nor was it a planned public policy. What distinguishes the Bolivian agrarian reform is its endogenous character, its strong roots in the indigenous identity, its outwardly redistributive orientation and the lack of clear public policies to support rural development" (Kay and Urioste 2007, 43).

16. One recalls the famous "paradox of value" that attempts to explain why diamonds are worth more in exchange than water.

17. A note on the Abuelas webpage (http://www.abuelas.org.ar/) says in hauntingly plain language: "If you were born between 1975 and 1980 and are unsure where you come from, contact us."

REFERENCES

Abers, Rebecca Neaera. 2000. *Inventing Local Democracy: Grassroots Politics in Brazil*. Boulder: Lynne Rienner.

Abers, Rebecca Neaera, and Margaret E. Keck. 2009. "Mobilizing the State: The Erratic Partner in Brazil's Participatory Water Policy." *Politics and Society* 37 (2): 289–314.

Alcañiz, Isabella, and Melissa Scheier. 2008. "New Social Movements with Old Party Politics: The MTL Piqueteros and the Communist Party in Argentina." In *Latin American Social Movements in the Twenty-First Century: Resistance, Power, and Democracy*, edited by Richard Stahler-Sholk, Harry E. Vanden, and Glen David Kuecker, 271–86. Lanham: Rowman & Littlefield.

Allegretti, Mary, and Marianne Schmink. 2009. "When Social Movement Proposals Become Policy: Experiments in Sustainable Development in the Brazilian Amazon." In *Rural Social Movements in Latin America: Organizing for Sustainable Livelihoods*, edited by Carmen Diana Deere and Frederick S. Royce, 196–213. Gainesville: University Press of Florida.

Alvarez, Sonia. 1990. *Engendering Democracy: Women's Movements in Transition Politics*. Princeton: Princeton University Press.

Alvarez, Sonia. 1998. "Social Movements and Social Relations." In *Cultures of Politics/Politics of Culture: Re-visioning Latin American Social Movements*, edited by Sonia E. Alvarez, Evelina Dagnino, and Arturo Escobar, 171–99. Boulder: Westview Press.

Alvarez, Sonia. 2009. "Beyond NGO-ization: Reflections from Latin America." *Development* 52 (2): 175–84.

Alvarez, Sonia, Agustin Lao-Montes, Jeffrey Rubin, and Millie Thayer. 2012. "Interrogating the Civil Society Agenda, Reassessing 'Un-Civic' Contention: An Introduction." In "Interrogating the Civil Society Agenda: Social Movements, Civil Society, and Democratic Innovation." Manuscript under review.

Arditti, Rita. 1999. *Searching for Life: The Grandmothers of the Plaza de Mayo and the Disappeared Children of Argentina*. Berkeley: University of California Press.

Auyero, Javier. 2004. "The Moral Politics of Argentine Crowds." *Mobilization* 9 (3): 311–26.

Avritzer, Leonardo. 2002. *Democracy and the Public Space in Latin America*. Princeton: Princeton University Press.

Avritzer, Leonardo. 2008. "Democratization and Citizenship in Latin America: The Emergence of Institutional Forms of Participation." *Latin American Research Review* 43 (2): 282–89.

Baiocchi, Gianpaolo. 2005. *Militants and Citizens: The Politics of Participatory Democracy in Porto Alegre*. Redwood City: Stanford University Press.

Baletti, Brenda, Tamara Johnson, and Wendy Wolford. 2008. "Late Mobilization: Transnational Peasant Networks and Grassroots Organizing in Brazil and South Africa." *Journal of Agrarian Change* 8 (2–3): 290–314.

Bobrow-Strain, Aaron. 2007. *Intimate Enemies: Landowners, Power, and Violence in Chiapas*. Durham: Duke University Press.

Collier, George A., with Elizabeth Lowery Quaratiello. 1994. *Basta! Land and the Zapatista Rebellion in Chiapas*. Oakland: Food First Books.

Crabtree, John. 2005. *Patterns of Protest: Politics and Social Movements in Bolivia*. London: Latin American Bureau.

Dagnino, Evelina. 2002. *Sociedade civil e espaços publicos no Brasil*. São Paulo: Paz e Terra.

Danaher, Kevin, ed. 2001. *Democratizing the Global Economy*. Monroe, ME: Common Courage Press.

Deere, Carmen Diana, and Frederick S. Royce. 2009. *Rural Social Movements in Latin America: Organizing for Sustainable Livelihoods*. Gainesville: University Press of Florida.

De Janvry, Alain, and Elisabeth Sadoulet. 2002. "Land Reforms in Latin America: Ten Lessons toward a Contemporary Agenda." Document prepared for the World Bank's Latin American Land Policy Workshop, Pachuca, Mexico, June 14. Online at http://are.berkeley.edu/~sadoulet/papers/Land_Reform_in_LA_10_lesson.pdf. Accessed February 3, 2010.

Desmarais, Annette Aurélie. 2009. "La Vía Campesina: Globalizing Peasants." In *Rural Social Movements in Latin America: Organizing for Sustainable Livelihoods,* edited by Carmen Diana Deere and Frederick S. Royce, 33–54. Gainesville: University Press of Florida.

Dezalay, Yves, and Bryant G. Garth. 2002. *The Internationalization of Palace Wars: Lawyers, Economists, and the Contest to Transform Latin American States*. Chicago: University of Chicago Press.

Dixon, Kwame. 2008. "Transnational Black Social Movements in Latin America: Afro-Colombians and the Struggle for Human Rights." In *Latin American Social Movements in the Twenty-First Century: Resistance, Power, and Democracy,* edited by Richard Stahler-Sholk, Harry E. Vanden, and Glen David Kuecker, 181–96. Lanham: Rowman & Littlefield.

Eckstein, Susan Eva, and Timothy P. Wickham-Crowley. 2003. *What Justice? Whose Justice? Fighting for Fairness in Latin America*. Berkeley: University of California Press.

Escobar, Arturo. 2010. "Latin America at a Crossroads: Alternative Modernizations, Post-Liberalism, or Post-Development?" *Cultural Studies* 24 (1): 1–65.

Fernandes, Bernardo Mançano. 2005. "The Occupation as a Form of Access to Land in Brazil: A Theoretical and Methodological Contribution." In *Reclaiming the Land: The Resurgence of Rural Movements in Africa, Asia, and Latin America,* edited by Sam Moyo and Paris Yeros, 317–40. London: Zed Books.

French, Jan. 2009. *Legalizing Identities: Becoming Black or Indian in Brazil's Northeast*. Chapel Hill: University of North Carolina Press.

French, John. 2009. "Lula, the 'New Unionism,' and the Brazilian Workers' Party: How Workers Came to Change the World, or at Least Brazil." *Latin American Politics and Society* 51 (4): 157–69.

Fung, Archon, and Erik Olin Wright. 2003. *Deepening Democracy: Institutional Innovations in Empowered Participatory Governance*. London: Verso.

Harvey, Neil. 1998. *The Chiapas Rebellion: The Struggle for Land and Democracy*. Durham: Duke University Press.

Hellman, Judith Adler. 1992. "The Study of New Social Movements in Latin America and the Question of Autonomy." In *The Making of Social Movements in Latin America,* edited by Arturo Escobar and Sonia Alvarez, 52–61. New York: Westview Press.

Hellman, Judith Adler. 2008. "Mexican Popular Movements, Clientelism, and the Process of Democratization." In *Latin American Social Movements in the Twenty-First Century: Resistance, Power, and Democracy,* edited by Richard Stahler-Sholk, Harry E. Vanden, and Glen David Kuecker, 61–76. Lanham: Rowman & Littlefield.

Houtzager, Peter, and Marcus J. Kurtz. 2000. "The Institutional Roots of Popular Mobilization: State Transformation and Rural Politics in Brazil and Chile, 1960–1995." *Comparative Studies in Society and History* 422: 394–424.

Karl, Terry Lynn. 2003. "The Vicious Cycle of Inequality in Latin America." In *What Justice? Whose Justice? Fighting for Fairness in Latin America*, edited by Susan Eva Eckstein and Timothy P. Wickham-Crowley, 133–57. Berkeley: University of California Press.

Kay, Cristóbal, and Miguel Urioste. 2007. "Bolivia's Unfinished Agrarian Reform: Rural Poverty and Development Policies." In *Land, Poverty, and Livelihoods in an Era of Globalization: Perspectives from Developing and Transition Countries*, edited by A. Haroon Akram-Lodhi, Saturnino M. Borras Jr., and Cristóbal Kay, 41–79. London: Routledge.

Keck, Margaret E., and Rebecca Neaera Abers. 2006. "Civil Society and State-Building in Latin America." *LASA Forum* 37 (1): 30–32.

Kurzman, Charles. 1996. "Structural Opportunities and Perceived Opportunities in Social-Movement Theory: Evidence from the Iranian Revolution of 1979." *American Sociological Review* 61 (1): 153–70.

Lehmann, David. 1990. *Democracy and Development in Latin America: Economics, Politics, and Religion in the Post-war Period*. Philadelphia: Temple University Press.

Leyva Solano, Xóchitl. 1999. "De Las Cañadas a Europa: Niveles, actores y discursos del Nuevo movimiento zaptista (NMZ) (1994–1997)." *Revista destacatos* 1: 56–87.

Mainwaring, Scott, and Edwardo Viola. 1984. *New Social Movements, Political Culture, and Democracy: Brazil and Argentina*. Notre Dame: Helen Kellogg Institute for International Studies, University of Notre Dame.

Martins, José de Souza. 2000. "As mudanças nas relações entre a sociedade e o Estado e a tendência à anomia nos movimentos sociais e nas organizações populares." *Estudos avançados* 14 (38): 268–78.

Medeiros, Leonilde. 1989. *História dos movimentos sociais no campo*. Rio de Janeiro: FASE.

Melucci, Alberto. 1989. *Nomads of the Present: Social Movements and Individual Needs in Contemporary Society*. Philadelphia: Temple University Press.

Navarro, Maryssa. 1989. "The Personal Is Political: Las Madres de Plaza de Mayo." In *Power and Popular Protest*, edited by Susan Eckstein, 241–58. Berkeley: University of California Press.

Oxhorn, Philip. 2001. "From Human Rights to Citizenship Rights? Recent Trends in the Study of Latin American Social Movements." *Latin American Research Review* 36 (3): 163–82.

Oxhorn, Philip. 2003. "Social Inequality, Civil Society, and the Limits of Citizenship in Latin America." In *What Justice? Whose Justice? Fighting for Fairness in Latin America*, edited by Susan Eva Eckstein and Timothy P. Wickham-Crowley, 35–63. Berkeley: University of California Press.

Peeler, John A. 2003. "Social Justice and the New Indigenous Politics: An Analysis of Guatemala, the Central Andes, and Chiapas." In *What Justice? Whose Justice? Fighting for Fairness in Latin America*, edited by Susan Eva Eckstein and Timothy P. Wickham-Crowley, 257–84. Berkeley: University of California Press.

Perrault, Thomas. 2006. "From the Guerra Del Agua to the Guerra Del Gas: Resource Governance, Neoliberalism, and Popular Protest in Bolivia." *Antipode* 38 (1): 150–72.

Perrault, Thomas. 2008. "Latin American Social Movements." *Geography Compass* 2 (5): 1363–85.

Postero, Nancy Grey. 2007. *Now We Are Citizens*. Redwood City: Stanford University Press.

Ramírez, Gloria Muñoz. 2008. *The Fire and the Word: A History of the Zapatista Movement*. San Francisco: City Lights Books.

Roberts, Kenneth, 2002. "Social Inequalities without Class Cleavages in Latin America's Neoliberal Era." *Studies in Comparative International Development* 36 (4): 3–33.

Saisari, Silvestre. 2009. "Toward a Real Agrarian Reform in Bolivia: The Perspective of the Landless Movement." In *Rural Social Movements in Latin America: Organizing for Sustainable Livelihoods,* edited by Carmen Diana Deere and Frederick S. Royce, 123–37. Gainesville: University Press of Florida.

Salazar Ortuño, Fernando. 2003. "El Plan Dignidad y el militarismo en Bolivia: El caso del Trópico de Cochabamba." In *Movimientos sociales y conflictos en América Latina,* edited by José Seoane. Buenos Aires: Consejo Latinoamericano de Ciencias Sociales (CLACSO).

Scherer-Warren, Ilse, and P. J. Krischke. 1987. *Uma Revolução no Cotidiano? Os novos movimentos sociais na América Latina.* São Paulo: Editora Brasiliense.

Scott, James C. 2009. *The Art of Not Being Governed: An Anarchist History of Upland Southeast Asia.* New Haven: Yale University Press.

Seed, Patricia. 2001. "No Perfect World: Aboriginal Communities' Contemporary Resource Rights." In *The Latin American Subaltern Studies Reader,* edited by Ileana Rodríguez, 129–42. Durham: Duke University Press.

Shiva, Vandana. 2004. Foreword. In *Cochabamba! Water War in Bolivia,* by Oscar Olivera. Cambridge: South End Press.

Sitrin, Marina. 2006. Introduction. In *Horizontalism: Voices of Popular Power in Argentina,* edited by Mariana Sitrin, 1–20. Oakland: AK Press.

Smith, Neil. 1993. "Homeless/Global: Scaling Places." In *Mapping the Futures: Local Cultures, Global Change,* edited by Jon Bird, Barry Curtis, Tim Putnam, George Robertson, and Lisa Tickner, 87–119. London: Routledge.

Spronk, Susan, and Jeffrey R. Webber. 2008. "Struggles against Accumulation by Dispossession in Bolivia: The Political Economy of Natural Resource Contention." In *Latin American Social Movements in the Twenty-First Century: Resistance, Power, and Democracy,* edited by Richard Stahler-Sholk, Harry E. Vanden, and Glen David Kuecker, 77–92. Lanham: Rowman & Littlefield.

Stahler-Sholk, Richard. 2008. "Resisting Neoliberal Homogenization: The Zapatista Autonomy Movement." In *Latin American Social Movements in the Twenty-First Century: Resistance, Power, and Democracy,* edited by Richard Stahler-Sholk, Harry E. Vanden, and Glen David Kuecker, 113–30. Lanham: Rowman & Littlefield.

Stahler-Sholk, Richard, Harry E. Vanden, and Glen David Kuecker, eds. 2008. *Latin American Social Movements in the Twenty-First Century: Resistance, Power, and Democracy.* Lanham: Rowman & Littlefield.

Svampa, Maristela, and Sebastian Pereyra. 2003. *Entre la ruta y el barrio: La experiencia de las organizaciones piqueteras.* Buenos Aires: Biblos.

Swords, Alicia C. S. 2008. "Neo-Zapatista Network Politics: Transforming Democracy and Development." In *Latin American Social Movements in the Twenty-First Century: Resistance, Power, and Democracy,* edited by Richard Stahler-Sholk, Harry E. Vanden, and Glen David Kuecker, 291–306. Lanham: Rowman & Littlefield.

Tarrow, Sidney. 1998. *Power in Movement: Social Movements and Contentious Politics.* Second edition. Cambridge: Cambridge University Press.

Tilly, Charles. 1978. *From Mobilization to Revolution.* Reading: Addison-Wesley.

Tiney, Juan. 2009. "For Life, Land, Territory, and the Sovereignty of Our People: The Latin American Coordinator of Rural Organizations." In *Rural Social Movements in Latin America: Organizing for Sustainable Livelihoods,* edited by Carmen Diana Deere and Frederick S. Royce, 79–86. Gainesville: University Press of Florida.

Touissaint, Eric. 1999. *Your Money or Your Life!* London: Pluto Press.

Van Cott, Donna Lee. 2000. *The Friendly Liquidation of the Past: The Politics of Diversity in Latin America.* Pittsburgh: University of Pittsburgh Press.

Vuletin, Guillermo. 2008. "Measuring the Informal Economy in Latin America and the Caribbean." IMF Working Paper WP/08/102. Online at https://www.imf.org/external/pubs/ft/wp/2008/wp08102.pdf. Accessed July 1, 2014.

Walton, Michael, 2004. "Neoliberalism in Latin America: Good, Bad, or Incomplete?" *Latin American Research Review* 29 (3): 165–83.

Wampler, Brian. 2007. *Participatory Budgeting in Brazil: Contestation, Cooperation, and Accountability.* University Park: Pennsylvania State University Press.

Weyland, Kurt. 2004. "Neoliberalism and Democracy in Latin America: A Mixed Record." *Latin American Politics and Society* 46 (1): 135–57.

Williams, Raymond. 1973. *City and Country.* Oxford: Oxford University Press.

Wolford, Wendy. 2007. "Land Reform in the Time of Neo-Liberalism: A Many Splendored Thing." *Antipode* 39 (3): 550–72.

Wolford, Wendy. 2010a. "Participatory Democracy by Default: Land Reform, Social Movements, and the State in Northeastern Brazil." *Journal of Peasant Studies* 37 (1): 91–109.

Wolford, Wendy. 2010b. *This Land Is Ours Now: Social Mobilization and the Meaning(s) of Land in Brazil.* Durham: Duke University Press.

Wolford, Wendy. Forthcoming. "From Mosquitoes to Marx: The Changing Dynamics of State and Social Movements in Brazilian Land Reform." *Latin American Research Review.*

Womack, John Jr., ed. 1999. *Chiapas: The Historical Reader.* New York: New Press.

Wright, Angus, and Wendy Wolford. 2003. *To Inherit the Earth: The Landless Movement and the Struggle for a New Brazil.* Oakland: Food First Publications.

Yashar, Deborah J. 1999. "Democracy, Indigenous Movements, and the Postliberal Challenge in Latin America." *World Politics* 52: 76–104.

Yashar, Deborah J. 2005. *Contesting Citizenship in Latin America: The Rise of Indigenous Movements and the Postliberal Challenge.* Cambridge: Cambridge University Press.

Zibechi, Raúl. 2003. "Los movimientos sociales latinoamericanos: Tendencias y desafíos." *Observatorio social de América Latina (OSAL)* no. 9 (January): 185–88.

Figure 3.1a. San Cristóbal de Las Casas, "the Ladino town," 1968. Photo © Jan Rus.

Figure 3.1b. San Cristóbal de Las Casas, majority indigenous city, 2005. Photo © Jacob Rus.

3

THE URBAN INDIGENOUS MOVEMENT AND ELITE ACCOMMODATION IN SAN CRISTÓBAL, CHIAPAS, MEXICO, 1975-2008

"TENEMOS QUE VIVIR NUESTROS AÑOS"
"WE HAVE TO LIVE IN OUR OWN TIMES"

Jan Rus and Gaspar Morquecho Escamilla

IN THE EARLY 1970s, the population of the colonial city of San Cristóbal, Chiapas, Mexico, and the small highland valley that surrounds it stood at barely twenty-five thousand—numbers that had grown only slowly in more than a century. Nearly all residents were Spanish-speaking ladinos—the term in Chiapas and neighboring Guatemala that glosses everyone who is not indigenous. Although the city had been passed by since it lost the state capital to Tuxtla Gutiérrez in the nearby lowlands in the late nineteenth century, San Cristóbal was still the local capital for Chiapas's Central Highlands, a region that also encompassed fourteen indigenous *municipios* containing approximately 140,000 Tsotsil- and Tseltal-speaking Mayas.

From colonial times, San Cristóbal had been both a necessary and a proscribed space for the indigenous. On the one hand, they had no choice but to come to the city to visit government and church offices, to go to the region's major market, and to secure contracts and advance payments for the migratory agricultural labor that was their principal source of income. On the other, despite this close relationship—or rather, given the necessity of maintaining the privileges and control of a nonindigenous minority in an overwhelmingly indigenous region, because of it—the city maintained a strict ethnic exclusion of indigenous people, almost a kind of apartheid. Still in the 1960s, by custom if no longer by law, indigenous people who found themselves in San Cristóbal at nightfall tried to get off of the streets and find a secure place—a church court-yard or the open patio of a patron—until morning or run the risk of being jailed for the night.[1] Because of the rigor of this exclusion, indigenous people avoided going to the city any more than was necessary. Those who did move into town, typically as servants, soon abandoned indigenous clothing and as much as possible spoke Spanish; they became ladinos.[2]

Turning to the San Cristóbal of today, we find a city of more than 188,000, 40 percent of them—approximately 80,000 people—speakers of Tsotsil and Tseltal who inhabit some eighty *colonias,* or shantytowns, ringing the old, tile-roofed city.[3] In some ways, the rural-urban migration embodied in this "new" city replicates that of other Latin American cities since the mid-twentieth century. Superficially, the only difference is that the Chiapas highlands came late to the transformation, becoming perhaps the last major region to urbanize. A closer look, however, reveals some sharp distinctions between San Cristóbal's urbanization and that elsewhere.[4] During its first three decades, right through the end of the 1990s, San Cristóbal's ladinos continued in general to resist what they perceived as the indigenous "invasion" of their city. In response, indige-nous people, driven out of the countryside by demographic and economic pres-sures not unlike those elsewhere, were compelled to develop extraordinarily coherent, militant forms of organization, first to push their way into the city and acquire land and then to secure urban services and eventually political representation and a share of power.

From a distance, some of this coherent organization appears to be a carry-over from the historical pattern of dyadic ethnic division: ladinos resisted the indigenous presence *as* ladinos, and the urban indigenous organized on their side as indigenous. In fact, however, there were profound organizational inno-vations on both sides. The indigenous migrants, most of whom at the beginning were Protestant converts, soon developed independent political and economic organizations that were at first aligned with their new religious denominations but soon transcended those boundaries and came to represent entire neighbor-hoods and groups of neighborhoods and eventually assumed the functions of labor unions as well. At the same time that the members of these organizations were transcending their religious denominations, they were uniting across former boundaries of community of origin and even linguistic divisions. What emerged was a new kind of secular, "pan-indigenous"—or, as people had come to say by the 2000s, a "Maya"—political and social organization and, increasingly, identity.

Meanwhile, concomitant changes were reshaping the ladino side of the dyad. Against the backdrop of a tourist boom that had begun in the 1980s, and then the Zapatista Rebellion in 1994, increasing numbers of San Cristóbal's ladino entrepreneurs and politicians realized they could not have the peace they needed with their Maya neighbors unless they themselves altered their own views and actions. The economic accommodation appears to have come first. As the city's economy accelerated through the 1980s, ladino businesses of all kinds—construction companies, supermarkets, hotels, and restaurants—expanded, and the owners gradually began to appreciate the ready supply of workers represented by the formerly reviled indigenous colonias. By the second half of the 1980s, some politicians had also realized that the urban colonists' multineighborhood associations made it possible to exchange urban services and benefits for votes in a systematic way. Initially, both of these relationships, economic and political, were largely obscured by a rhetoric of exclusion, even by those ladino entrepreneurs and politicians who participated in them. Following the 1994 rebellion, however—in particular, the Maya rebels' several-day occupation of San Cristóbal—the urban Maya became more assertive. The ladino elite eventually responded by ceding more economic and political space to them in return for more predictable, at least formally democratic, decision making. Such economic and political accommodation allowed the ladino elite to maintain its control, while Maya leaders believed it would eventually permit them to take over (Morquecho Escamilla 2000).

The chapter explores this thirty-five-year process of movement through conflict toward increasing coexistence historically, and shows how the actions of each side led the other to modify its organization and rhetoric as they both learned to pursue their group and individual goals in an increasingly complicated urban environment. Through interviews, eighteen representative leaders from both sides of this struggle, ten ladino and eight indigenous, look at what has happened over these years, at what part each has played in both the struggle and the accommodation, and where each foresees relations between the two ethnic groups going in the future.[5] Men and women on both sides consider this now generation-long process a watershed in the city's history; in retrospect, they recognize that before the 1970s, San Cristóbal was little more than a big Spanish-speaking town, and that by the early twenty-first century it had become a complex multiethnic, multilingual city.

Nearly everyone interviewed organized his or her thoughts into a series of "befores" and "afters," specific dates of major changes that essentially provide a common periodization for talking about what has happened in San Cristóbal. Building on this inherent periodization, the chapter is essentially a collective oral history. All of those we interviewed talked about the changes in the city, in the relationship between its ethnic groups, and the consciousness within each group—as well as within themselves as individuals. The chapter does not provide an economic or political history, nor even a social and cultural history, although it attempts to incorporate elements of all of those into the explanations of what separates one period from the next. Rather, it is an account of recent history as it is popularly remembered by those who lived through and acted in it. Some might think this is a loose reconstruction of the past, limited by the memory of the participants with all of their own and their groups' blind spots, prejudices, and self-justifications. However, the construction of the past by leading individuals (and through them, by their groups) tells us what they think their experience means, and thus what lessons they—as ongoing leaders—carry into the future.

A note about the interviewees: Although today San Cristóbal has some 188,000 inhabitants, many are new arrivals and the city is in effect still a relatively small place.[6] As a result, most of our collaborators are leaders in more than one area. On the indigenous side, the same individuals could be Protestant pastors or Catholic catechists (these were perhaps the only two functions that were mutually exclusive, or at least were not held simultaneously—some catechists have been pastors and vice versa), founders and political leaders of colonias and unions, elected members of the *ayuntamiento* (city council), and prominent merchants. On the ladino side, the leaders also tend to be multifaceted: university, health care, and civil administrators are also members of prominent commercial and/or landholding families and may be merchants and/or landholders themselves.[7] In several cases, the same people were also columnists or contributors to the local media. San Cristóbal is a smaller place than the settings of most of the other case studies in this book, and its leading families have deep historical roots and still dominate most sectors of local society. Perhaps this accounts for the fact that it is harder than elsewhere to distinguish a separate "private sector" elite from leaders in other facets of economic and political life. In other respects, however, this case does follow a model similar to the others examined in this book. There is an activist, almost insurgent movement from below in the social structure, and a local elite who has been largely responsible for setting the pace in accommodating the activists' thrust.

A last note: We have tried to make our interviewees as anonymous as possible. Unfortunately, a side effect of that effort is that it obscures the fact that quite often those speaking about political decisions are not just providing third-person accounts but are describing decisions for which they were themselves responsible.[8]

THE ORIGINS OF URBANIZATION IN HIGHLAND CHIAPAS, 1952–1982

Ladinos' historical exclusion of indigenous people was of course an expression of a deeper economic and political reality. Most things that were privately owned in highland Chiapas right to the present—land, buildings, businesses, and machinery—belonged to ladinos. Ladinos also filled all state, federal, and even religious offices; as late as the end of the 1990s, for example, in the five centuries since the arrival of Spaniards, there had never been an indigenous Catholic priest. Indigenous people, for their part, lived in and held land as communities, each marked by a distinctive style of dress and characterized by a slightly different dialect of Tsotsil or Tseltal. Most men worked as migrant agricultural laborers, and women spent the greater part of their lives within the spaces of their communities, caring for households and raising children.

The first significant breaches in the barriers separating indigenous people from ladinos began appearing in the 1950s, and not in the city but the countryside. In 1952, the Instituto Nacional Indigenista (INI), a federal agency dedicated to bridging the differences that divided indigenous people from other Mexicans, opened its first experimental center in San Cristóbal and quickly founded the first of what would eventually be scores of primary schools in native communities. As a result, by the early 1960s, the highlands had its first generation of significant numbers of indigenous people who were bilingual and literate. As INI-promoted roads spread throughout the region during the same period, indigenous entrepreneurs, also with the help of the INI, eventually began to purchase trucks and commercialize their products beyond San Cristóbal. By the end of the 1960s, there was an increasingly ambitious "nationalized" elite of young adults in municipios throughout the highlands.

The biggest break in the traditional roles of, and balance between, indigenous people and ladinos, however, came in the mid-1970s, when for the first time since the early colonial period Tseltals and Tsotsils, still wearing their traditional dress and speaking not only Spanish but their own languages, began to take up residence in the confines of the valley of San Cristóbal. Ironically,

these indigenous migrants to the city were a by-product, although an unantici-
pated one, of INI's efforts to promote development within the native municipios
themselves. As more indigenous people became bilingual, literate, and aware
of their rights as Mexican citizens, they eventually came into conflict with
their communities' political bosses, or *caciques*, who had long held a monopoly
as go-betweens with the national society and government—a monopoly that
had also become an economic stranglehold in most municipios. At stake were
such things as the right to own stores and trucks, to hold political offices, and
to be employed by the state (Rus 1994 and 2005). Younger people wanted a
share of these goods, and in most communities the old elite blocked their way.
As conflicts between the sides hardened, after a while they took on a religious
tint—the caciques using traditional religion to discipline the upstarts, and
some of the young turning in response to liberationist Catholicism and then
Protestantism to define themselves and seek outside allies. Eventually, by the
late 1960s, this religious schism overshadowed all other divisions in many of
the communities of the highlands. After several years of internal violence,
in the mid-1970s some of the biggest, most conflicted municipios began to
expel the dissidents. Although the exiles were often economic innovators and
political dissidents, they were banished for religious apostasy, which in turn
probably explains the great violence that was often involved. Their nonconfor-
mity, their supposed disrespect of traditional beliefs, was said by the caciques—
and believed by their neighbors—to place entire communities at risk of divine
punishment, and they were often purged in convulsions of communal violence
that lasted for days.[9]

The first colonia of such *expulsados* in San Cristóbal was founded in late 1976,
its residents Protestant refugees from the nearby Tsotsil-speaking municipios
of Chamula and Zinacantán. By 1982, there were five such colonias with a
total population of something less than three thousand (Rus and Vigil 2007).
The presence of these initial indigenous urban migrants was tolerated in the
historically exclusivist ladino city because they were refugees from religious
violence, and it was understood that they had nowhere else to go (Gossen 1989
and Rus 2005).[10] Their entrance to the city was thus perceived as a limited,
onetime event. Moreover, they had purchased the land on which they settled,
typically with the assistance of Mexican and international Protestant denominations. Not only did this benefit local landowners, who in every case sold them
marginal, unproductive lands, but they established their modest settlements
in far corners of the San Cristóbal valley, away from the area occupied by
ladinos. Finally, they were considered orderly and inoffensive. A common
(and racist) compliment paid by ladinos to the refugees in these early years

was that they were magnificent servants: hardworking, "less obtuse than most indigenous people" (many were of the educated elites of their communities), and "more honest than most"—a quality attributed to their fervent, converts' Protestantism.

Despite appearances, however, over time—and perhaps even at the beginning—rural-urban migration in highland Chiapas was not only, or even principally, driven by religion. As elsewhere in Latin America, it was the end of a process of dispossession in rural communities as a result of a declining agricultural economy, a rapidly growing population, and the ensuing conflicts within communities over limited resources. What makes this case distinctive, though, is that perhaps only such an extreme series of events as religious expulsions could have overcome the caste barrier, the cultural exclusion, that coincided with the rural-urban division in the Chiapas highlands (Cantón Delgado 1997, Rus and Vigil 2007, and Viqueira 2009).

From the beginning of their urbanization, the refugees were highly organized. In each colonia, early residents belonged to single religious denominations, and their first buildings, even before everyone had a formal house, were churches. Beyond their religious organization, all of the original colonias were also mobilized politically against those who had expelled them—the traditionalist caciques in their home municipios. Their principal goal was to return home, and they began staging demonstrations in San Cristóbal and the state capital of Tuxtla Gutiérrez within weeks of the first massive expulsions in the late summer of 1974. When the state government and official party, the PRI (Partido Revolucionario Institucional), lined up behind the caciques—both the state and party in fact depended on the caciques for their own control of the indigenous population—the refugees eventually began to organize against them as well. This pivot from opposing just their own caciques to opposing the apparatus of the state occurred so quickly that the shift went almost unperceived. After maintaining sit-ins against their expulsion and demanding the right to go home through 1975, by 1976, about the time the first "permanent" colony appeared in San Cristóbal, the expulsados realized that the state government not only did not support their claims but was not likely to. That same year, they sent representatives to begin a long-term sit-in in the central plaza of faraway Mexico City; they also continued their marches and sit-ins in Chiapas.

From 1976 through 1982, the number of indigenous people and colonias in San Cristóbal grew only slowly. The violence of expulsion from their homes, and the dislocation of coming into the city, hardly made urbanization an attractive option. With the decline of world oil prices in 1981 followed by the collapse of the Mexican financial system in 1982, however, the country entered a deep depression. Over the next half year, plantation agriculture, which had provided the seasonal, migratory jobs that fed three-quarters of highland Chiapas's indigenous households and which had already been stagnant since the mid-1970s, contracted sharply. Construction jobs in infrastructure development, which had employed many younger indigenous men, fell even more abruptly as funding was cut off from one day to the next in response to austerity measures imposed by the United States Treasury and the International Monetary Fund. Throughout the highlands, for the first time in generations, large numbers of people were suddenly without a way to make a living (Cantón Delgado 1997, Rus and Vigil 2007, and Viqueira 2009).

Despite the energy they continued to pour into their struggle with the caciques and government, the expulsados had by this time made niches for themselves in the city's markets, in construction, and as workers in the budding tourist industry. Seeing their success, rural indigenous people began to perceive traditionally hostile and racist San Cristóbal as a possible refuge. By early 1983, scores of new migrants were arriving every month; by the mid-1980s, hundreds. By 1988, there were eighteen colonias in the valley of San Cristóbal, and the indigenous population had ballooned to more than fifteen thousand.

YEARS OF DEPRESSION AND RADICALIZATION, 1982–1994

If the ladinos of the city had resigned themselves to the presence of a few hundred indigenous refugees in the late 1970s, from 1982 and 1983 on, they were increasingly alarmed at the rapid growth of San Cristóbal's indigenous population. Not only did their new neighbors erect scruffy colonias that were increasingly visible from the roads entering and leaving the city—and after 1983, with the first colonia that climbed the northern hillsides, from everywhere in the valley—but throngs of them soon filled sidewalks, plazas, and even church courtyards, where they sat down to sell artisan goods and food or just to visit. In the evening, even larger crowds gathered in the main plaza and at the market to relax. Unlike the first scared, isolated refugees, as the numbers of urban indigenous people grew, they made themselves at home in every corner of the city. This "invasion" of the city's space by "indigenous hordes" (la indiada), as our ladino interlocutors remember seeing them at the time, was blamed on a laundry list of factors.

According to "Professor" (to ensure anonymity, we've come up with such descriptors for the interviewees; see chapter notes for additional details), the fault lay, simultaneously and somewhat contradictorily, with Protestant missionaries and Catholic liberation theology, both of which had "destroyed the age-old harmony" of "traditional" native communities, leading to social dissolution. "Store Owner," meanwhile, blamed rural schools and other government programs that had "made indigenous people too lazy to continue working in agriculture." While "Civil Servant" said the fault lay with government construction projects that had supposedly drawn "indigenous people looking for an easy life" permanently into the city. Falling back on a sort of mythical-traditional vision of highland Chiapas as a series of exclusive ethnic spaces, these and other ladino leaders recalled that well into the 1980s it was still universally believed that San Cristóbal was the ladinos' municipio—that the Chamulas had Chamula, the Zinacantecos Zinacantán, and the ladinos San Cristóbal. Everyone should go back where they belonged, and not intrude unwanted in spaces that were not theirs. (Truth be told, until plantation agriculture began to stall in the 1970s, forcing many ladino landowners, overseers, and store owners to retreat to San Cristóbal from an increasingly conflictive countryside, ladinos had never before considered that *they* were excluded anywhere.)

Under the influence of the rapidly increasing resistance to the indigenous migrants of these years—a resistance redoubled by the economic crisis that also left many San Cristóbal ladinos in economic distress even as they were being obliged to share "their" space with impoverished indigenous people—the city began putting up roadblocks to further immigration. Attempts were made to deny colonies of new migrants access to water, electricity, roads, schools, police protection, and work. These last two points were often one and the same: from 1983 on, municipal police, directed by the city's leading officials, were regularly used to drive away and arrest indigenous street vendors, to break up indigenous artisan markets, to harass indigenous truck and *colectivo* (minivan) drivers, and in general to make life in the city as unpleasant as possible for the newcomers. In response, the city's already existing indigenous associations began reorganizing to fight the ladino city for space, services, and representation. These associations included Protestant churches, Catholic base communities, and residential groups based in the colonias—groups that heretofore had focused their political energies on campaigns against rural caciques and the federal and state officials who supported them but which had also come together to provide lodging and work for new migrants, for example, or to share medical expenses or to pool resources to start businesses. The era of circumspect urban migrants who felt themselves guests, and barely welcome ones at that, was over.

The first non–religiously based, united indigenous front organization in San Cristóbal, formed by Protestant and Catholic refugees from Chamula in response to a new wave of violent religious expulsions from that municipio in

1982, was the Comité de Defensa de los Amenazados, Perseguidos y Expulsados de Chamula (Committee for the Defense of the Threatened, Persecuted, and Expelled of Chamula). Comité goals were to put an end to the destruction of the property and murder of religious converts still in Chamula, to ensure the right of return for all the refugees, and perhaps most of all, to secure recognition from the state and federal governments of their civil rights as Mexican citizens. The civil right that had concerned them for the longest time was the freedom to choose their own religion, but in 1982 and 1983, their most urgent demand was the right to be safe from arbitrary official violence. At first, this demand was asserted with respect to their home municipio and its caciques, with the Comité organizing marches and demonstrations outside of government buildings and demanding meetings with officials in San Cristóbal and Chiapas's capital of Tuxtla Gutiérrez. Within months of the Comité's founding, however, equal rights and treatment before the law became an explosive issue in San Cristóbal as well (Morquecho Escamilla 1992, 23–32).

In their efforts to stop or slow urbanization, San Cristóbal's legal remedies were limited. The municipal government was unable to prevent the migrants from forming new settlements because the migrants themselves were buying the land, and there were no zoning or other laws to say they could not do with it what they wished.[11] The city could, however, deny the colonias official recognition, and with that, since legally the colonias did not exist, such urban improvements as streets, sidewalks, sewers, and water—all of which were under local control—could also be denied. Connection to electricity—a federal service—was more complicated. The city could not deny it, but because the new colonies could not afford to pay for installation of power lines without government help, lack of official recognition typically left them in the dark. Finally, the city could also cut off (or try to) street vending, perhaps the most common entry-level source of work in the city.

Indigenous people could solve some of these obstacles to making their homes in the city independently. Electricity could be siphoned off by hooking up to power lines directly, for instance, and through the 1980s and 1990s there were men in the colonias who for a moderate fee would climb the nearest power pole and attach a home connection. Water was more problematic, but some colonias around the city's northern side eventually made contracts with neighboring indigenous settlements and installed independent water systems. Finally, street vendors of artisan goods found at least a partial remedy when after being driven away by the municipal police, Dominican priests and sisters offered them the grounds surrounding the Dominican church for a permanent *tianguis* (open-air market).

But such solutions were ad hoc and partial. The larger problems of receiving the services due them as citizens, and simply of being recognized as legitimate residents of the city, remained. After consulting with independent political organizers, the democratic teachers union, and the growing indigenous movement in the countryside, in 1984 the Comité de Defensa disbanded and reformed as the Consejo de Representantes Indígenas de los Altos de Chiapas (CRIACH, Council of Indigenous Representatives of Highland Chiapas). In addition to Chamulas, indigenous migrants to the city from throughout the highlands were represented in this new group. While the leaders were still typically Protestant pastors and Catholic catechists from Chamula, and although religious rights and the struggle against those who had expelled them from their home communities remained on their agenda, with the founding of CRIACH, these were no longer the only goals.[12] Rather, their struggle was recast as a battle against the racism and exclusion suffered by indigenous people in general, and now they would fight as well for the improvement of their concrete living conditions and status as residents of San Cristóbal.[13]

From 1982 to 1994, with only two exceptions, successive ladino municipal presidents (mayors in Mexico are called *presidente municipal*) spent their terms of office fighting an escalating, and often contradictory, war with CRIACH and the dozens of unions of street vendors, market sellers, transport owners and drivers, religious congregations, and organized colonias that gathered under its umbrella. Item: From 1984 to 1986, for instance, harassment of street vendors continued, and although several hundred eventually wound up selling permanently on the grounds of Santo Domingo, hundreds of others were periodically driven off the streets by municipal police. At the same time, tourist information about the city prominently featured the presence of indigenous artisan sellers as one of the city's attractions. Item: From 1986 to 1988 and then from 1990 to 1992, a serious proposal was placed before the city government to acquire land outside of the Valley of San Cristóbal and relocate all of the unrecognized indigenous colonias, by force if necessary, to what would supposedly be "more natural environments" for them. Yet at the same time, during his campaign, the municipal president elected in 1988 had also acceded to—some say encouraged—CRIACH and its affiliated unions of market sellers to invade a large vacant lot near the city market to make more room for indigenous peddlers. In return, CRIACH voted as a bloc for his election (Morquecho Escamilla 1992 and 2002).

Beginning at the end of the 1980s, local politicians regularly traded concessions for votes. But whatever their temporary electoral alliances, each time the city government acted against indigenous interests, it was met by CRIACH and its affiliates with road blockages, sit-ins in government buildings, and marches. What until 1984 had been separate, worksite-by-worksite, colonia-by-colonia claims for services and rights now became common demands, backed by an organization that spanned the entire city and was tied to the growing indigenous movement in Chiapas's hinterland. Indeed, by the second half of the 1980s, CRIACH made a point of noting that its cause was the same as that of other surging indigenous and peasant organizations around the state. In response to the economic crisis, these organizations were increasingly militant in demanding the resolution of delayed agrarian reform claims, fair agricultural prices, state authorization for indigenous cooperatives to possess truck and bus routes, and release from prison of peasant leaders jailed on trumped-up charges.[14] After 1994, the Zapatistas would sum up these urban and rural claims as "the right to have rights."

Three decades later, memories of this period from the early 1980s by indigenous activists and members of the San Cristóbal elite mirror each other. As one indigenous leader put it: "In the early years, there wasn't that much trouble with the ladinos. I sold popsicles out of a cart, and the ladinos didn't seem to care, they didn't pay much attention to me. Later [in the early to mid-1980s], it was like they hated us. They didn't want us to sell anything, they didn't want us to be here at all. Maybe it was because there weren't so many of us at first" ("Activist," summer of 2008). On the ladino side, meanwhile, still in 2008 there were some who looked back on their attitude in the 1980s and reaffirmed the ways they had felt and acted then. "Store Owner," for example, a woman from a family of traditional plantation owners, said bitterly: "They aren't from here—this is not their municipio, it is ours. There's no reason they should stay here. They are invading our space."

But others, while honestly describing the battles they had fought with CRI-ACH and the indigenous migrants, recognized that times had moved on. "PRIísta," who held positions in local government beginning in the 1990s, recognized that through the 1980s and early 1990s he remained unalterably anti-indigenous and opposed to the colonias; he was one of those who wanted them razed. He now admits, however, that his family construction business had begun to benefit from the presence of indigenous laborers in the city as the business grew with the first small boomlet of tourism from the mid-1980s on. Even "Journalist," although now a well-known social activist, recalls that in the 1970s and early 1980s, at the same time that her parents were becoming outspoken supporters of Chiapas's liberationist bishop Samuel Ruiz and participating in nongovernmental organizations (NGOs) for the benefit of the poor, at least some of her relatives would not have indigenous people in their houses. As a child, she recalls, it had not been easy for her to accept that indigenous people were truly equal.

Meanwhile, more enlightened members of San Cristóbal's elite appear from their actions during the 1980s to have accepted early on the reality of a multicultural city, and to have done what they could to keep the city functioning despite the resistance of a vocal share of its leaders. While the city's government was trying to deny water, sewers, and roads to the new settlements, for example, some local delegates of state and federal agencies made a continuous effort to make the city livable. "Physician," for example, against the policy of local officials through most of the 1980s, went in person to the colonias and where possible allocated federal resources to remedy such threats to public health as standing water, rats, and unsanitary conditions in local markets. Similarly, "Builder" served on the local boards of NGOs affiliated with the Catholic Church. During a period at the end of the 1980s when he served in the municipal government, he did what he could to extend public services to all of the city's inhabitants. These actions on his part appear to have been motivated by a sense of humanism as well as public-spirited foresight, rather than a desire for indigenous votes or personal commercial interests. Among "Builder's" complaints was that throughout the 1980s, the city did not receive nearly enough appropriations from the federal government for its exploding population, which stymied the efforts of those who *were* willing to plan for a more rational growth. Waste disposal, potable water, open space—these are limited goods, he recalls, and the city government failed to get ahead of them in the 1980s. Because of the stubbornness of much of the city's elite and the stinginess of the national treasury, city government has been running behind ever since. From his description of his actions, it is apparent that he perceived early in the crisis years that indigenous migration to the city was only going to increase, and that he used the various forums in which he participated to make strong, technocratic arguments for planning to keep the urban environment livable.

Despite these counterexamples, however, where they could and for as long as they could, the city's leaders attempted to prevent more colonias from forming, denying services to new settlements, attempting to break up indigenous markets and run off street peddlers, and using the police and other officials to harass indigenous immigrants.

THE ZAPATISTA REBELLION, 1994–1998: "WHEN EVERYTHING BEGAN TO CHANGE"

When the Zapatistas seized San Cristóbal on New Year's Eve of 1994, indigenous people in the valley of San Cristóbal, no matter what their religion or politics, were for the first week and a half afraid the military's response would be turned against them.[15] That response could be seen throughout the valley in the form of the Mexican air force shooting rockets into supposed Zapatista strongholds just over the valley's southern rim. Indeed, from our interviews, it is clear that many of the EZLN troops who occupied San Cristóbal took their ski masks and uniforms out from under their beds in the city's indigenous colonias and walked into town where they joined the troops coming from the jungle.

Even before 1994, however, tension on both sides of the ethnic divide in San Cristóbal had been reaching a crescendo. The five-hundredth anniversary of Columbus's landfall was to have been celebrated internationally on October 12, 1992, as the "Encounter of Two Worlds," but indigenous protests erupted all over the Americas in response. In San Cristóbal, a massive indigenous demonstration, led it later turned out by the Zapatistas, pulled down and sawed into souvenirs the bronze statue of Diego de Mazariegos, leading officer of the Spaniards who had established the city in 1528. A few months earlier in 1992, fifteen truckloads of Chamula traditionalist men had attacked the city's most activist Protestant colonia and stronghold of CRIACH, La Hormiga, at dawn one morning. Using machetes, steel pipes, and rods as well as fire, they fought a pitched battle with the *colonos* that lasted through midday. La Hormiga's (and other colonias') Protestant expulsados had been slipping back into their old hamlets to visit their former homes and fields and proselytize their old neighbors—actions that escalated their never resolved conflict with the caciques. In the case of Chamula, the bosses intended to end these provocations once and for all. During the attack, residents of San Cristóbal heard the shouting, horns, and eventually a handful of gunshots; certainly they saw the smoke from burning houses. But the police and authorities never intervened.

Confronted on one side by San Cristóbal's hostile ladinos and on the other by the caciques of their communities of origin, a group of the colonias' leaders met secretly in February 1994 with Subcomandante Marcos and the Zapatistas inside San Cristóbal's cathedral during a break in the internationally covered peace talks with the national government. Accounts of the meeting say that Marcos advised them to arm themselves, and to be prepared to respond with equal or greater violence if violence were employed against them. Newly armed and emboldened, over the next several years the expulsados, now colonos, did indeed fight back—with many killed—every time the caciques of their home communities confronted them.[16]

Meanwhile, taking heart from the Zapatistas, the colonos were increasingly confident and aggressive in their struggle for rights and space in the city as well. In the summer of 1994, they elected one of CRIACH's founders as their first member of the state legislature. At roughly the same time, in open defiance of state authorities who had largely excluded the urban indigenous from taxicab licenses, growing numbers of indigenous entrepreneurs acquired passenger cars and began to operate them as taxis in San Cristóbal. From only one hundred taxis in the early 1990s, all owned by ladinos, by the end of the decade San Cristóbal had more than one thousand, most of them unlicensed indigenous *"piratas"* (pirates). The new taxi owners feared that the state police or other authorities might seize their vehicles. At the same time, the taxis themselves were the objects of a good deal of crime. As a result, by 1995 and 1996, the indigenous cabs were increasingly interconnected by CB radio, and most drivers had begun carrying weapons. Because San Cristóbal's municipal police, when they weren't repressing the indigenous, had always refused (or been afraid?) to attend calls for help from indigenous colonias or to provide more than pro-forma assistance to indigenous victims of crime (not to mention their nonresponse to violence like the 1992 attack on La Hormiga), it should perhaps come as no surprise that by 1996, when indigenous people needed help from police, they increasingly called for an indigenous taxicab. Over the next half decade, the indigenous taxi fleet essentially became an alternative indigenous police force—and in much of the city, the *only* police force: when called, they came in numbers, and when the authorized municipal officers saw them, they invariably veered away (Rus and Vigil 2007).

Finally, before 1994, all eighteen of San Cristóbal's indigenous colonias had been founded on land purchased from ladino landowners. After 1994, and through the beginning of the new millennium, every new colonia began as either a refugee camp for those fleeing rural violence (three cases) or an organized land invasion (ten cases). While San Cristóbal's indigenous people recall the Zapatista uprising and the years immediately after with pride as the moment when they finally "won" a little, not surprisingly, San Cristóbal's ladinos remember the period quite differently. All of the members of the elite whom we interviewed spoke of this period (1994–98) as a time of lawlessness, physical threat, and personal and social confusion. Beyond that, however, their reactions were much more mixed than might have been expected, reflecting not only that over time many had reconciled themselves to indigenous people's presence in the city, but that they had become increasingly willing in the aftermath of 1994 to consider policies and politics that accommodated all of the city's people.

The most stridently anti-indigenous feelings were expressed by "Store Owner," who conflated the Zapatista invasion of San Cristóbal with the presence of indigenous people in general. At the same time, she did not believe indigenous people could have planned and executed the Zapatistas' seizure of the city without the help of nonindigenous "outsiders"; she was especially bitter about the role of the Catholic Church and its "outsider" bishop, Samuel Ruiz (head of the diocese of San Cristóbal for forty years, from 1960 to 2000) with his liberation theology, for inciting "our indios against us." Although she did not admit to belonging to them herself, "Store Owner" spoke admiringly of the group Auténticos Coletos ("coleto" is the nickname for the traditional ladino population of San Cristóbal). The Auténticos, as they came to be called, formed in the spring of 1994 when they perceived that among the supposedly white/mestizo population of San Cristóbal, the "outsiders" could not be counted on to demand sufficiently harsh measures to restore ladino order in San Cristóbal and to crush the Zapatistas in the countryside. Over the next several years, the Auténticos organized occasional demonstrations against the bishop and the EZLN (including marches in which their indigenous servants carried signs denouncing Ruiz and Marcos equally). Some among them are credibly reputed to have helped organize the paramilitary gangs that fought for control of rural Chiapas in the late 1990s.

"Civil Servant" was also deeply offended by what he called the "indigenous reign" from 1994 to 1998. What he focused on was not the indigenous assertion of their power when they had the chance, but the government's weakness, the unwillingness—or inability?—of the state, on all levels, to reassert control. A forest reserve for which he was a trustee was lost to an invasion in 1995, and the fact that no government authority was willing to risk conflict with the invaders—and with an indigenous movement whose size and strength were still at that point not fully known—to dislodge them still infuriated "Civil Servant" thirteen years later. Equally aggravating was that when the state began indemnifying private owners and "regularizing" invasions in succeeding years—a common campaign ploy just before elections to win indigenous votes—the lost reserve was never given a second thought. It was considered already "public property" and could thus be disposed of for the public good. "Civil Servant" also shared a story about his own wife being detained on the road by the "taxi police" for several hours in the late 1990s after an indigenous-owned and -operated vehicle crashed into her. No civil authority ever appeared to free her, and he was forced to negotiate a settlement on the road by himself under the view of a phalanx of armed taxi drivers. This abdication of the rule of law he could not forgive, and his anger appeared equally great at the indigenous "who don't know any better," who were just "taking advantage," and the cowardly politicians who abandoned the city to them for the first several years after 1994.

Of the other interviewees, "PRIísta," the "Hotel Owners," and "Professor" also expressed dissatisfaction with the 1994–98 period, with descending levels of anger. "PRIísta" was at the time known for his support of the Auténticos, a fact he freely admitted. In retrospect, however, he also recognized that he increasingly relied on indigenous labor during the years immediately following the rebellion, and that by sparking interest in Chiapas in the rest of Mexico, the United States, and Europe, the Zapatistas paradoxically played a large role in the tourism boom after 1994 from which he and the merchant class have profited handsomely. The "Hotel Owners" were conflicted. While acknowledging the justice of many indigenous complaints—both are from local families but were educated outside of Chiapas—they were clear that the disorder that followed the 1994 rebellion could not be allowed to continue. The city needed planning, needed to be inclusive of all of its citizens, and needed investment and jobs; the "Hotel Owners" felt that all of these goals were postponed during these four years after the rebellion. Finally, "Professor" said that although he and his household did not personally experience any of the aggressiveness of the city's indigenous people after 1994, they did partake of the air of uncertainty and threat. People moved about less, "Professor" recalled, locked themselves in at night, and generally lived in fear. That said, he also noted that a sister-in-law who owned a store that sold household goods (inexpensive pots and pans, plastic plates, buckets, plastic sheeting, and so on) on the city's northern edge adjacent to the largest colonias did a booming business with those who started new households in the land invasions. Personally, she never had any trouble with any of them: "They were also quite respectful with her."

The last three of our interviewees demonstrate again the difficulty of generalizing about "ladino," "elite" responses to indigenous people, the Zapatistas, and the urban indigenous movement. While certainly not condoning Zapatismo, "Builder" called attention to the fact that efforts to govern in a way that embraced all the city's residents and that adequately planned for a common future were "pathetic" before 1994. Now they have become "more energetic," he said. Perhaps, he suggested, the city had to go through the fire of the decade after 1994 for there to emerge a politics that takes all into account. More than that, "Builder" noted that before 1994 the city never received sufficient federal or state funds to deal with its many problems. After 1994, the city became the recipient of significant public investment by the Mexican government, not to speak of money from international banks and NGOs. This flow of aid and investment began soon after January 1994 and continued at a relatively high level for the next decade and a half because Chiapas, and with it San Cristóbal, had come to be recognized as a "foco rojo" (flashpoint) that could upset the stability of a much larger region. "Builder," looking at the years after 1994 as a whole, considered that the entire period has been better in terms of urban planning and infrastructural investment than any that preceded it.

"Journalist's" family, unlike those of all of our other interviewees, was enthusiastically pro-Zapatista from the beginning. As social activists, her parents had predicted for some time that the mistreatment of indigenous people and the failing rural economy were going to lead to an explosion, and the rebellion of January 1994 was in a way a vindication. Over the succeeding years, even as many ladinos (e.g., the Auténticos) plotted against the Zapatistas, "Journalist's" family openly attended Zapatista gatherings, welcomed Mexican and international supporters into their home, supported political parties and candidates that opposed the PRI, and in general were known as some of the principal nonindigenous Zapatistas in Chiapas. Perhaps as a result of this background, "Journalist" brushed quickly over the years of conflict immediately following 1994, which for herself and her family were a period of estrangement from many in San Cristóbal.

Last, and most remarkable, is our interview with "Physician." From the oldest, perhaps most distinguished family of all of the interviewees, he described loading his car with medical supplies during the fighting in January 1994 and going to the battle site on the southern and eastern edges of San Cristóbal, where he treated the injured without asking whether they were Zapatistas, federal soldiers, or civilian bystanders. To do this, he had to talk his way through the army's lines, using his federal health credentials. In the months immediately following the revolt, he worked with the International Red Cross to get food and health supplies to communities that had been cut off, again without respect to their politics, and helped find accommodations for refugees who had made their way to San Cristóbal. Like most other interviewees, "Physician" lamented the disorder after 1994, and while not talking directly about the organization of the urban indigenous movement—strikingly, none of our ladino interviewees did—he felt that there were indigenous leaders in the city who had manipulated this disorder for personal gain. This being his only, albeit indirect, mention of the secular organization of the urban movement, the impression that remains is somewhat negative.

RESTORING ORDER: 1998–2002

From 1994 on, state violence in the northern, more indigenous half of Chiapas—which includes San Cristóbal—was continuous and high. Throughout these years, some one-third of the Mexican army, more than sixty thousand men, was stationed in the region. Most worked from new rural bases and camps scattered around and through the Lacandón Forest, but there was also a major headquarters base on the eastern edge of San Cristóbal. The state police also had large "strike" forces throughout the region, and there were shadowy paramilitary groups armed by landowners and the state, trained by regular soldiers seconded to the state police. Some of the well-known acts of repression during these years include the December 1997 massacre in the Tsotsil hamlet of Acteal, in a straight line, just ten miles north of San Cristóbal, which is the most infamous.[17] Despite this continuous violence, however, and an atmosphere that almost crackled with the threat of violence, during the first four years after 1994, repression in San Cristóbal itself was not as high as elsewhere. Although conservative urban elites clamored throughout this period for the state to restore law and order ("*un estado de derecho*"), there continued to be land invasions, and the pirate taxi fleet—much of it armed—flourished. Seizure of spaces in markets, plazas, and on sidewalks by indigenous peddlers also continued. These activities were organized by a handful of indigenous unions and political organizations, and most of them were interlocking: taxi drivers protected the invasions of market spaces by members of their own unions; land invasions were organized by the same unions; and groups of allied unions supported the first urban colono candidates for state political office in 1994.

If the army and other armed groups were conducting a campaign to suppress the rebellion in the countryside, why did the same forces not act decisively to reimpose control in San Cristóbal itself? The theory at the time, and it is probably true, is that there was already enough turmoil in Chiapas without risking an explosion in the cities. Better to go softly, at least for a while. Certainly there were officials who knew the details of the urban indigenous organizations; indeed, the organizations were widely believed by indigenous people themselves to have been riddled with informants. As for why San Cristóbal's municipal police didn't do more, most civilian ladinos were unable to distinguish the local unions, with their concrete, economic, and political goals mostly limited to San Cristóbal, from larger, statewide organizations, including the Zapatistas. They were cautious on those grounds of taking on too big an adversary by themselves. As we saw in 1992 and January 1994, there *were* overlapping memberships between the Zapatistas and the urban organizations. Perhaps the army and the police did well to be careful.

The harshest rural repression in the central highlands began in the spring of 1997, with numerous confrontations in the municipios north of San Cristóbal, eventually culminating in the massacre at Acteal. More decided repression in the city began soon after. In the spring of 1998, there was a predawn raid on La

Hormiga by a mixed force (ominously known as a BOM, Brigada de Operación Mixta) of the national army, the PGR (Procuraduría General de la República, or General Prosecutorial Service of the Republic), and the state police. Supposedly the raid was to search for high-powered weapons, drugs, and stolen vehicles. Doors were smashed, and men—including our interviewee "Leader"—were taken away in handcuffs. All that was found were two pistols and a number of possibly stolen cars (later returned to their owners in the colonia when it was verified that the cars had not been stolen). Nevertheless, in the aftermath both Domingo López Ángel and Manuel Collazo, leaders of the colonia movement, were sent to state prison, where they remained until after the 2000 elections.

Later in 1998, a strict law-and-order PRI candidate, Mariano Díaz Ochoa, was elected municipal president of San Cristóbal. With the backing of a stridently anti-Zapatista interim governor who took office at about the same time, over the next three years Díaz Ochoa cracked down on the "excesses" of the urban indigenous. Although several hundred new licenses were granted for indigenous taxis, "flying roadblocks" were established and improperly registered (i.e., presumably stolen) cars were confiscated, as were weapons in cars. By the end of the three years, pirate taxis were being stopped and fined (although not confiscated: that was considered too explosive a tactic). Unauthorized vendors in the space around the market were also violently removed and their stalls destroyed, and smaller land invasions were dislodged, typically with great violence. The status quo before 1994 was not reestablished, but by 2002 many ladinos felt that for the first time in a decade the balance had shifted back to them.

Most of our ladino interviewees did not talk much about this period, jumping instead from the "lawlessness" after 1994 to the relative stability of the years since 2003. "Builder" believed that possibly the passage from the chaos of the mid- to late 1990s and the reestablishment of more order around the turn of the millennium had been necessary for the city's diverse populations to become reconciled to each other . . . or at least, more reconciled than they were before. "Physician," whose valor was widely recognized in the city after 1994 and who was known as a sympathetic ladino in the colonias, became a department head in the municipal government from 1997 to 2000—that is, from the end of the administration before the one that imposed order until the middle of the law-and-order regime. Similarly, one of our indigenous interviewees, "Norteño," became in 1998 the first Chamula ever elected to the city council (ayuntamiento) of San Cristóbal. Along with several other officials, he resigned in 2001, just before completing his term, because of what he considered the arbitrary treatment of indigenous people in the city by the political slate that had invited him to run for office and of which he had been part. Nevertheless, the fact that even relatively conservative ladino politicians had felt the need to include a Chamula in their slate (an example followed by all subsequent candidates for municipal president and their parties), and that he had served, represented a powerful break with the city's exclusionist past. "Civil Servant" also served in the municipal government during this period, and his general comment on the entire run of years from the late 1990s to the present (during which he worked for two of the four municipal presidents) was that the indigenous colonies demanded a far disproportionate share of the government's energy. But order and legitimacy had to be restored, even if he lamented they were essentially being bought.

THE HIGHLAND CANCÚN: 2002–2010

Beginning at the very end of the 1990s, but with increasing clarity after 2001 and 2002, San Cristóbal was in an economic upswing, even boom. In addition to the government, international organization, and NGO funds, which had begun flowing into the region after 1994, there were three important new sources of income. First, chronologically, was tourism. Growth in the number of tourists, and services to tourists, had been steady since the 1980s, and ironically, appears to have been spurred by the 1994 rebellion. But after 2001 it surged. By 2008, there were more than a hundred one- to five-star hotels in the city, including representatives of the Holiday Inn, Roadway Inn, and La Misión chains, for a total of more than twenty-six hundred rooms. There had been only three hotels in 1970, all quite rustic; these numbers increased slowly to fourteen in 1985, but still came to only twenty-eight as late as 1999.[18] After 2000, particularly after 2004 and 2005, the growth was meteoric. There was a concomitant explosion in nightclubs, restaurants, fashion boutiques built around indigenous artisan goods, and tour and travel agencies. Chamula, which was a mere four miles away, had been accessible only with four-wheel drive in 1970; now the community had more than twenty luxury tour buses in its parking lot on market mornings.

The second and perhaps even greater income stream came from the remittances of undocumented workers. Essentially, there were no migrants from Chiapas in the United States as late as 1997. By 2008, there were more than four hundred thousand; from 2005 on, Chiapas was the leading sending state in Mexico (Nájera Aguirre and López Arévalo 2009). Precise numbers from the colonias of San Cristóbal and the immediately surrounding municipios are not available, but rough calculations are that 20 percent of indigenous men from sixteen to thirty-four years of age, some forty-five thousand to sixty thousand in all, were in the United States in 2007 and 2008. If each sent home a hundred dollars per month (an extremely moderate estimate), and an important part of those funds eventually found their way to the stores and markets of San Cristóbal, the figure would have been approximately five million dollars a month.[19] The third income stream, even harder to calculate, is from various forms of contraband. San Cristóbal is an organizing point for smuggling of migrants and drugs from Central America to the North. As a major tourist destination, San Cristóbal has also become a drug market in its own right. But again, it is hard to calculate the economic importance of these activities.

Under these circumstances, the city was much less tense beginning in approximately 2002 and 2003 than at any time in perhaps a generation. The unemployed young men of a decade ago were now often away, either in the United States or other regions of Mexico. Employment locally had also surged. In addition to the new businesses that serve tourism, national and international franchises have flooded into the city since 2002 and 2003; among them, MacDonald's, Burger King, Radio Shack, Kentucky Fried Chicken, Dr. Simi pharmacies, a Cinépolis multiscreen movie theater, as well as Chedraui, Sam's Club, and Soriana superstores. All of these businesses not only offered new jobs—to indigenous and ladino workers alike—but with their growth, the construction and reconstruction/remodeling industry has boomed to service them. More than that, businesses from "outside," by treating all customers equally—not forcing indigenous people to wait while ladinos were served, for example—have had a profound social and cultural, and ultimately economic, impact. To remain competitive, locally owned businesses also became more open, increasingly reaching for customers from the half of the city's population that is indigenous. By 2008, most businesses, even those owned by the city's most conservative families, were hiring indigenous employees to service these new customers in their own languages.

The benefits of all the fresh activity are, of course, badly distributed, and conflict perhaps lies ahead. Most of the profits have gone to the owners of the best new hotels and tourist business as well as to the holders of franchises—and a large percentage of both groups are not originally from San Cristóbal. Of the old ladino elite, probably only those who own "*pisos*" (urban land and buildings that they can rent to the new commerce) are really doing well. The number of indigenous elites, who have profited from lending for migration (and perhaps contraband), is also rising. Not doing as well are the old ladino merchant class whose businesses have fallen behind, and much of the old ladino working class, which has been forced to compete with ambitious indigenous immigrants and newcomers from elsewhere in Mexico. At the same time, it would be a mistake to think urban indigenous migrants are all doing well. Those who do not receive remittances or who do not work for the better-paying franchises, for example, live lives as precarious as ever.

As for politics, after the repressive municipal presidency of 1999–2001, the candidate elected for 2002–4 was an "outsider," a radio broadcaster from another region of Chiapas who had a morning program popular in the indigenous colonias. During his term, the harassment of indigenous street vendors ceased, and roadblocks to catch pirate taxis also disappeared (such vehicles were rechristened *taxis no-autorizados*, and the police now limited themselves to issuing warnings against carrying passengers without authorization). By this time, there had been almost a decade of indigenous representatives to the state legislature from rural districts with overwhelmingly indigenous populations. But no party had nominated an indigenous candidate for one of the larger encompassing federal deputyships. In 2003, however, the indigenous pro-PRI elite of the municipios surrounding San Cristóbal—almost all of whom had second homes in San Cristóbal—did just that. The PRI candidate for the federal congress in 2003 was a Chamula.[20] To the surprise of no one, save perhaps the supporters of the candidates of the old ladino elite, the indigenous elite contributed more money to their candidate (one hundred thousand dollars from the leaders of Chamula alone), ran more radio ads, had more posters—and won. For the first time in history, the highest elected official from Chiapas's central highlands was a Tsotsil. It must be noted that he was not a member of the urban indigenous movement, but a member of the younger generation of Chamula's local elite—the caciques who had expelled the Chamula Protestants a generation earlier. But it should also be noted that the people of the colonias of San Cristóbal voted for him.[21] Is this apparent indigenous electoral unity only temporary? What does the division between "caciques" and "expulsados" mean now that the sons of the caciques live in the colonias founded by expulsados? What are the future politics of the city if the emerging indigenous majority, at least for the immediate future, votes as a bloc? Will fuller political participation by indigenous people lead to a new polarization?

Whatever the eventual answers to these questions, our ladino interviewees, on all sides, agree that there is more *convivencia*, more spirit of coexistence, in the city in the past few years than a decade ago. They do not agree about the reasons for the new peace, however. "Store Owner," "Civil Servant," and to some extent "Professor" credit the crackdown of the late 1990s. "Builder," "PRIísta," the "Hotel Owners," and "Anchorman," on the other hand—all of whom have business relationships with indigenous people—call attention instead to the increased prosperity of the city and the growing economic interdependence between its ladino and indigenous populations. Interestingly, "Physician" and "Journalist," who start from very different places politically— the first characterized by a sort of noblesse oblige, the second imbued with the radicalism of her parents—agree that as indigenous people and ladinos have cohabited over the past thirty-five years, they have come to know each other better and see each other more as humans. After repression and prosperity, this sort of humanistic drawing together is perhaps a third explanation for why the city is less tense, less polarized than in the recent past.

EPILOGUE

As we wrote at the beginning, this chapter offers a collective oral history of indigenous migrants' struggle since the mid-1970s for rights and space in formerly all-ladino San Cristóbal. Constructed from the memories of leaders on both sides, the city's old ladino residents, and its new, insurgent indigenous population, it has attempted not so much to present a detailed account of these decades as to outline the thrust of the struggle in each period, to recapture what those on each side remember as their goals, what they were learning about the other, and ultimately how they were able to arrive at a state of relatively peaceful coexistence. Like all histories, however, San Cristóbal's is open at both ends. It could be extended further into the past and finishes whenever we decide to stop. This chapter's end point was the year we conducted our interviews, in 2008, and perhaps a little more to account for the time it took us to write the text. But now that more time has passed, the story has another end point. Like the rest of the world, the economy of highland Chiapas went into crisis in late 2008. Sectors of it had gone into crisis almost a year and a half earlier. So far, the modus vivendi forged by the city's diverse populations as of 2008 has held. But it is fraying, and to many on all sides, the city again seems on the edge of serious conflict.

The first impact of the crisis that began in the United States was felt by the tens of thousands of young indigenous men who had migrated north without documents between the end of the 1990s and 2006. When the mortgage and then the construction crises began in the United States in mid-2006, some million and a quarter construction workers lost their jobs. As they moved to lower-paying jobs to find work, unemployment rippled down through the labor force. Eventually, many of those squeezed out at the bottom were the newest, least-educated undocumented migrants. By early 2007, new migration from Chiapas had stalled; by the summer of 2008, many of the migrants gave up on the United States and began returning home. In the colonias of San Cristóbal and the surrounding indigenous municipios, if there had been forty-five thousand to sixty thousand migrants at the highest point, by 2012 according to surveys, more than two-thirds of these migrants had returned to Mexico. Equally serious is that those who remained in the United States were sending smaller individual remittances, so that the total amount coming to the highlands had declined by as much as 80 percent.[22] Obviously, this meant families in the region of San Cristóbal had much less to spend in the city's stores. It also meant that there were now larger numbers of young men around the city without work—undoubtedly, a destabilizing factor. There was also a significant jump in the number of street vendors, especially single women struggling to make enough to feed their families.

The second impact was on tourism. The year 2008 was the high point of foreign tourism in San Cristóbal, as in Mexico in general. With the economic crisis, the number of foreign tourists fell almost 20 percent in 2009. Observers point out that the swine flu scare in the spring of 2009, which began in Mexico, and the adverse publicity of the country's escalating drug war also affected foreign tourism. But economics undoubtedly was, and still is, the major reason for the decline. Numbers recovered slightly in 2010 and slightly more in 2011, but the 2008 peak has still not been reached. To some extent, San Cristóbal and Chiapas weathered this crisis by beginning to cater to national (Mexican) tourists. In 2009, the state secretary of tourism rolled out a national advertising campaign with the slogan "Chiapas, el México que tu recuerdas" (Chiapas, Mexico as you remember it). The pictures that accompanied the commercials were of Maya ruins, waterfalls, and colonial cities. But not lost on anyone was the underlying message that crime rates were lower in Chiapas than the rest of Mexico, that narco-crime was almost nonexistent, and that people still walked the streets and plazas in the evenings. As a result, hotels were often full in San Cristóbal on national holidays. But instead of relatively big-spending Europeans and North Americans, most of the guests were Mexicans who arrived in their own cars, ate mostly in economy restaurants, and spent relatively little in boutiques and artisan markets. The surges of visitors were enough to keep businesses going, but most hotels suffered from long periods of vacancy; business for everyone else was extremely slow.[23]

Under these circumstances, two negative tendencies have reappeared in San Cristóbal since 2008 and 2009. First, the city government has renewed its efforts to sweep itinerant peddlers off the streets and to clear plazas, particularly in the city's center. On the one hand, hard-pressed merchants resent the competition from indigenous sellers of artisan goods, sweets, and fast food.

On the other, hotel owners and the city's hotelier-friendly local government worry that large numbers of clearly impoverished people crowding the center to sell things will give the city an image of disorder and, by extension, of lack of safety. The second tendency, in a sense indigenous pushback against the ladino center's pushback, is that land invasions and invasions of public markets have begun to recur. Beginning in 2010, invasions of park land and small ranches on the outskirts of the city, each time involving dozens of indigenous families seeking a place to live, have been a slow but constant drumbeat. Sometimes the invaders are dislodged, sometimes not. But as an example of the dangers inherent in each invasion, consider the events of October 2012.

On October 5, 2012, several hundred indigenous men, women, and children broke into and squatted on a small ranch belonging to a nonresident foreigner. Eventually, at the end of the month, they were violently dislodged by a force of several hundred federal, state, and local police. In the meantime, however, ladino civilians in the center of San Cristóbal began a petition drive and then held a march against the "continuing invasion of space in the city, both private and public." Lost on no one was that the land invasion, which even many urban indigenous people felt destabilized a precarious peace, was being linked to the unwanted presence of indigenous vendors in streets and plazas throughout the city. Unable to end the land invasion immediately, in mid-October the municipal police were able to seize the property of, and drive away, three hundred indigenous women who for almost a decade had held an afternoon and evening *tianguis* in the square in front of San Cristóbal's greatest symbol of indigenous-ladino coexistence: the Cathedral of Bartolomé de Las Casas and Samuel Ruiz.[24] Peaceful relations between San Cristóbal's indigenous residents—no longer now newcomers but an ever larger share of them born in the city—and its ladinos are once again tense, and still tensing. Where will this history go next? Like all history, we shall have to wait and see.

NOTES

1. For more on the legal disabilities and formal rules of exclusion affecting indigenous people until the Instituto Nacional Indigenista (INI) began the legal fight to overturn them in the early 1950s, see Villa Rojas 1976.

2. The difference between "ladino" and "indio" is thus one of ethnic identity and ascription, not "race" in a phenotypical sense. The "ladino" category includes people whose ancestors would have been whites, mestizos, mulattos, and indios. As for indios, many speakers of native languages who are classified as indios clearly have mixed ancestry as well. See Sulca Báez 1997 and Bermúdez nd.

3. In fact, the effective population of the city, especially the indigenous portion, is certainly much greater, perhaps fifteen thousand to twenty thousand more than these figures. Because they receive government benefits in their communities of origin, many Tsotsils and Tseltals who work in the city continue to live in the surrounding municipios—or have even moved back to those municipios in recent years—and commute to the city on a daily basis. The greatly expanded network of paved roads and the hundreds of taxis and minivans in the surrounding countryside facilitate this movement.

4. Juan Pedro Viqueira (2009) has written of the extraordinarily delayed nature of Chiapas's urbanization, which he attributes to the state's externally organized export economy; the fact that its communications networks were always oriented outward; and its cycles of boom and bust in which no region—or town—became dominant until late in the twentieth century.

5. It should be noted that a third group, whose importance to the balance of power in the city has grown dramatically during the 2000s, is that of the "outsiders" (i.e., Mexicans and foreigners alike), who increasingly control the business of central San Cristóbal.

6. According to the 2000 census, the population was a little over 130,000, of whom 46,000 were indigenous (INEGI 2001). Although the 2010 census raised the total population to 188,000 (INEGI 2011), based on house counts and other measures, officials in the city government claimed the resident population in 2010 may have been as high as 220,000.

7. We have avoided the terms "business" and "businessman/-woman" to designate the members of our elite. In part, this is explained by the entwined nature of the landowning, professional, political, and business elites in San Cristóbal. Even for those who are primarily entrepreneurs, however, we have avoided the term. The reason is that given Mexico's often adversarial relationship to the United States, and a century of revolutionary rhetoric, the English words "business" and "businessman" have a pejorative, foreign ring to many Mexicans. That same revolutionary rhetoric has even made the terms "negocios" and "hombre de negocios," used elsewhere, suspect to many. Instead, following our interviews, we substitute the terms "entrepreneur," "private sector," or "private initiative" ("emprendedor," "sector privado," and "iniciativa privada").

8. To ensure anonymity, we include the following descriptions of our interviewees:

Ladino leaders: I. Private sector: (1) **Builder**: owner of a construction company, former *presidente municipal* (mayor) of San Cristóbal; (2) **PRIísta**: businessman, former presidente municipal of San Cristóbal; (3) **Store Owner**: owner of a major tourist store, daughter of a coffee plantation owner father and a mother who operated an Indian trading post in San Cristóbal; (4, 5) the **Hoteliers**: husband and wife owners of a small hotel, both from well-known and respected families of San Cristóbal merchants.

II. Journalists, culture workers: (6) **Anchorman**: radio personality on regional programs; (7) **Journalist**: newspaper reporter, daughter of ladino social activists, including a father who was presidente municipal and ran for governor; (8) **Professor**: ex–university administrator, retired professor, owner of a dairy, and member of an important commercial family;

III. Public servants: (9) **Physician**: retired administrator of hospital and government health service, descendant of a family of major landowners; (10) **Civil Servant**: lawyer, retired administrator of civil servant programs, teacher.

Indigenous leaders: (1) **Activist**: originally exiled from his community in 1974, sells artisan goods in the market, and is an organizer of market union; (2) **Catequista**: exiled in 1974, Catholic catechist, member of the Asamblea Popular de las Colonias Indígenas; (3) **Norteño**: Chamula from a rural colonia of San Cristóbal, five years an undocumented worker in the United States, urban political activist; (4) **Lideresa**: exiled in 1974 as a Protestant, now a Muslim, owns a store in her colonia, political activist; (5) **Saleswoman**: activist daughter of a family of indigenous activists, born in the late 1970s in San Cristóbal; (6) **Leader**: exiled in 1974, participated in the foundation of several colonies, both by purchase and invasion, jailed several times for his activism, now a Muslim activist; (7) **Pastor**: Protestant pastor, participated in the foundation of indigenous colonias and organizations, jailed multiple times for his activism; (8) **Street Vendor**: exiled in 1977 for Protestantism, organizer of indigenous street vendors.

9. For a fuller explanation of the recent politics of the highland communities, see Rus and Collier 2003, and Rus 2005 and 2012. On the religious wars in Chamula, the first and most violent case, see Rus and Wasserstrom 1979, Gossen 1989, Sterk 1991, Cantón Delgado 1997, and Rus 2005.

10. Gutiérrez Gutiérrez 1996 takes credit for San Cristóbal's "selfless generosity" in "taking in" the refugees but then emphasizes the refugees' negative cultural impact on the city and their ingratitude for all San Cristóbal had supposedly done for them.

11. The fact that the landowners selling the migrants the land were members of the local elite, profiting handsomely while disposing of stony hillsides and perpetually soggy pastures (later recognized as important wetlands) brings up another contradiction in the city's response to these early immigrants. See Gutiérrez Gutiérrez 1996, Ruiz Ortiz 1996, and Bétancourt Aduén 1997.

12. In fact, although religiously based expulsions have continued into the 2000s, from 1984 on, an increasing percentage, and eventually a majority, of urban indigenous people were not *expulsados* at all but voluntary migrants who had moved to the city for complex reasons. These included better economic opportunities as well as such things as access to education, health care, and other services, or, in the case of many women, flight from abusive marriages. See Cantón Delgado 1997, Robledo Hernández 1997, and Kovic 2005.

13. Gaspar Morquecho, formerly of the MRP (Movimiento Revolucionario del Pueblo), was the principal adviser of the Comité de Defensa and then CRIACH and served as well as a link to other organizations. He was joined from the beginning by supporters of liberation theology within the Catholic Diocese of San Cristóbal—in particular, the Dominicans and the women's religious of the order of the Divino Pastor. After 1984, radicalized members of the nonindigenous Protestant clergy also took an increasing role in the movement. For a close description of the organizational struggles of the 1980s, see Morquecho Escamilla 1992. A masterful summary of the history of CRIACH and its successors through the early 2000s can be found in Hvostoff 2009.

14. Although it is beyond the scope of this chapter, it should be noted that if indigenous and peasant groups became increasingly militant, they were more than matched by the state and federal police, the army, and the armed guards of the landowners themselves. Collectively during the late 1970s and 1980s these forces murdered dozens of leaders of independent orga-

nizations and *ejidos* (communal lands granted under agrarian reform) in rural Chiapas. Urban migrants who joined forces with CRIACH had often experienced this repression firsthand (see Kovic 2005). In any case, it was widely reported and discussed among the indigenous people we knew. See Burguete Cal y Mayor 1987 and Harvey 1998 for excellent summaries of the rural organization and repression of this period.

15. The Tsotsil phrase common at the time was "xlik sjelav skotol" (when everything began to change). For an indigenous report on changes in the city beginning in 1994, see Peres Tsu 2002.

16. The best account of these confrontations is Aramoni and Morquecho 1997.

17. After a three-year reign of terror by anti-Zapatista paramilitary gangs in indigenous communities of the highlands, forty-five Tsotsils, mostly women and children, were murdered by assault rifle and machete at a chapel in the hamlet of Acteal on December 22, 1997 (see Hernández Castillo 1998).

18. The 2008 hotel and room count come from the websites for Chiapas's one- to five-star and boutique hotels (http://www.zonaturistica.com/chiapas/san-cristobal-de-las-casas/). Not counted are 115 more youth hostels and rooming houses (*posadas*), offering several hundred more beds (http://www.hostelworld.com/findabed.php/ChosenCity.San-Cristobal-de-las-Casas/ChosenCountry.Mexico). The 1970 figure is from the *South American Handbook* (London, 1971); the 1985 figure is from the *Directorio de Hoteles* (Asociación Hotelera, San Cristóbal, 1985); and the 1999 figure is from *Lonely Planet, Mexico* (Lonely Planet Guides, Oakland, 1999). See also Van den Berghe 1994, 45–58.

19. The income for Chiapas as a whole from tourism in 2007 was slightly more than five hundred million dollars, and from remittances $906.3 million. See Rus and Rus 2008, Villafuerte Solís and García Aguilar 2006, Nájera Aguirre and López Arévalo 2009, and López Arévalo 2010.

20. Morquecho Escamilla 2000, and interviews with Lic. María Eugenia Herrera of the San Cristóbal office of the Instituto Federal Electoral, August 2008.

21. Before the 2006 congressional elections, the indigenous municipios north and east of San Cristóbal were consigned to a new district that, significantly, also included many of the indigenous colonias on the north side of the city. Meanwhile, the ladino center of San Cristóbal was connected by a thin neck to the largely ladino valley of Teopisca, thirty kilometers to the south. Its ladino majority thus restored, in subsequent elections San Cristóbal has again been represented by ladinos in congress.

22. See Cóporo 2013, and Rus and Rus 2014. Between 2007 and 2011, according to the Banco Nacional de México, overall remittances to Chiapas fell by 37 percent, from 906.3 million dollars to 573 million (reported in López Arévalo 2010, and *Cuarto poder* [Tuxtla Gutiérrez], July 11, 2011, "Disminuyen remesas hacia Chiapas"). Based on the direct surveys in Cóporo 2013 and in Rus and Rus 2014, the percentage fall in the indigenous highlands was much greater.

23. On the decline of tourism nationally, both by Mexicans and foreigners, see INEGI 2012, tables 17.4, 17.5, and 17.8. For notes on the trends in San Cristóbal, see the state newspaper *Cuarto poder* (e.g., May 21, 2009 ["Reactivar el turismo"], August 22, 2011 ["Afluencia turística a 70% durante el verano"], and October 11, 2012 ["Se desploma la actividad turística"]).

24. On land invasions, the repression of itinerant sellers, and the rising repression of indigenous people in the center of San Cristóbal in general, see Morquecho Escamilla 2012 and 2013.

REFERENCES

Aramoni, Dolores, and Gaspar Morquecho. 1997. "La otra mejilla . . . pero armada: El recurso a las armas en manos de los expulsados de San Juan Chamula." In *Anuario 1996*, 553–611. Tuxtla, Chiapas: CESMECA-UNICACH.

Bermúdez, Luz. Nd. "¿Categoría étnica? 'Los coletos' y la designación de procesos de identidad social. San Cristóbal de Las Casas, Chiapas (México)." Unpublished manuscript.

Bétancourt Aduén, Darío. 1997. "Bases regionales en la formación de comunas rurales-urbanas en San Cristóbal LC, Chiapas." Facultad de Ciencias Sociales, UNACH, San Cristóbal, Chiapas.

Burguete Cal y Mayor, Araceli. 1987. *Chiapas, cronología de un etnocidio reciente, 1974–1987*. Mexico City: Academia Mexicana de Derechos Humanos.

Cantón Delgado, Manuela. 1997. "Las expulsiones indígenas en los Altos de Chiapas: Algo más que un problema de cambio religioso." *Mesoamérica* 33 (June): 147–69.

Cóporo Quintana, Gonzalo. 2013. "Migración, pobreza y desarrollo: Estudio de casos en dos localidades del municipio de Chamula en los Altos de Chiapas." PhD dissertation, Centro de Estudios Superiores de México y Centroamérica, Universidad de Ciencias y Artes de Chiapas, San Cristóbal.

Gossen, Gary H. 1989. "Life, Death, and Apotheosis of a Chamula Protestant Leader." In *Ethnographic Encounters in Southern Mesoamerica*, edited by Victoria R. Bricker and Gary H. Gossen, 217–29. Albany: Institute for Mesoamerican Studies.

Gutiérrez Gutiérrez, José Antonio. 1996. *Infundios contra San Cristóbal de Las Casas*. Mexico City: Fundación Chiapaneca Colosio.

Harvey, Neil. 1998. *The Chiapas Rebellion: The Struggle for Land and Democracy*. Durham: Duke University Press.

Hernández Castillo, Rosalva Aída. 1998. *The Other Word: Women and Violence in Chiapas before and after Acteal*. Copenhagen: International Work Group on Indigenous Affairs.

Hvostoff, Sophie. 2009. "La comunidad abandonada: La invención de una nueva indianidad urbana en las zonas periféricas tzotziles y tzeltales de San Cristóbal de Las Casas, Chiapas." In *Chiapas después de la tormenta: Estudios sobre economía, sociedad y política*, edited by Marco Estrada Saavedra, 221–77. Mexico City: Colegio de México, Gobierno del Estado de Chiapas, Cámara de Diputados.

Instituto Nacional de Estadística, Geografía e Informática (INEGI). 2001. *Resultados preliminares del XII Censo General de Población*. Tuxtla Gutiérrez, Chiapas, and Aguascalientes: INEGI.

Instituto Nacional de Estadística, Geografía e Informática (INEGI). 2011. *Resultados preliminares del XIII Censo General de Población*. Tuxtla Gutiérrez, Chiapas, and Aguascalientes: INEGI.

Instituto Nacional de Estadística, Geografía e Informática (INEGI). 2012. *Anuario Estadístico de los Estados Unidos Mexicanos*. Aguascalientes: INEGI.

Kovic, Christine M. 2005. *Mayan Voices for Human Rights: Displaced Catholics in Highland Chiapas*. Austin: University of Texas Press.

López Arévalo, Jorge. 2010. "Familias chiapanecas dejan de percibir 2.5 mmdp al disminuir remesas de migrantes." *Expreso Chiapas* (Tuxtla Gutiérrez, Chiapas). February 3.

Morquecho Escamilla, Gáspar. 1992. "Los indios en un proceso de organización." Licenciatura thesis in social anthropology, Universidad Autónoma de Chiapas, San Cristóbal.

Morquecho Escamilla, Gáspar. 2000. *La Convención de Morelos: Una experiencia de autonomía desde la perspectiva de los indios priístas*. San Cristóbal, Chiapas: Ediciones Pirata.

Morquecho Escamilla, Gáspar. 2002. *Violencia en el Mercado Municipal de San Cristóbal, de las cuentas pendientes a las gotas que derraman los vasos*. San Cristóbal, Chiapas: Ediciones Pirata.

Morquecho Escamilla, Gáspar. 2012. *Los indios en San Cristóbal de Las Casas a 19 años del levantamiento Zapatista*. San Cristóbal, Chiapas: Ediciones Pirata.

Morquecho Escamilla, Gáspar. 2013. *Racismos: Tensiones interétnicas en el entorno de San Cristóbal de Las Casas*. San Cristóbal, Chiapas: Ediciones Pirata.

Nájera Aguirre, Jéssica, and Jorge A. López Arévalo. 2009. "Migración de chiapanecos a los Estados Unidos de América, una visión desde la Encuesta sobre Migración en la Frontera Norte de México." Paper presented to the Primer Congreso Internacional sobre Pobreza, Migración y Desarrollo, April 22.

Peres Tsu, Marian. 2002. "A Tzotzil Chronicle." Translation from Tzotzil by Jan Rus. In *The Mexico Reader*, edited by Gilbert Joseph and Timothy Henderson, 655–69. Durham: Duke University Press.

Robledo Hernández, Gabriela. 1997. "Disidencia y religión: Los expulsados de San Juan Chamula." Universidad Autónoma de Chiapas, San Cristóbal, Chiapas.

Ruiz Ortiz, Juana María. 1996. "Los primeros pobladores de Nich'ix, la Colonia de la Hormiga." In *Anuario de Estudios Indígenas*. Vol. 6, pp. 11–24. San Cristóbal, Chiapas: CEI-UNACH.

Rus, Diane, and Jan Rus. 2008. "La migración de trabajadores indígenas de los Altos de Chiapas a Estados Unidos, 2001–2005: El caso de San Juan Chamula." In *Migraciones en el Sur de México y Centroamérica*, edited by Daniel Villafuerte and María del Carmen García, 343–82. Mexico City: Miguel Ángel Porrúa Editores, Universidad de Ciencias y Artes de Chiapas, Facultad Latinoamericano de Ciencias Sociales (FLACSO)–Costa Rica, Organización Internacional de Migración, NCCR-Suiza.

Rus, Diane, and Jan Rus. 2014. "Trapped Behind the Lines: The Impact of Undocumented Migration, Debt and Recession on a Tsotsil Community of Chiapas, Mexico, 2002–2012." *Latin American Perspectives* 41, no. 3 (May): 154–77.

Rus, Jan. 1994. "The 'Comunidad Revolucionaria Institucional': The Subversion of Native Government in Highland Chiapas, 1936–1968." In *Everyday Forms of State Formation: Revolution and the Negotiation of Rule in Modern Mexico*, edited by Gilbert Joseph and Daniel Nugent, 265–300. Durham: Duke University Press.

Rus, Jan. 1995. "Local Adaptation to Global Change: The Reordering of Native Society in Highland Chiapas, 1974–1994." *European Review of Latin American and Caribbean Studies* 58 (June): 71–90.

Rus, Jan. 2005. "The Struggle against Indigenous Caciques in Highland Chiapas, 1965–1977." In *Cacique and Caudillo in Twentieth-Century Mexico*, edited by Alan Knight and Wil

Pansters, 169–200. Washington, D.C.: Institute for Latin American Studies, Brookings Institution Press.

Rus, Jan. 2012. "El ocaso de las plantaciones y la transformación de la sociedad indígena de los Altos de Chiapas, 1974–2009, Mexico City and Tuxtla Gutiérrez." Centro de Estudios Superiores de México y Centro América, Universidad de Ciencias y Artes de Chiapas, Consejo Nacional de Ciencia y Tecnología. (Original English is available at http://www.escholarship.org/uc/item/1s11164b).

Rus, Jan, and George A. Collier. 2003. "A Generation of Crisis in the Chiapas Highlands: The Tzotzils of Chamula and Zinacantán, 1974–2000." In *Mayan Lives, Mayan Utopias: The Indigenous People of Chiapas and the Zapatista Movement,* edited by Jan Rus, R. Aída Hernández, and Shannan Mattiace, 33–61. Lanham: Rowman and Littlefield.

Rus, Jan, and James D. Vigil. 2007. "Rapid Urbanization and Migrant Indigenous Youth in San Cristóbal, Chiapas, Mexico." In *Gangs in the Global City,* edited by John Hagedorn, 152–83. Urbana: University of Illinois Press.

Rus, Jan, and Robert Wasserstrom. 1979. "Misioneros y control político." *Revista Mexicana de ciencias políticas y sociales* 25 (July–September): 141–60.

Sterk, Vernon. 1991. "The Dynamics of Persecution." Doctorate of Missiology dissertation, Fuller Theological Seminary, Pasadena, CA.

Sulca Báez, Edgar. 1997. "Nosotros los coletos: Identidad y cambio en San Cristóbal." Centro de Estudios Superiores de México y Centroamérica. UNICACH, Tuxtla Gutiérrez, Chiapas.

Van den Berghe, Pierre L. 1994. *The Quest for the Other: Ethnic Tourism in San Cristobal, Mexico.* Seattle: University of Washington Press.

Villafuerte Solís, Daniel, and María del Carmen García Aguilar. 2006. "Crisis rural y migraciones en Chiapas." *Migración y desarrollo* 1: 102–30.

Villa Rojas, Alfonso. 1976. Introducción. In *El indigenismo en acción: XXV aniversario del Centro Coordinador Tzeltal-Tzotzil,* edited by Gonzalo Aguirre Beltrán, Alfonso Villa Rojas, et al. Chiapas, México, D.F.: Instituto Nacional Indigenista.

Viqueira, Juan Pedro. 2009. "Cuando no florecen las ciudades: La urbanización tardía e insuficiente de Chiapas." In *Ciudades mexicanas del siglo XX,* edited by A. Rodríguez Kuri and C. Lira. Mexico City: UAM-Azcapotzalco, El Colegio de México.

4

DEMOCRACY BY INVITATION

THE PRIVATE SECTOR'S ANSWER TO PARTICIPATORY BUDGETING IN PORTO ALEGRE, BRAZIL

Jeffrey W. Rubin and Sergio Gregorio Baierle

Figure 4.1. Participatory budgeting in action. Photo © CIDADE.

SINCE 1989, THROUGH MEETINGS run by formalized procedures of debate and voting, ordinary people in Porto Alegre, a city of 1.5 million people in southern Brazil, have made decisions about how the budget for infrastructure in their neighborhoods would be spent.[1] In addition, they have supervised the process of implementation and held municipal officials accountable for the results. As part of this oversight, officials in charge of such departments as housing and water have found themselves facing pointed and angry questioning at tempestuous late-night meetings in school cafeterias or church meeting halls far from their downtown offices. Ordinary citizens have discovered that they could change the face of their streets and the quality of life in poor *vilas* (shantytowns) by seeking out information, attending meetings, and bringing their neighbors along to speak their minds and vote. By the late 1990s, participatory budgeting in Porto Alegre had gained international acclaim for successfully turning over control of portions of the municipal budget to poor people in their own neighborhoods.

The officials who envisioned participatory budgeting, along with many domestic and international observers, saw the program as an embodiment of deliberative democracy, where citizens come together in the public sphere to debate, revise their views, and develop practical policies.[2] For militants of the Partido dos Trabalhadores (PT, or Workers' Party), which implemented participatory budgeting and governed Porto Alegre for sixteen years (1988–2004), the yearlong cycle of meetings, culminating in the formation of a citywide Participatory Budgeting Council, enabled the "voice of the people" to be heard and ordinary citizens to exercise decision-making power. The value of such a process, more collaborative and participatory than conventional representative democracy, lay not only in the possibility of producing efficient proposals for infrastructure and securing support for them. Its supporters saw participatory budgeting as more democratic as well, because of the ongoing decision-making role played by ordinary citizens in every stage of the budgeting process. Compared to the backroom deals for which the city council was known, participatory budgeting more fully recognized the dignity and subjecthood of individuals and their capacity to participate collectively in self-government.

Although tens of thousands of people in Porto Alegre's neighborhoods took part in participatory budgeting over two decades, achieving countless successful public works projects that bettered their lives, the businesspeople we interviewed for the Enduring Reform project were uniformly opposed to this process.[3] Although some businesspeople understood the basics of how participatory budgeting functioned and what it accomplished, all of the businesspeople interviewed rejected participatory budgeting outright as an undemocratic process controlled by the Workers' Party for electoral gain. They dismissed the capacities of ordinary people to collaborate in a budgeting process and insisted on the worthlessness of the participatory budgeting meetings held in neighborhoods throughout the city. In addition, businesspeople insisted that they had not been "invited" to participatory budgeting and that for this reason it was an exclusive and illegitimate process.

In the same interviews in which they spoke dismissively of participatory budgeting in Porto Alegre's vilas, several of the businesspeople interviewed presented narratives of places to which they had traveled and observed the characteristics of poor people. In these distant places, in Brazil's Northeast or in Porto Alegre in the past, the businesspeople found poor people to be competent and responsible, despite stereotypes to the contrary, so long as they were treated with respect and engaged in productive work. However, while acknowledging with these stories that direct experience could invalidate stereotypes of incompetence and laziness, businesspeople did not at any point question their own uniformly negative views of Porto Alegre's vilas and their inhabitants. Claiming that improving the lives of poor people required a greater say for business in urban affairs—and not participation for the poor themselves in budgetary decision making and oversight of capital investments—businesspeople supported modifications to participatory budgeting after 2004, when a centrist candidate won mayoral elections. These modifications favored practices of consultation with business as well as programs of voluntary corporate social responsibility. Thus, in Porto Alegre, businesspeople's perception and analysis of participatory budgeting, informed by their cultural understandings of politics and poor people, paved the way for the implementation, through electoral competition, of a counterproposal squarely in line with market-based ideas of economy and citizenship.

This chapter begins by explaining the origins and characteristics of participatory budgeting and presenting evaluations and critiques of the process in the words of participants and scholars, focusing on internal dynamics that limited the program's effectiveness over time. We then examine in depth the responses to participatory budgeting on the part of businesspeople, a group whose evaluations of the project have not previously been studied and whose responses directly impacted the manner in which participatory budgeting was reduced in scope after 2004, when the Workers' Party was voted out of power. Our interviews demonstrate that it was the democratic character of participatory budgeting—the fact that businesspeople could be outvoted in transparent processes of deliberation and decision making—that led businesspeople to act to limit the program's reach.

THE HISTORY AND ORGANIZATION OF PARTICIPATORY BUDGETING IN PORTO ALEGRE

In order to understand the significance of participatory budgeting in Porto Alegre, it is necessary to view it in the context of the political project in which it originated, known as state participatory management. After twenty-one years of military dictatorship in Brazil (1964–85), it seemed to a broad group of political actors on the left—the forces that came together in the Workers' Party—that the main cause of deepening social inequalities and the poverty of practically half of the country's population lay in the political exclusion of low-income classes and the lack of a representative parliamentary system that effectively expressed society's political will. The creation of management councils, starting at the neighborhood level and continuing through cities and states all the way up to the federal level, was seen as a way to give voice and vote to civil society in the everyday management of public policies, including social welfare issues such as health, education, and housing. The focus of a state-led participatory management project would be to give power back to the people, to transform institutions by starting from proposals built collectively in forums, councils, and conferences, as well as plebiscites and referenda, for subsequent consolidation into law.[4]

The emphasis on participation did not specify one particular method. Rather, the focus was on the constitution and the strengthening of collective subjects as political agents, combining pedagogical traditions inspired by Paulo Freire, methodologies of Situational Strategic Planning (or Planejamento Estratégico Situacional, PES), liberation theology's Christian base communities, and historical leftist organizational practices, such as party committees, popular councils, labor union federations, fronts, and social movements.[5] The left's embrace of these grassroots methods constituted a bet on the possibility of democratic hegemony for a participatory project, in the context of an ascending political party without a social base sufficient for achieving the presidency. Participatory budgeting in Porto Alegre was a manifestation of this broader approach. The groundwork for participatory budgeting in Porto Alegre was laid in a process of urban neighborhood mobilization in the 1970s and 1980s, during the final years of Brazil's military dictatorship and the first years of democratic rule. This mobilization drew attention to the needs of the city's poor, many of whom had been moved from central areas of the city during urban redevelopment projects, and culminated in 1983 in the formation of a citywide grassroots movement, the Union of Neighborhood Associations of Porto Alegre (or União das Associações de Moradores de Porto Alegre, UAMPA), which pressed for political voice and policy reform. The Workers' Party built on this organizational legacy when it won the mayor's office in 1988, moving rapidly to institute its proposals for participation.

The participatory budgeting idea, simultaneously simple and startling, was to turn over decision-making power for portions of the municipal budget to ordinary citizens in their neighborhoods. Equally important, the project made explicit the need to encourage people to participate and to develop the everyday skills necessary to make deliberation and the management of local projects into efficient and meaningful endeavors. This meant bringing municipal officials to the neighborhoods and insisting that they present accounts of what they had done, respond to residents' (often angry) questions, and puzzle together with residents over how to develop innovative solutions to entrenched problems. It meant a constant process of translation, by which technical concepts and jargon could become real and accessible to ordinary people and by which the concerns and proposals of those ordinary people could be accepted as intelligible and significant by officials, many of whom were accustomed to routinized, clientelistic politics and a menu of conventional technical solutions.

Upon taking office, the Workers' Party rapidly and successfully cleaned up municipal finances and raised property taxes as well as taxes on services. The government's ability to devote resources to neighborhood projects derived as well from decentralization carried out in the early years of Brazil's democracy, when constitutional reforms mandated that more federal funds be returned to cities, which were also given license to raise and retain several local taxes. The Workers' Party approached participatory budgeting as a radical project to be accomplished through a procedurally democratic process that depended on flexibility and innovation. The government divided up the city into sixteen regions and instituted a yearly cycle of meetings, connecting neighborhoods to regions and regions to a citywide participatory budgeting council that would produce the municipal budget. The participatory budgeting cycle was framed around two large meetings in each region, with several months of neighborhood meetings in between. At the first regional meetings, which were festive events that often included musical performances, the city government presented its accounts, going over what it had accomplished over the previous year and its plans for the coming one as well as explaining the procedures of the participatory budgeting process. At these meetings, delegates were elected to a regional forum (one for each of the sixteen regions) that would oversee the process of neighborhood deliberation in the region during the first months of the cycle and the implementation of projects there later on.

In the second set of large meetings (one in each of the sixteen regions), held approximately three months after the first, the Forum of Delegates presented its ranking of projects for the region.[6] In addition, those attending their regional meetings elected representatives to the citywide Participatory Budgeting Council, two from each of the sixteen regions and five thematic groups that constituted the budgeting public. The forty-two members of the citywide council then met for the next several months to aggregate the regional lists of projects and produce a master budget—tasks it accomplished in interaction with the various municipal agencies on the one hand and with the individual regions and subregions on the other.

In between the regional gatherings, which framed the process, the substance of participatory budgeting took place in weekly neighborhood meetings. This is where local residents came together to discuss their neighborhood's needs and assemble a list of projects, in order of priority, to submit to their regional Forum of Delegates. Projects might include potable water, drainage and sewage systems, pavement, and street lighting as well as health care posts, day-care centers, and schools. In the neighborhood meetings, people presented their problems, made their cases, argued fiercely with one another, formed alliances, and horse-traded—in short, did politics and became engaged citizens. The genius and success of participatory budgeting in Porto Alegre is that these meetings worked to produce well-developed lists of priorities—out of a process chock-full of need, emotion, argumentation, and rough-and-tumble politics, including an open mike at the beginning of meetings, an agenda thereafter, and strictly timed three-minute interventions throughout. In the meetings and the neighborhoods, tensions over gender and race, over who could speak with authority and effectiveness, and over desperation, crisis, and the sheer desire to speak were mediated by activists, representatives of the city government, and ordinary people themselves so as to produce concrete and feasible proposals (Damo 2005, Wilkinson 2007, Baiocchi 2005, and Abers 2000).

In addition to the cycle of meetings, the city government created a planning agency that turned infrastructural projects and preferences into practical plans and was required to explain those plans and gain acceptance for them. The government also established regional administrative offices and staff who coordinated the participatory budgeting process in the regions and acted as mediators between the municipal administration and the neighborhoods (there were administrative offices and staff in each of the sixteen regions). Throughout the participatory budgeting cycle, municipal officials were held accountable to neighborhood residents, first to provide information during the deliberative phase, at the neighborhood and regional levels, and later during the implementation phase of the projects that were selected.

One of the most extraordinary and innovative aspects of participatory budgeting, as a project of the left, is the emphasis on democratic procedure, on institutional construction and functioning, and on ongoing evaluation and innovation. The number and borders of regions were adjusted over time; the criteria for dividing the city budget among regions were revised to change the balance between level of participation and extent of need; five thematic issues, such as health and economic development, were given their own weight alongside that of the sixteen regions. Participatory budgeting proposed a reformist, within-the-system path to empowerment and the effective improvement of municipal services. As a result of its early successes, knowledge of participatory budgeting made its way around the world. The writings of one of its innovators, Tarso Genro—past Porto Alegre mayor (and current governor of Rio Grande do Sul, of which Porto Alegre is the capital) who emphasized the creation of a "nonstate public sphere"—were translated into multiple languages and distributed by the World Bank, which also sponsored international conferences on the subject. Local activists applauded "the emergence of a new ethical-political principle," "a new type of citizen," and "a new relationship between the public and the private, constructed as a countercurrent to the capitalist modernization of Brazil."[7]

Similar claims were made by foreign researchers. Rebecca Abers (2000) focused her analysis on whether the participatory budgeting process privileges already skilled activists and neighborhoods, and she found that demonstration effects (when one neighborhood observes the successes of another) and processes of political learning (of participatory skills) led to an ebb, flow, and circulation of skills and benefits. Like Abers, Gianpaolo Baiocchi's (2005) observation of participatory budgeting meetings revealed the gives and takes, the pauses and heated exchanges, out of which infrastructural plans get constructed and visions of the common good emerged. "In Porto Alegre," Baiocchi (2005, 5, 4) observed, "a pre-figurative social movement innovation—norms of claims-making and collective access to the public good—became institutionalized and extended to a whole city" where militants and citizens "act[ed] in civic and cooperative ways." Boaventura da Sousa Santos (1998, 464) "define(d) the contribution of participatory budgeting as institutional mediation for the reinvention of democratic theory." For Peter Evans (2004, 44), who made use of the examples of Porto Alegre and Kerala, India, to argue against what he calls "institutional mono-cropping," participatory budgeting demonstrates "that deliberative development is not just a theoretical and philosophical imperative . . . but also a real possibility."[8]

Participatory budgeting came rapidly to be discussed in urban planning programs in the United States, such as those at Cornell and MIT, whose faculty visited and/or did research in Porto Alegre. Knowledge of the process became widely disseminated among European mayors, many of whom (including the mayors of Barcelona, Budapest, and Paris) attended a Local Authorities Forum that preceded the World Social Forum in 2002. For Olivio Dutra, then governor of Rio Grande do Sul, participatory budgeting served "to guarantee to the citizen the role of participant." For the mayor of Paris, Bertrand Delanoe, "it is democracy in our cities that can be the counterweight to globalization."[9] Even as participatory budgeting succeeded in holding the attention of mainstream observers, it remained a centerpiece of the vision of the Workers' Party and of groups on the left in Brazil and elsewhere through the late 1990s and early 2000s.

Thus participatory budgeting became the central axis of the participatory management project that had emerged on the left at the end of the military dictatorship. Participatory budgeting put poor neighborhoods in direct contact with the mayor and his secretaries, empowering residents of these communities to say face-to-face to authorities what neighborhood residents wanted and giving them the rules and power to achieve it. The striking effectiveness of this tool was fundamental in attracting the organized sector of the poorest part of the population. Through participatory budgeting, successive administrations of the Workers' Party in Porto Alegre (1989–2004) actualized a political commitment to the city's lower classes, linking increased tax revenues—obtained by using popular support to pressure the legislature to approve new tax proposals—to the implementation of works and services prioritized by participants and their delegates and counselors (Marquetti 2003). In so doing, however, participatory budgeting encouraged practically all grassroots community organizations to focus their attention and organizing on the government-created forums. Such a connection between once-autonomous organizations and city government brought risks that did not take long to emerge.

Although most scholarly writing about participatory budgeting in the 1990s and 2000s concluded that the process achieved its stated goals in a credible fashion, some evaluations of the project included cautions and critique. Zander Navarro (2002) noted the absence of explicit agreements or laws linking the elected city council to participatory budgeting, leaving the process without safeguards if the council or a new mayor decided to ignore it. Navarro also flagged early on the difficulty of moving participants, and the process as a whole, from immediate infrastructural demands to broader issues of economic and urban development. He found that the city's poorest residents tended not to attend participatory budgeting meetings and that much of the technical and professional personnel in city hall remained skeptical of closer and more open relationships with ordinary citizens (Zander Navarro 2002). Sergio Baierle (2003) pointed to the "politico-administrative monopoly" by which the Workers' Party maintained continuing control of participatory budgeting, including its very close relationship with local community leaders and the degree to which the process risked becoming an extension of the party's electoral politics.[10] Baierle (2003) also observed that the turn from providing infrastructure to regularizing the process of land ownership, which the city government undertook only reluctantly as a prerequisite to the provision of water and sewage to illegal squatter settlements, had blunted the radical impact of the participatory process; while squatters wanted titles to their land, attention to navigating complex legal procedures in order to secure ownership diverted energy from collective community projects.

Jeffrey Rubin (2003) emphasized the way participatory budgeting, even as it enabled and valued speech in some areas, relegated other kinds of needs and issues, such as race and religion, to the margins of participatory budgeting, off the political agenda. Mutual aid in a racially stratified *vila*, for example, was equated with bringing ideas about infrastructure to participatory budgeting meetings and attending those meetings, rather than with other forms of neighborhood cooperation. The emphasis on infrastructure and a particular form of participation, Rubin (2003) argued, wrote out culture and difference, with all citizens and neighborhoods evaluated solely in terms of their presumed infrastructural needs and attendance at meetings. Benjamin Junge (2007) showed that neither participation nor gender were neutral categories in participatory budgeting, with particular beliefs and practices of participation, including gendered forms of posture and speech, shaping people's understanding of politics and the power they could wield in meetings. Junge also discovered that many participants saw participatory budgeting meetings, which they valued for their democratic and infrastructural outcomes, as dangerous zones of *inveja* (envy) as well. Such envy, an integral part of the participatory process in participants' minds, was seen to cause bodily harm, prompting some participants to undergo religious cleansing rituals as a complement to participation in meetings or to forego meetings entirely (Junge forthcoming).

All of these observers, however, affirmed the successes of participatory budgeting on multiple levels: the infrastructural face of the city's poor neighborhoods was transformed, with some of those neighborhoods becoming accessible to the rest of the city for the first time; and new, more open relationships between government officials and ordinary citizens were forged. And then there were the meetings, which all of the researchers just cited attended; time and again, researchers watched moments of high emotion, seemingly uncontrolled outbursts, rejection of the needs and demands of others, and apparent disorder give way to judicious weighing of competing claims and effective programmatic action (Rubin 2003 and Baiocchi 2005).

PARTICIPATORY BUDGETING IN THE WORDS OF PARTICIPANTS

In the words of Cultural Promoter, a black activist, "Participatory budgeting is a tool in the struggle for democratization and citizen participation." One of the primary ways this democratic tool functioned was by encouraging people to reject conventional clientelist politics in their neighborhoods. In the beginning, neighborhood association presidents resisted participatory budgeting. This was the case for Street Activist, an emerging, tough community leader who had recently been sworn in as president of her neighborhood association when participatory budgeting started in 1989. "Participatory budgeting empowered anyone," she said. "The associations were left adrift. Before, it was the president [of the association] who wrote documents and demanded infrastructural services of the government departments." Once neighborhood residents realized that they couldn't achieve services in the traditional way, however, they decided to join participatory budgeting directly, rather than depend on the neighborhood associations. Before, being a community leader meant being selected to represent an organized population once every two years. Now, it was necessary to demonstrate ability to mobilize and encourage participation in meetings on an ongoing basis.

Political Activist, also president of his neighborhood association, was a teenager when participatory budgeting started. A militant in the high-school student movement, he was against participatory budgeting. "I preferred to continue counting on the help of politician friends," he recalled. His community ended up entering participatory budgeting from outside of its neighborhood association, around 1995, through street committees. "People saw infrastructural works in the whole region and evaluated participatory budgeting positively," Political Activist said; then the neighborhood association rushed in. Participatory budgeting resulted in street paving and sanitation, as had occurred in a well-known nearby vila. According to him: "In those days, OP was revolutionary. The process was simple and direct. People understood better how it worked. You felt like participating."

Community Leader related a similar account of the demonstration effects (Abers 2000) of successful participatory budgeting projects. His entry into participatory budgeting started in 1992, motivated by the possibility of replicating in the vila where he lived the same process of regularization, urbanization, and construction of new houses that was occurring in a nearby neighborhood. According to Community Leader's experience, there was no resistance from the neighborhood association: "When we entered, we really believed in it, because we saw that it worked." In 1997, through participatory budgeting, a new housing development was built, replacing the old vila. These two-story houses could accommodate all the residents and make space for social service facilities. All residents were able to remain in the same location, paying a monthly fee of twenty-five *reais* (in 2008): "And then we started building the spirit of solidarity of community movements by prioritizing the basic needs of the community, which were housing and land regularization. We managed to obtain the regularization of all the vilas in the Central region, including Vila dos Papeleiros—even though they did not participate in the meetings, through the solidarity of participatory budgeting delegates, of the people who created this collective consciousness in the region."

For Street Activist, who came from a history of fighting for the right of the women in her vila to work, doing volunteer work in child and teenage care, participatory budgeting took too long in getting to key issues, but it got there eventually. Later recognizing the democratizing benefits of participatory budgeting, Street Activist observed that early on in the project, "too much time was lost prioritizing only infrastructural works—paving, sewage, land regularization. The consciousness process is very slow." In reality, only in the 2000s was it possible to include income-generating projects and a day-care center for Street Activist's vila as participatory budgeting priorities.

The most significant aspect of participatory budgeting, recalled Street Activist, was the learning process, which usually occurred in specific situations. It happened, for example, when the Metropolitan and Regional Planning State Foundation (METROPLAN, or the Fundação Estadual de Planejamento Metropolitano e Regional) organized a training seminar putting planning technicians and community leaders in direct contact, as well as merging budgeting and urban planning, during the period when the Workers' Party governed at the state level (1989–2002). While technicians developed a global vision of problems, which turned out to be "one size fits all" and distant from daily life, community militants proposed more inclusive solutions, more adapted to individual neighborhood needs but also too attached to particular cases. The collaborative work of the two groups, combining technical skills with local priorities, resulted in securing ownership for hundreds of families occupying state-owned public lands in the neighborhood of Partenon. More than that, the work resulted in the appropriation of legal instruments to secure rights and in an agenda of land regularization and urban planning that endures to this day.

CRITIQUES OF PARTICIPATORY BUDGETING IN THE WORDS OF PARTICIPANTS

Participatory budgeting started as praxis, not as theory. The theories emerged after the experiences of participatory budgeting had begun to accumulate. Maybe because of the predominance of a procedural definition of democracy in the academic world, many observers and even participants came to consider participatory budgeting as a political project in itself, sometimes even as the expression of a new political regime. This generated a mechanical replication of participatory budgeting experiences—with its calendar, procedures, and yearly cycle—around the world, particularly after its inclusion in the World Bank prescriptions for development and good governance.

In Porto Alegre, many participants who value the achievements of participatory budgeting, including its ability to integrate technical knowledge and popular culture, have come to take a negative view of the relationship between politicians and community organizations. "Today neighborhood associations are in the hands of political parties," reported Street Activist. "The community movement is paralyzed. Some national [political] leaders have never been in a local leadership position. The movement lost its way with partisanship." This opinion, widespread among leaders of grassroots community organizations in Porto Alegre, is shared by Community Leader, who initially joined participatory budgeting to obtain land regularization and housing for his neighborhood: "The first step of the ladder to politics is the community. But I stayed put. I did not take the second step and promised to myself that I would never run for city council or anything of the sort, profiting from the community work. So much that I do not openly support any candidate, party, anyone." Taken to extremes, however, this rejection of political parties and representative institutions can backfire, becoming a way to isolate communities. In such a situation, the community-state mediation relationship, which functions best through dense networks, can be monopolized by a single person (Ruppenthal 2008), in effect returning to a new version of the clientelist politics of the past.

PT administrations declined to codify participatory budgeting procedures into law, claiming that the city's residents, now empowered as citizens and possessing this tool, would demand continuation of the process even under non-PT governments. In fact, the non-PT mayor who won office in 2004 promised to continue participatory budgeting and kept his word, but his centrist administration acted to dilute and sideline the process, recasting it as a contribution to "market driven development rather than citizenship" (Junge 2012). As this played out, critiques of participatory budgeting that had surfaced since the late 1990s came to seem prescient. Neighborhood activists have become particularly critical of participatory budgeting since 2004, when the new mayor instituted his own program, Governança Solidária Local (Local Solidarity Governance), alongside participatory budgeting. Governança Local was more open to consultation with business. "Until now," recalled Community Leader, "at least here in our region, it [Governança Solidária] hasn't worked. I mean, it works a little in regards to social welfare and the day-care center. This is a solidarity government, but there isn't solidarity with the disadvantaged communities, there's solidarity with businesspeople. We see DEMHAB [Departamento Municipal de Habitação, or the Municipal Housing Department] using their logo in constructions for people who earn more than five minimum wages. It's hard for those of us who fight for the poorer communities, for children and for teenagers."

Street Vendor, differently from the other interviewees, entered participatory budgeting after the Workers' Party administrations (post-2004). He was not motivated by any fascination with the project, as he already saw participatory budgeting as a tug of war in which "the one who mobilizes more, gets more." As leader of a street trade association facing the explicit intention of the government to remove street vendors from the city center, he made sure to attend all of the meetings where the proposal would be discussed. The government's solution was to build a shopping area in a bus terminal through a public-private partnership, collecting a monthly rent of 400 *reais* from the approximately eight hundred vendors who benefited from the project. The remaining vendors were excluded, with the aid of the state military police. Street Vendor recognized that participatory budgeting had opened up space for a more direct relationship between citizenship and government, but he judged the current participatory budgeting proposals to be very modest and, in the case of the new shopping area, exclusionary. To Street Vendor, there should be a much broader space in participatory budgeting for developing fair trade projects through alternative processes of production and marketing, along with "securing professional training and skills for street vendors."

THE RESPONSES OF BUSINESSPEOPLE TO PARTICIPATORY BUDGETING

Businesspeople in Porto Alegre also emphasized the centrality of professional training and skills for improving the lives of poor people but not through participatory budgeting. Their discussion of the program revealed understandings of democracy different from those of the program's architects and characterizations of meetings and poor people at odds with day-to-day life in the city's vilas. Most strikingly, businesspeople feared being outvoted in the transparent democratic process that lay at the heart of participatory budgeting. Out of these intertwined understandings and fears, businesspeople across ages, sectors, and genders critiqued participatory budgeting in very similar terms. They also agreed on the superiority of corporate social responsibility in promoting economic inclusion.

Several of the businesspeople interviewed interpreted the main outlines of participatory budgeting much as the Workers' Party and international observers did. In the words of a leading real estate developer in the city: "Participatory budgeting . . . destined a certain amount of money for projects that would be voted on by the population, and the population would meet up and choose their priorities." Another, the owner of a midsize company that produced flooring, flagged the deliberative aspect of the process by describing what it would mean to enter participatory budgeting to secure a neighborhood need: "I need to get a street paved, for example, so I go to participatory budgeting and say 'listen, this street needs paving for this, this, and this reason.'" Participatory budgeting thus involved giving reasons. It was also, as several interviewees frankly noted, about power. In the view of a conservative, older businessman who emphasized his own gut instincts and ability to get what he wanted in politics: "All the power was turned over to lower-class people" who now had not only "the power to implement works" but the power to decide which projects were most necessary and which less compelling.

Two of the businesspeople interviewed had attended participatory budgeting meetings themselves, in each case to secure pavement for the street in front of their newly constructed homes. Both found the process mildly disagreeable. They resented having to attend weekly meetings for more than a year to secure something to which they felt any taxpayer should be entitled, and they found the places where the meetings were held to be unpleasant. The meeting halls were "bare," "poor," and "really bad"; they were without "structure" but filled with "a crowd of people." At the same time, these two businessmen described a process that was open to them and worked smoothly. Each went to participatory budgeting meetings, figured out how the process worked, and put his needs on the table, and in the end both of their streets were paved. When asked if it was difficult to have their projects put on the master list, one—the older man with the gut instincts—said he had waited six months before speaking in the meetings, to learn the language and procedures of the budgeting process. After that, the regional coordinator of participatory budgeting put his street on the list of potential projects. The other businessman who went to participatory budgeting, the chief executive of a family trucking business, said that the street in front of his house also provided access in and out of the adjacent vila. Therefore, at the participatory budgeting meetings he made common cause with the people who lived in the vila and had no trouble getting the pavement project put on the master list and approved.

Many of the interviewees said they see something of value in the aspect of participatory budgeting that involves the city government's becoming aware of people's needs. A leading industrialist characterized this as "listening to the client," which businesspeople agreed contributes to effective policy making. For a high official in the Federação das Indústrias do Rio Grande do Sul (FIERGS)—arguably the second most important statewide business association in Brazil, after that of São Paulo state—"listening to the poor population is important, especially because they live in deprivation." Furthermore, in the view of this official, also the CEO of an industrial firm, participatory budgeting made poor people visible: "Participatory budgeting taught everyone that there is a poor population that not only needs to be served, but also listened to."

To the co-owner of the local branch of a prosperous international franchise, participatory budgeting was responsible for bringing basic necessities to Porto Alegre's vilas, where "sanitation infrastructure was nonexistent." According to the franchise co-owner, without participatory budgeting the provision of a minimum standard of living, to which everyone has a right, would never have happened in Porto Alegre, and people would still be living in subhuman conditions. Today, if you go to a vila, he said, you don't see sewage in the streets; there is potable water and pavement. This was important for the whole city, he insisted, because improving material conditions decreases violence. As a result of these improvements to the basic standard of living in vilas in Porto Alegre, elite businesspeople in the city don't need to drive around in armored cars, the way rich people do in other major Brazilian cities.

While none of the businesspeople quoted so far were supporters of participatory budgeting, each of them characterized its basic procedures accurately at times and discerned some value in the process. Significantly, none of the interviewees accused participatory budgeting of corruption, and none claimed to have been harmed by the process in either business or personal life. These responses suggest a story of progressive reform accepted, albeit with discomfort, by the private sector. In this view, participatory budgeting, understood and tolerated by the private sector and promoted by community movements and leftist parties, would function simultaneously within neoliberalism and within a more progressive project of citizen empowerment and material redistribution. A terrain of significant actual and potential reform, participatory budgeting might continue to shift and reconfigure power relations between economic elites and the residents of Porto Alegre's working-class and poor neighborhoods over time, thereby enduring and deepening as a reform.

However, although these ideas were expressed by a range of businesspeople, this is not the account they voiced most of the time. What preoccupied businesspeople in Porto Alegre was another set of concerns, a very different telling of the story of participatory budgeting and their own place in it. This analysis of participatory budgeting, shaped by the businesspeople's cultural understandings of politics and poor people, promoted actions to undermine the program rather than to develop the reformist potential within it. During the years when the Workers' Party was in power and participatory budgeting at its most vibrant, most businesspeople rejected it outright as undemocratic, because it deliberately bypassed the elected city council in formulating policy.[11] They dismissed the participants in participatory budgeting, who were disproportionately working class and poor, as lazy people who had time to go to meetings because they didn't work but had nothing to contribute to the meetings because they were uneducated. "Since I have to be productive," the developer said, "I have no time to go." By characterizing participatory budgeting in these ways, businesspeople ignored the innovative characteristics that had garnered global acclaim: through codified, democratic procedures involving written agendas, the giving of reasons, and conclusions reached through voting, ordinary people engaged in savvy and productive debate and reached effective decisions concerning budgeting and urban development.

Instead of identifying these characteristics of participatory budgeting, businesspeople asserted that the process was controlled and manipulated by the Workers' Party. Even the co-owner of the franchise, who spoke eloquently about basic economic rights and the material success of participatory budgeting in building infrastructure in vilas, insisted that it was all top-down control: "What was the 'participatory'? They transferred the power from the government, and passed it on to half a dozen people who decided what would be done, and brought people to vote on what they thought would be good. So, in reality, they transferred the decision making to other people." Worse still, according to the wife of the developer, who was also his business partner and a lawyer, the elite in Porto Alegre had not been "invited" to enter participatory budgeting. If she herself had gone to a participatory budgeting meeting and said she wanted to participate, the people at the meeting would have said, in her words, "Ha, ha, you don't enter." The notion of invitation, and of their not having been invited, permeated the responses of businesspeople to participatory budgeting in interviews. In the words of the statewide trucking business owner, "They never came to my house." They never said, "Come participate. Let's build a good environment for everyone." For the lawyer, participatory budgeting was "a closed club." The female owner of a successful, upscale clothing store said, "They never came over to ask or tell me anything."

These responses are both disingenuous and true. Although participatory budgeting meetings were public, advertised, and open to all, elites were not sought out for participatory budgeting or encouraged to participate. Participatory budgeting was seen by its leftist creators as a means to redistribute, to a modest but discernible extent, both political power and urban goods and services. While the Worker's Party government took great pains to maintain the economic dynamism and attractive investment climate that had long made Porto Alegre one of the most prosperous cities in Brazil, the participatory budgeting project itself worked to elicit and sustain the participation of poor people, not the middle classes or elites. The government official who designed Governança Local, the business-friendly program instituted in 2004 to complement participatory budgeting, aptly characterized the discomfort that came from having access in the technical sense but not being invited or welcomed: "In the logic of participatory budgeting, the participation of businesspeople was strange. It didn't fit in, you know?"

The two businessmen among the interviewees who went to participatory budgeting meetings to get their streets paved reported no difficulties in finding their way to the meetings or participating in them, beyond the fact that they didn't like the surroundings and needed to learn the procedures and language before speaking. When pressed, the same interviewees who complained deeply and at length about not having been "invited" acknowledged that businesspeople themselves rejected the participatory budgeting process. "They didn't invite us," the trucking business owner explained, "but neither did we go there to say, 'Here we are.'" According to the developer, "They didn't make any effort to bring in outsiders." But despite his wife's insistence that she would have been prevented from entering a participatory budgeting meeting, he added, "I don't know of any businessperson who wanted to go and was turned away." (He also said that neither he nor anyone in his economic or social circle had ever attended a meeting.)

Nearly every time an interviewee spoke about not having been "invited" to participatory budgeting, he or she laughed in a way that defies easy analysis. Did this laughter mean that they knew there was something suspect about what they were saying, that it didn't match the facts of open, accessible meetings, where common cause could be made with vila residents and facilitators made sure that agendas were open to all? Did businesspeople laugh because they were aware that it is others who are usually excluded, not themselves? Others who don't speak the language of the places where decisions are made, who don't feel comfortable in those places and aren't invited anyway, except in the most impersonal way, during business hours, if they travel to the city center and wait in line?

Or did the businesspeople laugh because they were uncomfortable feeling excluded? Because they were embarrassed that this could happen? Did the laughter signify fear? What if businesspeople continued to be excluded in just the same way, by not being invited ever again? What if they had to keep going to places they found repugnant, having to learn new procedures and languages to get their basic needs satisfied? According to the older businessman accustomed to getting his way, "These meetings happened at night, sometimes in places annoying to get to . . . so it wasn't pleasant, it was better not having to go, but there was no other way." When he went to participatory budgeting meetings to get his street paved, the people there had nothing to fear from him. For this reason, in a curious recasting of elite fears of lower-class violence, he himself had no concerns about his own safety when he went to participatory budgeting meetings in vilas: "There was no physical rejection, no . . . But it's also true that I always went with only two or three people along and they went with fifty! If a vila wanted sewage, or something, they took fifty people—once even playing the drums [batucada, an Afro-Brazilian musical form]—so they really filled the space. We didn't pose any risk to them, you know?" Because the "ordinary" people could outvote him fifty to three, they had no need to act violently toward him.

The boss-like businessman was not the only one who recognized the power of democracy. The family trucking business owner, the other person among the interviewees who had actually attended a participatory budgeting meeting, said it outright: "Businesspeople are scared of the following: for every business-person that goes there, ten ordinary people also go . . . and those ten are going to vote." In this analysis, poor people use violence when they cannot claim democratic citizenship, while elites fear democracy because where democracy functions, they can be outvoted. "At the time," the savvy boss told me, "I feared that from then on everything would function like that." If the absence of violence was notable, along with the lack of formal invitations, so was the inability of businesspeople to see or name what lay in front of their eyes. It wasn't democracy that occurred at participatory budgeting meetings, the trucking owner explained, because people had to fight for what they wanted. Democracy, he said, means the government brings you solutions, and you support them.

In saying this, the trucking owner expressed the preference for representative rather than direct democracy common among businesspeople. This is complicated by businesspeople's frank admission that representative democracy in Porto Alegre favored elite interests and their insistence that transparent procedures of direct democracy were undemocratic by their very nature. The developer rejected participatory budgeting as undemocratic because, he said, democracy means electing a city councilperson who will look after your needs. The owner of the flooring company understood this situation perfectly. He said that he elects a city councilperson who should be responsible for his community—but he acknowledged that councilors appear only at election time, when they go to vilas to buy votes from poor people, whom they won't see again until the next election. Asked if participatory budgeting wasn't created for this reason (to establish a responsive democratic institution and replace the clientelistic city council), he agreed, observing that participatory budgeting "occupied the space that the city council left void." But then he repeated the observation with which he had begun our discussion of participatory budgeting: that it was completely manipulated by the Workers' Party.

In fact, participatory budgeting opened up new spaces for democratic participation and at the same time was used by the Workers' Party for political gain. PT officials designed participatory budgeting procedures, informally mediated community disputes, favored party supporters at times, and campaigned on the program's successes, even as those successes were real, in terms of empowering ordinary people and securing infrastructure for poor neighborhoods. Researchers and activists on the left criticized the PT's willingness to influence participatory budgeting for partisan purposes, and this critique deepened over the years. The difference between the businesspeople's accounts and those of leftists critics is that the leftist critics discerned the coexistence of popular empowerment and partisan manipulation and made judgments about the balance. To businesspeople, in contrast, organizing, discussion, and voting in vilas *could not* be democratic. For the trucking owner, participatory budgeting is not democratic precisely because people had to go to it and fight for what they needed. It was not democratic because it came from the participants themselves: "We, the population, had to go . . . but OP didn't come to us, you know? It was a struggle . . . We got together and we fought. It was not a democratic thing . . . because it had to come from us."

Thus, using formal procedures of speech and voting to fight for material rights and needs is not democratic at all. In this view, it seems that the organizing and mobilizing strategies of social movements and community groups are by definition not democratic, precisely because they involve organizing and mobilizing—"com[ing] from us" rather than policy making on the part of government. Indeed, from this perspective, any effort on the part of poor people to expand their participation in politics beyond voting in elections or "being heard" in the most passive sense, and that comes from within the community, "from us," cannot be democratic either.

In addition to being undemocratic because they are places of action and struggle, businesspeople saw participatory budgeting meetings as a place of fantasy and disorder. In the analysis of the developer, who had never been to a meeting and didn't know anyone who had, the serious and the crazy went into the same budget: "OP put together a bunch of people, and those people decided the craziest things; some important and serious, but some were pure fantasy. And everything was included in the budget." To the international industrialist, the formalized rules of the participatory budgeting process, printed in handbooks and enacted at each meeting, literally did not exist, because they had not been enacted by the city council: "I want criteria! Transparency! I don't want assembly-ism [which leads to 'political demagoguery']. . . . I want definitions, straightforward discussions; clear legislation. . . . Things need order . . . discipline . . . as it happens within the legislative chamber." The places the industrialist had never visited, where actual meetings were held, could not in his view be transparent and could only be places of demagoguery, not democracy, which was the province of the elected city council.

Participatory budgeting meetings take place all over the city, from the city center to public buildings in lower middle-class neighborhoods or poor vilas. In the business imaginary, however, all participatory budgeting occurs in the vilas, which are places of disorder. " I know they had that in the vila," the shop owner said, " but it never came near me." Just imagining participatory budgeting, she sighed at the thought that "one of the vilas chose what it wanted": "This is not the way it should be! There has to be a macro plan. Someone has to sail this boat. Not one vila deciding one thing and the other something else. . . . It is not through votes. Less democracy. Let's make a plan and someone takes the lead." In their very way of describing reality, businesspeople denied the possibility of that which already existed. They wielded ignorance as a form of power, keeping the reality of participatory budgeting, of the competence of ordinary people, an "open secret"—something that everybody knew on one level but that could be denied for the purposes of politics and policy making, social interaction, and cultural representation on the level of everyday elite life and politics. Were the "open secret" to be openly acknowledged, the terrain of politics would shift to one of more even-handed contestation over reform.

The interviewees rarely referred to vilas by names, identifying them as places of deprivation and little else. Some of the interviewees said that the needs of vila residents needed to be heard. The franchise co-owners spoke forcefully about basic human rights, characterizing ending poverty and providing health care and education in vilas as "a basic prerequisite." The younger of the two officials of the business association, himself the CEO of an industrial firm, understood that the Workers' Party had invested great political effort in the vilas, "in the power of the vila," and that rather than buying the support of vila residents with money, as most politicians do, the party had created an idea there, sold a project, "a social idea of citizenship." In saying this, the business official offers an understanding of the Workers' Party and participatory budgeting compatible with both business development and enduring socioeconomic reform. However, he explained, when the new city government took power in 2004, the whole wave of activity created in the vilas receded—"The political pressure of the PT in the vila does not exist"—and with it the potential of participatory budgeting to continue to promote an alternative political project.

The owner of the flooring business, it turned out, had taught school in a vila to fund his education, returning year after year during college and winning "honored teacher" awards. If there were public commitment to change today, he said (as if participatory budgeting did not constitute such a commitment), "I would go to the vilas . . . and I would do some work there." He would also, he said (if he were to go there, which he didn't), treat the people there "like normal human beings. Not as excluded people." What he would do there is not stimulate popular participation in managing the city budget but train people for jobs: "Train people. That's what's important." In saying this, the flooring entrepreneur sets the context for corporate social responsibility. As soon as he mentioned the vilas in his city, near to where he lived, but where he had not ventured since college, the flooring company owner traveled immediately in his thoughts to Brazil's northeast. In many of the interviews, in fact, businesspeople turned without prompting to other locations, from the interior of Rio Grande do Sul to the northeast of Brazil, to explain what they had learned about poor people there. This is the imaginative, cultural move that enables corporate social responsibility, by skipping over the participatory budgeting that exists and works in the city to imagined elsewheres where otherwise unruly people are disciplined and contented by job training and work.

The developer's wife, a lawyer, told a story of traveling to Mato Grosso, in central Brazil, with her elderly mother, to attend to land her father had purchased there fifty years ago. The land had recently been turned over to her family after a decades-long legal dispute. When she learned of the legal victory, the lawyer said immediately that she would go see the land, but everyone told her, "No! Go there? Are you crazy? You'll get shot!" But the lawyer insisted, wanting to see this reality for herself and to take her mother along: "'Mom, we'll go there just to get to know the place, okay?' And we did go in March. But we were scared stiff!" The reality was nothing like what she expected, however; instead of confronting violence and laziness, she discovered a booming economy where "everybody wants to work, to do things, to grow." The lawyer found herself enchanted by this place of dynamism and growth.

She returned to criticize the elite of Porto Alegre for their "horrible prejudices" toward the people of the center and northeast of Brazil; she criticized the elite themselves for living off their money without working. She leveled this charge almost as strongly as she criticized participatory budgeting for not inviting her to have a seat at the table. "People should always work, should always do something. . . . I think every person has to do something with their life, it doesn't matter what, but you have to do something." The lawyer found common ground with evangelicals on this score; she took her daughter out of the elite school where she and her husband had been educated, putting the daughter instead in an evangelical school, because the students there have to do social service. By working in a day-care center, her daughter's class learns about the real world. As with her own trip to Mato Grosso, she recalled: "Experiencing something yourself is very different from reading about it in a book, isn't it?"

What was the lawyer saying, with this long story of travel, confrontation with reality, and return with fresh eyes? The same woman who could speak only with disparagement about participatory budgeting and the vila across the street from her house (which she had never entered and from which she was protected by numerous guarded doors and barbed wire) had traveled across Brazil to cut through the prejudices of her culture and class and learn about reality through direct experience. She had discovered that the *vagabundos* there, the violent and lazy people who would shoot her on sight, were in fact hard workers building new cities. However, although she could talk about this insight once she was back home, she could not apply it to the vilas of Porto Alegre.

The owner of the flooring company, who had taught school in the vilas decades ago, when he was in college, but never returned, told a related story. He talked about the direct, human connection he had made with his students in the vila—a place to which he had traveled and learned directly about reality. But when asked if participatory budgeting perhaps fostered the same kind of connections and education today, he responded that participatory budgeting is all about manipulation, with the PT playing with marked cards. And immediately, with no prompting, he went on to talk about Brazil's northeast, much as the lawyer had brought up Mato Grosso. Until recently, the flooring company owner told me, the people in the northeast were vagabundos, they didn't want to work, and this made it difficult to set up businesses there. Investors from Rio Grande do Sul went there to set up factories, but workers didn't show up when they were supposed to. But then, what did a creative corporation do? The man continued: "They started to treat people with dignity." And what happened? "The moment people started believing they had dignity, the productivity level of companies in the northeast became the highest [in the country]."

What was the flooring entrepreneur communicating, by linking his story of working in a vila thirty years ago to learning about Brazil's northeast today? This man talked about participatory budgeting as a deck of marked cards; yet he had traveled daily to a vila in Porto Alegre thirty years earlier to teach a class that two prior teachers had already abandoned. Because he needed money for college, the flooring entrepreneur had gone to the vila and learned about the everyday lives of people there. By getting to know his students and treating them with dignity, he led them to educational success. Similarly, if people in the northeast appeared to be vagabundos, he observed, it was not because of who they were but how they were treated. As with the lawyer who had traveled to Mato Grosso, direct knowledge countered stereotypes. The flooring entrepreneur was indicating that he knew popular prejudices about poor people could be tested—and shown to be false—through experience. He related all of this in direct response to questions about participatory budgeting, a project he rejected in its entirety on the basis of little or no evidence. Something about going to an "elsewhere" distant in time or geography to learn about reality was valuable and appropriate; going down the street was unthinkable. To go down the street would mean to accept some of the claims and successes of participatory budgeting and to act on the terrain of the reform itself; to look elsewhere, however, allows the development of a counterproposal and the closing down of existing reform.

These businesspeople dismissed participatory budgeting wholesale, without any sense of the richness and rough-and-tumble of the process, the give-and-take, the commitment to hard work, the fitting of great emotions into an agenda of three-minute speeches and carefully counted votes, the grilling of municipal officials and the originality of new solutions. Because they made of participatory budgeting and of the vilas the local equivalents of the vagabundos of Brazil's center and northeast—but took no steps to dispel the myths locally—they failed time and again to recognize that participatory budgeting carried out many of the tasks and functions the businesspeople themselves thought most relevant to business growth and social good. In neglecting or refusing to notice that participatory budgeting provided much the sort of education, training, and experience they felt poor Brazilians needed, businesspeople set the stage for replacing participatory budgeting with a more congenial alternative: corporate social responsibility. With this idea, companies themselves would carry out focused social programs, generally designed to provide educational opportunities to their own workers or to selected young people in the neighborhood in which the business was located. In so doing, they would replace a reform that could work within both neoliberal and progressive frameworks (participatory budgeting) with one narrowly compatible with an individualist market notion of economy and citizenship (corporate social responsibility).

Without unduly romanticizing participatory budgeting, it is fair to say that many of the people who participated in the yearly cycle of meetings learned to speak in public, present their cases, and evaluate the alternatives. They learned to lobby and maneuver in democratic settings, harness (and lose hold of) passion and outrage, make (and break) alliances and coalitions, abide by the results of voting, and return (or not) to fight another day. In addition, they learned to seek out information, apply lessons from one time period or neighborhood to another, communicate across the city's different regions, and hold municipal officials accountable.

All of the businesspeople interviewed in Porto Alegre cite education as the single biggest problem and challenge facing the country. Among them, however, they have no evaluations or proposals concerning public education, beyond the claims that more is needed, that education costs money, and that all of the funding necessary to improve education can be found by fighting corruption. At the same time, not one person among the business interviewees suggested that an educational process might be occurring in participatory budgeting, which had involved more than a hundred thousand adults of all ages, across the length and breadth of the city, over the course of twenty years, garnering national and international acclaim.

The franchise co-owner explained that participatory budgeting provided infrastructure in poor neighborhoods, but it didn't provide skills. To the suggestion that participatory budgeting activists would say that the budgeting process provided skills in citizenship, this man responded: "But when I want to hire a maid, I want to know what she can do: What can you do? Can you do the laundry? Can you iron? Can you cook?" Pressed further with the question, "Does she know how to participate in meetings?" the franchise co-owner concluded that "participating in meetings doesn't matter" because "a few leaders really manipulated participatory budgeting, but they didn't create the tools, the means to give professional advice to disadvantaged adolescents . . .

[who might then say,] 'Listen, I want to be a construction worker,' 'I want to be a carpenter,' 'I want to be a mechanic.' ' I want to be an auto electrician.' ' I want to be a metalworker.'" The savvy boss added: "The only people doing that in Brazil are businesspeople."

The Workers' Party was voted out of office in 2004 and replaced by the administration of centrist Jose Fogaça, who had promised throughout the campaign to continue participatory budgeting but to make city government more open to businesspeople.[12] The transition to a "lighter" participatory budgeting, with more invitations issued to businesspeople, was facilitated by the dismal—and hidden—state of the city's finances under the last PT government: the city was in debt and could not pay for many of the past several years of projects that had been approved through the participatory budgeting process (Junge 2012, 410). In the time it took to balance the books and catch up on the backlog of projects, the vigorous, mobilized participatory budgeting that was grounded in the force of the vilas gradually retreated. In the words of the developer, "The issue died naturally. . . . It was basically like that, that simple." A cautionary tale arose, strongly supported by the city's media, which had long opposed and denigrated participatory budgeting. "What good does it do," wondered an elderly housebound woman, who splits her time between news and telenovelas, "to approve projects that exceed the capacity of the budget? It only leaves people disappointed." Thus was participatory budgeting reduced to accounting, despite years of impassioned and procedurally democratic local decision making, ongoing and (with the significant exception of the final years of PT administration) transparent budget keeping, and infrastructural projects that transformed the face of the city.

As participatory budgeting continued, with less force and a lot less money, the Fogaça administration instituted a new program, Governança Local, that focused on the idea of partnerships rather than open meetings. Governança Local sought especially to bring the private sector into the development and administration of capital investments in a way that would make businessmen feel comfortable as one of three equal groups: government, business, and community-based NGOs.[13] The lawyer, who had complained so bitterly about not being invited to participatory budgeting, felt included in Governança Local, as she and other lawyers with whom she worked attended meetings with government officials. "Today," she said, when you have a problem, "you go there and your voice is heard!" "Businesspeople like that," said one of the officials who designed and implemented the new program. "It's a piece of cake for them."[14]

Governança Local favors projects designed in partnerships with business and focused on "productive capacities." The development of a shopping mall complex in the southern, waterfront area of Porto Alegre brought together city government, the largest mall management company in Brazil, an NGO to provide housing to those displaced by the mall, a recycling center run by the NGO, and, in the form of the mall itself, a new cultural space and jobs (Junge 2012, 412). The partnership suggests clear tasks to promote growth and inclusion, according to the official who designed the program: a shopping mall will be built, young people living nearby will be trained in construction. If wealthy people live near the water, young people shall be trained to work on boats and repair them. If computers are being thrown out by businesses, recycle them. In just this way, "young people start gaining skills." This is considered a natural process, without the conflict and disagreement of participatory budgeting: "Governança is something natural, something that flows naturally."

The problem with participatory budgeting, the official who designed Governança Local told me, was that it was democratic, and democracy polarizes people. What was needed, in contrast, was "a more advanced concept of democracy," and this was to be found in "social responsibility"—an idea that comes from the private sector." Indeed, the private sector in Porto Alegre had sponsored think tanks and conferences to oppose participatory budgeting ideologically and develop alternatives; the private sector supported Fogaça's electoral campaign and provided the architects of Governança Local with philosophical grounding and concrete ideas. As a result, in the official's view, Governança Local transcended democracy: "There's no voting with Governança, you don't vote. . . . Governança is only by consensus." The consensus process works, the official told me, because it has been "scientifically proven," that "the more plural the group, the easier the consensus. . . . The difficulty of consensus is when there is polarization of a few—a group holds one position and another holds a different one."

Based on these differing understandings of democracy, one could tell the story of participatory budgeting and Governança Local this way: when the Workers' Party in Porto Alegre, coming from a radical leftist tradition that had previously favored hierarchical decision making, embraced procedural democracy and insisted that decisions must be made by vote in open meetings, the right dismissed this as polarizing and called for decision making by consensus, behind closed doors. In the current postdemocratic moment, with meetings convened by invitation, businesspeople feel comfortable and problems are solved easily: "If you get people from the community together to discuss what is best for our community, it takes little time to reach an agreement, very little time. . . . It works like that. It works easily." Whereas participatory budgeting was, and continues to be, a citywide program, Governança is smaller and functions as a model. What it models—and reflects—is corporate social responsibility. When asked whether the private sector had any responsibility for dealing with pressing social problems, businesspeople answered either that their business offered aid to several social service projects in their area or that they ran a training program for a group of disadvantaged youth in the neighborhood. Several of the businesspeople interviewed did this through Projeto Pescar, which teaches young people at risk "how to fish" by placing them in an enterprise-based training program where they learned both skills and good work habits.

FIERGS, the statewide business association, spearheaded the turn to corporate social responsibility by establishing a collection of "social banks" under the motto, "Transforming Waste into Social Benefit." Located a few kilometers from FIERGS's state-of-the-art conference center and auditorium, the half-dozen "banks" occupy huge warehouses where surplus or discarded food, textiles, furniture, building materials, and computers are collected, repaired, and then distributed to schools, day-care centers, and service programs around the city. In addition, each "bank" provides classes in the creative use of its products— from cooking nutritious meals to crafting wedding gowns from patchwork-style scraps of material. The banks are impressive in both the scope of their distribution and the success with which they are transforming philanthropy into a socially respectable activity that is deemed necessary and appropriate by Porto Alegre's business elite.

The businesspeople interviewed did not worry that inequality would lead to crisis, and they did not speak of poverty when asked about serious problems facing Porto Alegre and Brazil. This is striking in a country of great poverty and inequality. Equally striking, especially from the perspective of the subsequent global economic crisis (as well as from the protests that rocked Brazil in 2013), was that they had come to take Brazil's economic boom for granted and saw no pressing economic problems on the horizon. It did not seem to occur to businesspeople in Porto Alegre, at the time of the interviews, that popular discontent could engender threatening social or political disruptions. The perceived absence of crisis facilitated their dismissal of participatory budgeting. The proper responses to exclusion, all the businesspeople agreed, were education and economic growth. From this view, there is no problem to which participatory budgeting—which recognizes the capacity of ordinary people to know, name, and shape the world—might be an answer.

Despite their lack of interest in participatory budgeting, however, almost to a person, the businesspeople interviewed were concerned with improving social conditions and having an impact on those around them. They value evangelicalism for motivating people to find purpose in their lives and work. They offer no analysis of the conditions and structures that produce and reproduce inequality, but some of them wrestle with the issue of how to do social good in a market system. In this regard, the international industrialist has taken a prominent public stand for voluntary acts of community service. The industrialist acknowledged that he could take a purely market view, which holds that "maximizing capitalization generates more jobs, and more jobs solve social problems. This rule is correct." However, he found that "in reality, I don't want to spend another day with children starving to death right next to me." This brought the industrialist to the idea of citizenship as individual acts of community service: "Everything is citizenship, everything is citizenship. Each person does it in his own way."

Just as acts of community service are individual, the expression of need can be individual as well. While participatory budgeting was right about the need to listen to people and learn their needs, to "listen to the client," in the words of the industrialist, this could be done electronically, without meetings or discussion: "Participatory budgeting is an option. Is it good or not? It's an effort, an attempt. But I would say that today, using electronic means, in theory I could work with thousands of modern communication systems, right?" The international industrialist was the only one among the interviewees who talked about hunger: "Two hundred meters from here, people live absolutely destitute. I cannot accept that." But for him addressing hunger had to occur within a competitive market system, and he found no satisfactory solution: "The very notion of social responsibility, within the classical liberal thinking, is an issue not satisfactorily solved." He lived, therefore, with a sense of both pride and disquiet.

Corporate social responsibility has turned the private sector's gaze to voluntary community service during just the two decades when market liberalism flourished, global corporations and entrepreneurial giants spearheaded philanthropy, and, in Porto Alegre, participatory budgeting made the vilas visible. The Enduring Reform interviews suggest that corporate social responsibility involves, at least in part, good-hearted intentions that demonstrably help poor individuals in increasing numbers. Robust programs of corporate social responsibility may be a long-term legacy of participatory budgeting in Porto Alegre. However, this constitutes a shift from collective efforts of democratic self-government through citizen participation to individual voluntary acts within a framework of market-driven development (Junge 2012, 410). Everyone can do something, the international industrialist said: "Help somehow, exercise their own rights, the enforcement of the law." "As a socially responsible citizen," the creator of Governança Local recounted, "I don't litter the streets, right? I don't throw my trash in Arroio Dilúvio. I care about kids, I treat animals well, I care if there's someone starving." In these matters, "everybody has something to offer." In the words of the flooring company owner: "It's a grain of sand, each one doing his part."

These are disaggregated efforts that we might perhaps call the invisible hand of social responsibility: exercise your rights, obey the law, don't litter, and be kind to children and animals. These are precisely the kind of microefforts that businesspeople reject when they think of the large-scale planning neces-sary for the success of the private sector in the global economy. In contrast to their rejection of the government's sponsorship of participatory budgeting, the businesspeople interviewed combine an emphasis on market-based economic growth with frank recognition of the importance and capacity of government planning and action to promote this growth. In order for such a process of plan-ning to succeed, in their view, the private sector needs to come up with its own proposals that can be launched in the public sphere, and it needs to have access to high government officials. In a sense, businesspeople need their own by-invitation-only version of participatory budgeting at the national level.

Ironically, this is what the left under Presidents Lula and then Dilma Rousseff has offered to business since 2002 and where the real learning process of recent years on the part of businesspeople has occurred. In the words of the younger official of FIERGS, the business association: "You have to work a lot more politically, not in order to stop this or that, but to come up with your own proposals . . . because in the end, the broad dialogue with the government is done by the elites. . . . We need to be able always to create better situations, so that the economy improves." The older FIERGS official, an active player in Brazilian industrialization since the 1950s, spoke enthusiastically about the access the private sector gained under Lula. He can go to Brasilia himself, he said, and discuss trade policy with the relevant ministers whenever he needs to, making suggestions and collaborating smoothly to create and fine-tune policies. He and other executives formed a national business association to work with the government on trade issues: "So, today this coalition is heard; the government today does not make any decisions without listening to the corporate area, without listening to the Brazilian business coalition." In the days of military rule, the official told me, the generals sponsored grand projects, but they communicated with businesspeople only on the macrolevel, about broad goals. "Macrovisions did happen," he acknowledged, "but the dialogue that we have today, no, it absolutely did not exist, no . . . not this day-by-day of 'let's carry out an operation, and I go there, here, and let's discuss the best way to do this.'"

When Lula took office, businesspeople worried that a leftist government would be a "closed government." They were certain that a PT government "would not look at the entrepreneurial side, would jeopardize decades of development and sacrifices." Instead, the left at the national level has offered to the private sector exactly the day-to-day autonomy, discussion, and influence over decision making that the private sector rejected in participatory budgeting: "Today there is real understanding and complete openness. . . . I go four, five times, three times at least, to Brasília to discuss." Businessmen in Porto Alegre endured participatory budgeting for sixteen years, then limited and channeled it by offering new proposals that won votes in democratic elections. In achieving these changes, they have played by the rules of democracy, furthering their own visions and interests while building on tensions and dissatisfactions within the participatory budgeting process itself (Junge 2102, 419). At the same time, participatory budgeting endures today, providing mechanisms for poor people to define their own priorities and supervise the selection and implementation of infrastructural projects. However, the reach of participatory budgeting has been circumscribed, with Governança Local and corporate social responsibility assuming some of its functions, and its empowering dimension limited. Businesspeople need no longer fear being outvoted, because the kinds of projects that are voted on have been limited and the resources devoted to them cut, with businesspeople invited to participate on equal terms with community organizations in Governança Local's partnerships and consultations. Porto Alegre's businesspeople, to their surprise and satisfaction, have gained a participatory voice under Presidents Lula and Dilma and in their own city as well. They are invited and welcomed. The people in Porto Alegre's vilas, in contrast, got corporate social responsibility, which, if they are lucky, will transform waste into social benefit.

NOTES

1. Participatory budgeting applies to the portion of the municipal budget dedicated to various forms of local infrastructure. This proportion varied between 4 percent and 11 percent of the total city budget over the course of twenty-five years. Most of the city budget, in contrast, goes toward fixed expenses, such as salaries. See Wilkinson 2007, 205, for discussion of how the relatively small size of the participatory budget's allotment has been downplayed in scholarly accounts.

2. On deliberative democracy, see Gutmann and Thompson 2004, and Habermas 1985.

3. Fifteen prominent businesspeople were interviewed by Rubin, from businesses of a range of sizes and economic sectors. We have not used names in this text and, in addition, we have changed the identities of the interviewees, although we have broadly maintained

characteristics of age, gender, and economic sector. Five activists were interviewed in depth by Baierle for this chapter, which also draws on the authors' far-reaching experience with participatory budgeting and its participants.

4. After considerable grassroots mobilization and national deliberation, parts of this program were adopted in the Brazilian Constitution of 1988 (see Júnior 1988).

5. A book about the planning dilemma during the Allende administration was very influential at the time (Matus 1987).

6. Changes in 2002 substituted one regional meeting, near the end of the process, for the original two.

7. Sergio Baierle (1998, 135), coauthor of this chapter and cofounder of a Porto Alegre NGO that supported participatory budgeting, has since become one of the few serious scholarly critics of the program. For critiques of Genro's concept of a "nonstate public sphere," see Avritzer 2002 and Wampler 2009.

8. See Walker 2013, 202–5, for an excellent summary of participatory budgeting approaches and experiences around the world.

9. Both quotations are from Jeffrey Rubin's notes of the sessions of the Local Authorities Forum in 2002.

10. The phrase and concept "politico-administrative monopoly" were developed by Pedro Prieto-Martín (2010).

11. The city council votes the final participatory budget up or down at the end of the participatory budgeting cycle but for most of the program's years could not amend the final budget. It has been commonly agreed since the initiation of participatory budgeting that the council has no viable option but to approve the budget, because of the budget's widespread legitimacy.

12. Fogaça was reelected in October 2008 with 60 percent of the vote, to the PT candidate's 40 percent. Fogaça (2008) stated in an interview that the most significant achievement of his administration was "pacifying the city and getting partisanship out of community life."

13. See Junge 2012 for a thorough description of the origins and priorities of Governança Local.

14. The exact phrase he used was "sopa no mel," which translates as "a piece of cake in honey"; several Brazilian colleagues thought the best translation is "The businessmen have it made in the shade."

REFERENCES

Abers, R. 2000. *Inventing Local Democracy: Grassroots Politics in Brazil*. Boulder: Lynne Rienner.

Avritzer, L. 2002. *Democracy and the Public Space in Latin America*. Princeton: Princeton University Press.

Baierle, S. 1998. "The Explosion of Experience: The Emergence of a New Ethical-Political Principle in Popular Movements in Porto Alegre, Brazil." In *Cultures of Politics, Politics of Cultures: Re-Visioning Latin American Social Movements,* edited by S. Alvarez, E. Dagnino, and

A. Escobar, 118–138. Boulder: Westview Press.

Baierle, S. 2003. "The Porto Alegre Thermidor: Brazil's 'Participatory Budget' at the Cross-roads." *Socialist Register* 39: 305–28.

Baiocchi, G. 2005. *Militants and Citizens: The Politics of Participatory Democracy in Porto Alegre.* Redwood City: Stanford University Press.

Cretella Jr., J. 1990. Comentários à constituição brasileira de 1988. Rio de Janeiro: Forense Universitária.

Damo, A. 2005. "A Peça Orçamentária: Os sentidos da participação política a partir do OP Porto-Alegrense." In *Etnografias da participação*, edited by Claudia Fonseca and Jurema Brites, 136–83. Santo Cruz do Sul: Editora da Universidade de Santa Cruz do Sul.

Evans, P. 2004. "Development as Institutional Change: The Pitfalls of Monocropping and the Potentials of Deliberation." *Studies in Comparative International Development* 38 (4): 30–52.

Fogaça, J. 2008. Interview. *Voto: Política e negócios* 46.

Gutmann, A., and D. Thompson. 2004. *Why Deliberative Democracy?* Princeton: Princeton University Press.

Habermas, J. 1985. *The Theory of Communicative Action.* Vols. 1 and 2. Boston: Beacon Press.

Junge, B. 2007. "Citizenship Appeals: Leftist Political Representation and Experience among Grassroots Community Leaders in Porto Alegre, Brazil." PhD dissertation, Emory University, Atlanta, GA.

Junge, B. Forthcoming. "The Energy of Others: Narratives of Envy and Purification among Former Grassroots Community Leaders in Porto Alegre, Brazil." In *Lived Religion and Lived Citizenship in Latin America's Zones of Crisis*, special issue, *Latin American Research Review.*

Junge, B. 2012. "NGOs as Shadow Counter-Publics: Grassroots Community Leaders' Perceptions of Change and Continuity in Porto Alegre, Brazil." *American Ethnologist* 39 (2): 407–24.

Marquetti, A. 2003. "Participação e redistribuição: O Orçamento Participativo em Porto Alegre. In *A Inovação Democrática no Brasil: O Orçamento Participativo*, edited by L. Avritzer and Z. Navarro, 129–56. São Paulo: Cortez Editora.

Matus, C. 1987. *Adiós Señor Presidente.* Caracas: Fundación Altadir

Navarro, Z. 2002. "'O Orçamento Participativo' de Porto Alegre (1989–2002): Um conciso comentário crítico." In *A Inovação Democrática no Brasil: O Orçamento Participativo*, edited by L. Avritzer and Z. Navarro, 89–128. São Paulo: Cortez Editora.

Prieto-Martín, P. 2010. "Las alas de Leo. La participación ciudadana del siglo XX, Asociación Ciudades Kyosei." Online at http://www.ckyosei.org/docs/LasAlasDeLeo.pdf.

Rubin, J. 2003. "Porto Alegre and Participatory Budgeting: Toward a Politics of Decentered Representations (Fighting with Words)." Paper presented at the meeting of the Latin American Studies Association, Dallas, March.

Ruppenthal, F. 2008. *Orçamento Participativo: A "unidade" do FROP da Região Centro.* Porto Alegre: UFRGS.

Santos, B. d. S. 1998. "Participatory Budgeting in Porto Alegre: Toward a Redistributive Democracy." *Politics and Society* 26 (4): 461–510.

Walker, A.P.P. 2013. "Embodied Identity and Political Participation: Squatters' Engagement in the Participatory Budget in Brazil." *Ethos* 41 (2): 1548–52.

Wampler, B. 2009. *Participatory Budgeting in Brazil: Contestation, Cooperation, and Accountability*. University Park: Pennsylvania State University Press.

Wilkinson, M. 2007. "Participatory Politics and Social Inclusion in Porto Alegre, Brazil." PhD dissertation, Columbia University.

Figure 5.1. Production in a worker-owned factory. Photo © Graciela Monteagudo.

5

RECUPERATED FACTORIES IN CONTEMPORARY BUENOS AIRES FROM THE PERSPECTIVE OF WORKERS AND BUSINESSMEN

Carlos A. Forment

WHEN I ASKED RICARDO why he and some of his coworkers at Ghelco, a medium-sized food-processing plant, had decided in May 2002 in the midst of Argentina's worst socioeconomic debacle, to "recuperate" their factory after the owner had terminated them and filed for bankruptcy, he responded: "If we had not done so, we would have been unemployed, and at our age [late forties to late fifties] it would have been impossible to find another job. . . . Anyone who is jobless is treated like garbage; look at the *piqueteros* [picketers]. . . . Restarting the factory enabled me to regain my dignity."[1] After pressing Ricardo several times to clarify the meaning of this last phrase, he replied: "Whenever I talk to the piqueteros in my neighborhood, they always tell me that they should have stayed put and recuperated their factory. . . . All of them are now receiving *planes* [welfare relief] from the government, but this makes them feel like shit, like real nobodies. . . . They lost their place [in public life] the moment they abandoned their factory." Many of the workers whom I interviewed used strikingly similar terms rooted in civic recognition and political belonging to describe their own situation as well as the plight of unemployed piqueteros (Merklen 2005).

This chapter examines, from the perspective of each group, how workers in recuperated factories and owners of small privately owned firms in the greater metropolitan area of Buenos Aires influenced each others' practices in the course of transacting business.[2] In Buenos Aires as in many other regions across South America, recuperated factories and small firms have played a central role in challenging neoliberalism and advancing an alternative model: that is, "social economy" (Roitter 2008). These factories and firms have contributed to this model by generating jobs and providing stable employment to large numbers of citizens; reviving national "light" industry, generating local and regional markets for domestically produced durable and consumer goods; and stimulating consumption and investments among the middle classes and the working poor. Although scholars have not yet studied the relationship between this emergent social economy and the electoral victories of "pink" governments across the region—especially in Argentina, Brazil, Ecuador, Uruguay, and Venezuela—there is no denying that recuperated factories and similar enduring reforms elsewhere challenge the logic of neoliberalism from within.

Scholars and public intellectuals of all stripes have been quick to recognize the significance of these governments. One of the first to do so is the distinguished Mexican scholar-intellectual Jorge Castañeda, who in an influential essay developed a typology classifying these governments in dichotomous terms as "populist" or "pragmatic," with the government of President Hugo Chávez of Venezuela an example of the former and the government of President Luis "Lula" de Silva of Brazil exemplifying the latter (Castañeda 2006). More than a decade after Castañeda published his article, scholars continue to use his typology and focus on "high politics" to understand the sociopolitical changes under way in the region, including in Argentina under the governments of presidents Nestor Kirchner and Cristina Fernández de Kirchner.

This chapter provides an alternative account of the current situation in Argentina. It does so by exploring the socioeconomic interactions in daily life between workers in recuperated factories and businesspeople in small firms, underscoring the ways that workers and businessmen influenced and made sense of each others' practices. This relationship cannot be understood by relying on Castañeda's (2006) typology. Some of the factories that I studied, for example, rationalized production in response to the pressures that were placed on them by capitalist-owned firms; likewise, several of the firms adopted a "synergistic" or flexible approach to business life in response to the practices of factory workers. Instead of using Castañeda's typology, I have relied on the experiences of workers and businessmen to understand everyday life in the social economy. This gap in interpretive categories raises a much larger issue; though I do not discuss it anywhere in the chapter, this reality underlies it: the links between social economy and institutional politics is far more flexible than some political sociologists admit.

After providing an overview of the socioeconomic context from which worker-owned factories emerged in Buenos Aires, I survey the various ways that Argentina's democratic institutions expelled factory workers from public life, thereby making it difficult for them to establish business ties with small firms. Next, I describe some of the communitarian practices that surfaced in the worker-owned factories in relation to the social economy, and the concerns that some of these practices generated among businessmen. I then focus on how their relations with worker-owned factories transformed commercial life for the business firms. Finally, I underscore the main point: daily life in the social economy cannot be understood in dichotomous terms as either pragmatic or populist.

EMERGENCE AND DEVELOPMENT OF RECUPERATED FACTORIES

Beginning in the mid-1980s, the Argentine state—under intense and sustained pressure from the International Monetary Fund (IMF), the World Bank, and the so-called Washington Consensus—implemented a series of wide-ranging policies aimed at transforming the country into a market-centered society. This was accomplished far more thoroughly and in a shorter span of time than in any other South American country, including Chile. Wage workers in the Buenos Aires greater metropolitan region were among the first to experience the full force of this transformation (Instituto Nacional de Estadísticas y Censos 2002, 2003, 2004, and 2005).[3] By the end of 2003, roughly 25 percent of workers in the region were jobless; another 10 percent were underemployed; and no fewer than 35 percent of those who still had jobs now worked in the informal sector. Between the early 1990s and mid-2000, real wages plummeted by 50 percent; roughly 60 percent of citizens were poor while another 27 percent were indigent. Relative inequality reached record-breaking levels, representing the single largest transfer of wealth from the lower to the upper sector of society since the 1970s, when systematic data of this type began to be collected (Lozano 2005).

Despite such dire conditions (because of the lack of an opportunity structure), Argentine workers throughout the country restarted no fewer than 283 shuttered factories between 2000 and 2009. The majority of them were organized before 2005, the worst years of the crisis; nearly all of them were small and medium-sized firms (twenty to fifty workers) in the industrial (metallurgical, food processing), manufacturing (textile), and service sectors (tourism, printing) (Rato 2009 and Fajn et al. 2003). As of 2009, no fewer than 90 percent of these factories remained productive and profitable, providing their workers with salaries that were the same as or slightly above what their counterparts earned in privately owned firms. Eighty percent of all factories are concentrated in the greater metropolitan region of Buenos Aires (figure 5.2), the country's most urbanized, populated (2.7 million), and industrialized area. It is also the region hardest-hit by neoliberalism during the governments of Carlos Menem (conservative, 1989–95, 1995–99), Fernando de la Rua (social democratic, 1999–2001), Eduardo Duhalde (centrist, 2002–3), Nestor Kirchner (populist, 2003–7), and Cristina Fernández de Kirchner (populist, 2007–) (Kulfas 2003, 9–19). Prior to the debacle, 75 percent of all small and medium-sized factories in the country were located in this region; by 2004, roughly 45 percent of these factories had vanished from the landscape (Kulfas 2003, 9–19; and Donato 2005). Among the 55 percent that remained afloat, some of the privately owned factories among them developed commercial ties with recuperated factories despite considerable opposition from other businessmen. Whether unemployed workers from the other five thousand shuttered factories across the country will be restarting them in the coming years remains to be seen (Moreno 2009).

No one knows with any degree of certainty, including researchers in the Ministry of Labor, the number of workers in these worker-run factories; the most recent and credible estimate puts them at twenty-two thousand.[4] These workers are typically family men and women between the ages of forty-six and sixty-five; somewhat skilled, having completed several years of secondary or technical school; and without any significant experience of activism in labor unions or militancy in any political party or social movement (Rebón 2007, 63–72).[5] In addition to providing for their own spouses and children, most of these workers are also financially responsible for their aged parents, their in-laws, and increasingly their (fatherless) grandchildren. These additional 154,000 people who depend on these factories for their livelihood bring the grand total to 176,000. Clearly the significance of these worker-run factories has less to do with their social or economic preponderance than with their capacity to provide local residents with an opportunity to reconfigure the institutional boundaries between the region's social and market-centered economies.

Democratic Forms of Exclusion and Invisibilization

The expulsion and invisibilization of factory workers from public life could not have been accomplished without the support of the judicial wing of the state, labor unions in civil society, parties in political society, and newspapers in the

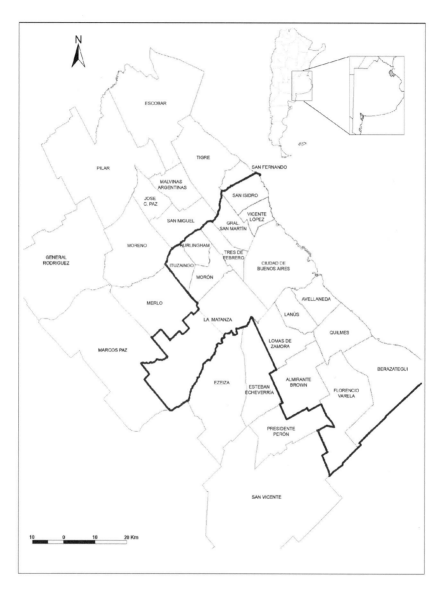

Figure 5.2. Greater metropolitan region of Buenos Aires.

public sphere. In other words, it could not have happened without the support and endorsement from the same institutions that in democratic regimes are responsible for ensuring that citizens, especially the most vulnerable and disenfranchised, are able to exercise the right to have rights. In 1995, Domingo Cavallo, minister of economics under President Menem, secured congressional approval for his Law of Insolvency and Bankruptcy (24.522). This signaled to international investors and agencies that the Argentine government now had the legal mechanism, in addition to the political will and economic instruments, to turn the country into a market-centered society.[6] Pedro Kesselman, who in 1994 contributed to reforming the national constitution, summarized the consequences that Law 24.522 (hereafter, the New Law) had on labor-capital relations: "Our civil and commercial judges are concerned solely with property rights; they view them as sacrosanct, as if the rights of creditors are the only ones worth defending. These judges ignore the rights of workers who, after all, have suffered the most in cases of insolvency and bankruptcy" (Kesselman as quoted in Vales 2008). Neoliberal notions based on property rights now became the language of juridical life, forcing judges, lawyers, plaintiffs, and defendants, including factory workers, to speak in these terms.

IMF and World Bank advisers considered the "cram-down clause" to be the most "innovative" aspect of the New Law because it had the potential of radically restructuring property relations across economic society (Rodríguez 2002 and World Bank 2007, 29). Under the terms of this clause, bankrupt businessmen were granted a two-year moratorium on their debt; during this time, they were also allowed to retain ownership of their factories, but in return they had to transfer their firm to a court-designated trustee who assumed responsibility for managing it. Keeping the factory productive and profitable benefited everyone: workers, owners, and creditors. If at the end of the second year of "cram-down" the owners remained insolvent, the court magistrate auctioned their factory and used the money to compensate creditors.

Cram-down was designed to assist distressed owners to retain their factories; however, many of them used the clause to hasten their own bankruptcy. Before surrendering their factory to the court, these businessmen established an "offshore" or "phantom" company, enabling them to disguise their legal identity at state-organized auctions and regain their embargoed firms. Small wonder that between 1994 and 1996, the years that immediately preceded and followed the New Law, the annual number of bankruptcy (and insolvent) cases soared from 1,400 to 2,450; during the next decade, the number of cases continued to climb steadily, though not as steeply as before (Magnani 2003, 36–37). Instead of promoting "creative destruction" in Schumpeter's sense, the

New Law contributed to generating a "habitus of impunity" across economic society (Fajn et al. 2004, 35, 102–3).

The judiciary, like all the other wings of the state, slashed its budget and reduced its personnel under neoliberalism, requiring judges to outsource and privatize the task of dispensing justice. Judges subcontracted accountants to serve as "trustees" and relied on them to implement cram-down. In addition to managing embargoed factories, trustees were responsible for maintaining a detailed inventory of all the machinery, tools, and stock in each plant (in the event that it was sold by the courts). A team of experts from the World Bank visited Argentina to evaluate the performance of trustees and concluded: "The sharpest criticism [that we heard during our investigation] was leveled against the 1995 bankruptcy law for privatizing insolvency proceedings by allowing . . . them to be administered by persons [trustees] outside the judiciary" (World Bank 2002, 11). "[M]any creditors complain . . . that trustees often acted in collusion with debtors" (World Bank 2007, 29). Businessmen routinely bribed trustees so that they would omit from their inventory stock and equipment from the embargoed factory. Before the auction, trustees allowed owners, under cover of night, to enter their plant and remove much of its machinery, tools, and stock. The New Law atrophied the state's already diminished capacity to protect the property and social rights of all its citizens, especially factory workers.

Before the debacle, workers in Buenos Aires had a long history of acting and speaking as citizens inside and outside their factory (James 1988). In Argentina more than in any other salaried society across the globalized South, populist unions had been relatively successful (until the military dictatorship, 1976–83) in ensuring that workers enjoyed all the civil, social, and political rights accorded to them in the 1947 national constitution. During the crisis, the most powerful labor confederation, the Confederación General de Trabajadores (CGT), under pressure from the minister of labor, instructed shop stewards to discourage the rank and file from recuperating their factories and to accept the meager financial compensations the owners were offering them (Fajn et al. 2003, 23–25). Businessmen in the meat, textile, and metallurgical sectors exerted additional pressure; they threatened to discontinue deducting monthly dues from the paycheck of workers if any local affiliate provided medical coverage to workers in recuperated factories. They often chanted slogans and displayed banners denouncing the CGT and its local affiliates at street marches and demonstrations.

Workers in recuperated factories were also expelled from the political field. In the upper and lower chamber of the national congress, the three most important parties—the Peronist (Justicialistas), the Civic Radicals (Union Cívica

Radical), and the Front for Victory (Frente para la Victoria)—blocked any bill that favored the factories from becoming law ("Fábricas recuperadas" 2011).[7] Paul O'Neill and other high-ranking IMF officials had already warned the Argentine government that if it decided to annul the New Law, the country would not receive an additional thirteen million dollars in credit that it had requested (Vidal and Eichelbaum 2002). Like many other factory workers in Buenos Aires, Damian Giordano, a metallurgist from Constituyentes (Villa Martelli), followed closely the monthlong debate between the Argentine government and the IMF. He concluded: "Instead of spending their day reading faxes from the IMF . . . , legislators should convene all [the recuperated] factories so that we can begin to discuss what we need to salvage them" (Giordano as quoted in Palomar 2002). Factory workers now accused government officials of representing the IMF rather than its own citizens and the "national interest." This was the first time that many of them gained an understanding of how the IMF and other international agencies undermine democratic politics within the nation-state.

Leftist parties misconstrued the factories, depicting them in Leninist terms, the new vanguard of Argentina's labor movement, which was "poised to lead the national struggle against capital and the state" (Heller 2005, 46).[8] During the first wave of recuperations, these parties sent their most experienced militants to colonize a number of factories, including Brukman (textile), Sasetru (food processing), and Unidos por el Calzado (footwear) and win over the rank and file to "revolutionary socialism."[9] Roberto Salcedo recalls: "When we began, several political parties came and offered us assistance; at first we accepted it, but then we realized that they were doing this in order to claim our factory as their war trophy. Soon after this, we told them they had to leave and we regained control of our plant" (Salcedo as quoted in Magnani 2003, 165–66). By 2002, the few factories that had any contact with leftist parties had severed them, although the conservative media (radio, television, newspapers, magazines) claimed otherwise and continued to exaggerate their significance.

In its editorials, *La Nación*, the country's most prestigious daily, continued to invoke Manichean, anachronistic images from the recent past, portraying workers as "occupiers," "usurpers," and worse, and describing factories as "soviets," "a menace to the constitutional order" and so on: "The occupation and control of these factories by workers is a violation of property rights, and annuls one of the central precepts enshrined in our constitution. The right of workers to make demands on their employers and on our government must never be allowed to prevail over the right to private property."[10] Some of the terms and phrases used by *La nación*'s editor to describe factory workers were mnemonic devices and served as a reminder to its readers that the last time that this had occurred, the armed forces had stepped in and implanted a bloody dictatorship that led to the "disappearance" of thirty thousand citizens. *La nación*'s "news" coverage was so biased that La Vaca, an alternative news service staffed by professional journalists, brought formal charges against the daily to the Inter-American Commission on Human Rights (La Vaca 2007, 112).

La Nación's middle- and upper-class readers began to use a "reactionary rhetoric," borrowing from Albert Hirschman (1991), in talks shows and at public forums, creating a "moral panic" and hostile "climate of opinion" against the factories. Commercial and criminal judges responded by launching a campaign against the factories; between 2002 and 2003, they routinely ordered the gendarme and special antiriot police to retake them and arrest their workers. This continued until several human rights groups and distinguished jurists, including Raul Zaffaroni, a member of Argentina's supreme court, denounced these actions and came out in defense of the workers by arguing that the constitution protected their right to strike and to engage in other forms of public protest (Zaffaroni 2003). These democratic forms of exclusion influenced the imaginary and real practices of businessmen and workers in daily life, playing a key role in structuring the type of relationship they developed.

SOCIAL ECONOMY AND FACTORY-BASED COMMUNITARIAN PRACTICES

Workers have generated a variety of communitarian practices in their factories that are themselves rooted in Buenos Aires's social economy. Nearly all of them are at odds with formal, market-centered forms of life that prevail in capitalist-owned firms. This section surveys some of these practices and includes, whenever possible, the judgment that small businesspeople have of them.

Restarting Factories and Reconfiguring Selfhood

When the recuperations started, 60 percent of workers followed the advice of their shop stewards and abandoned their factory; the remaining 40 percent decided to remain in the plant and restart production (Rebón 2007, 60–63). Pierre Bourdieu's (1998) account of neoliberalism's corrosive effects on social relations remains useful for making sense of the first group: "Casualization profoundly affects the person who suffers it by making the whole future seem uncertain; it prevents all rational anticipation and, in particular, the basic belief and hope in the future that is needed in order to rebel, especially collectively, against present conditions." These workers, without knowing so, had transformed their sense of collective uncertainty into individual insecurity, leading many of them to sever ties and became "disaffiliated" from their families, friends, and neighbors, to recall Robert Castel's (2002) work. Although neoliberalism had stripped them of their rights, these workers contributed to the spread of the market across Buenos Aires in the same way that "possessive individualists" played a key role in transforming seventeenth-century England into a market-centered society.

But how do we make sense of the other 40 percent of workers who recuperated their plant? Most of them experienced the same degree of uncertainty and anguish as their counterparts. However, they followed a different path.[11] Their experience goes against Bourdieu's rationalist-strategic account. In the course of interviewing Aníbal and some of his coworkers at the metallurgical plant Union y Fuerza, an alternative interpretation emerged:

> We never had much to do with each other [prior to recuperating the plant]; we came to work, did our job and went home. . . . We spent eight or ten hours daily, but we hardly knew each other. . . .
>
> When we heard that the owner was about to close the plant, we began to meet and talk amongst ourselves about the situation. . . . We were scared shitless. . . . We visited several recuperated factories nearby; their workers encouraged us to do the same. After months of discussion, we restarted the factory; most of us didn't believe we would be able to pull it off. . . . We lived from day to day without knowing what would happen next. . . . We kept returning to the plant, day after day, although we really did not think that we would be able to keep this going.

From whence did Aníbal and his coworkers get their motivation to recuperate their factory?

Family relations, as I discovered, played a crucial, albeit indirect, role in instilling trust and encouraging mutual recognition among these workers. Enrique, a skilled printer at Chilavert, explained the process:

> Our families supported us; this was very important. . . . [During the recuperation], they came and brought us food, and when we went home to rest every few days or at the end of the week, they recharged our batteries. . . . Seeing each other's family in the plant and visiting each other [at our homes and neighborhood events] made all of us

realize that we were in this together, there was no turning back . . . because this was not only about us, the factory, or even a job; this was primarily about our family, about all our families.

In contrast to the salaried middle and professional classes, the notion of "family" among these factory workers is as much an institution of "public" as it is of "private" life, putting into question Hannah Arendt's rigid separation between "social and economic necessity" and "political freedom" (Pitkin 1998, 10–18, 177–225).

From the perspective of the workers, the single greatest challenge was to find a way of remaining in the plant without violating the property rights of the owner; in cases where workers had done so, commercial and criminal judges had sent antiriot special police units to evict them. In front of court magistrates, workers justified their presence in the factory in neoliberal terms by describing themselves as the plant's "permanent guard," committed to upholding the New Law and preventing owners from stealing machinery. After the Argentine government had slashed its budget for police protection, the phrase "permanent guard" acquired special meaning and was often used by small businessmen in reference to private security agencies they contracted to guard their firms. Although they remained uneasy and skeptical, many judges decided to allow workers to remain in their factories knowing that they could not rely on court-appointed trustees to enforce the New Law (Blanco 2002).

Recall that 60 percent of all workers had abandoned the factory; they had to be replaced immediately because it was imperative to restart production and generate profit. But hiring such a large number of workers in such a short period of time threatened to undermine factory life from within; these newcomers had not participated in recuperating the plant nor were they committed to self-management. Many factories resolved this dilemma in the only way they could: hiring family members (nuclear, consanguineal, affinal), friends, and neighbors. Roughly 45 percent of all new hires were of this type; nearly all of them were unskilled (Fajn et al. 2003, 185–218). This hiring practice seems clannish, an urban version of A. V. Chayanov's (1996) peasant community; however, it was a late modern communitarian solution to the public problem of disaffiliation brought on by neoliberalism and which remained unattended by the state rather than a resurgence of "atavistic" practices rooted in the distant past.

There were other reasons for hiring friends, neighbors, and family members. After President Menem's government in 2002 privatized public education and closed hundreds of technical schools, an entire generation of working youth—among them the children, nieces, nephews, and grandchildren of factory workers—were left without the opportunity to acquire specialized training ("Crear el espacio" 2007, 4–6). And since most of them were raised in households where the parents were unemployed, these young adults had never experienced the "culture of work" (Lobato 2001). Older factory workers assumed the responsibility of teaching these neophytes technical skills; they also instilled in them the work ethic (discipline, efficiency, honesty) and taught them democratic practices (participation, mutuality, fairness, equality). These young workers disseminated their newly acquired predispositions and practices in their own neighborhoods, repairing the socio-moral fabric of working-class institutions (kinship networks, sports clubs, church groups, neighborhood associations, and so on), which were in an advanced state of disrepair because of neoliberalism's corrosive effects. Moreover, these young factory workers were now earning a wage, and in the moral economy of Buenos Aires's working class, they were expected to provide relatives with financial relief in the same way that they had received assistance from other family members when they were in need. Subaltern groups relied on this family-centered system of welfare to supplement the state's relief programs, which were underfunded and, in any case, morally repulsive to many.

The rest of the newly hired factory workers were relatively skilled; however, few of them had any personal ties to their older coworkers. These skilled workers played a key role in altering daily life on the shop floor, eroding whatever patron-client relations had existed among friends and family members and instilling both groups with practices rooted in efficiency, collegiality, and meritocracy. Over time these practices eroded the hierarchical ties of dependency in the factory among friends and family members and prepared the way for the emergence of egalitarian, collegial relations. These practices altered authority relations inside the plant and across poor, working-class neighborhoods throughout Buenos Aires.

Delegitimizing Injustice and Inequality: Workers' Self-Authorization

Before becoming bankrupt, authority relations between owners and workers in small family firms had been intensely personal and clientelistic. In a desperate attempt to rescue their insolvent firms, capitalist owners appealed to the loyalty of their workers, most of whom agreed to accept a 40 to 50 percent reduction in salary with the understanding that, in the words of Samuel, a textile worker:

> We had a special relationship. . . . When he [the capitalist owner] informed us of the problems confronting the firm, he told us that if we stuck together, it would survive. . . . In fact, the owner had already filed for bankruptcy, and was getting ready to sell the machinery and to terminate us without any compensation. We worked here for two decades, but he thought nothing of dumping us. . . . We could not allow that. Later he tried to negotiate with us (after we found out what was going on and confronted him). We needed the money and wanted to keep our jobs, but we already had made our decision to recuperate the factory.

Many of the workers in small family-owned firms who eventually restarted them felt humiliated and dishonored by the owner. This is what motivated them—more so than any formal, abstract concept of the "rights of workers" or an "employment contract"—to resist.

Factory workers transformed their own personal experience of humiliation into a broad-minded criticism of social inequality and institutional injustice in public life. Bank officers and commercial judges almost always discouraged workers from restarting their firms, reminding workers that they were "blackies" (*negritos*) and lacked the education and entrepreneurial skills required to manage a factory.[12] Facundo, who works at a metallurgical plant, recalled:

> They are partly right; we are workers and have never managed a firm. However, this is not the real point; what none of them want to recognize is that all of them—who went to the university and own businesses—failed miserably; otherwise we would not have four million unemployed and our country would not be falling apart as it is. Why is it that the Banco de la Nación [a state-owned public bank] lends them millions of pesos—all of which are now gone, but refuses to give us a small loan? How come it invested huge sums on these coat-and-tie businessmen, but refuses to take a small risk with us blackies? This country has always taken care of the rich at the expense of the poor. I am not saying that we will succeed, all I am saying is that they already failed and that we should be given an opportunity to prove ourselves.

The sense of mistrust and disdain for public officials, including commercial judges, was so intense that during a court hearing, Poinciano, who works in a printing and binding shop, scolded the magistrate for not visiting the plant to collect the information he required to make an informed decision on their case. He was called to order and nearly evicted from the chamber.

None of Buenos Aires's privately owned or state-owned public banks were willing to provide loans and credit to recuperated factories, as noted earlier. In order to restart them, workers had to invest a large portion of their severance packages and unemployment insurance to pay for several months' worth of accumulated utility bills (electricity, water, gas, telephone) that the ex-owner had left behind. Once these factories achieved a certain level of productivity and were generating profit, they provided interest-free loans to newly restarted firms so that they would be able to pay their bills, purchase stock, and repair their old or buy used machinery. Restarting and managing production instilled workers with a sense of authority and self-confidence that they never had before.

Transforming Social Relations and the Meaning of Work in the Plant

In addition to regaining their sense of dignity and place in public life, factory workers experienced several other changes that contributed to altering their relations with businessmen in the region. Perhaps their most important transformation was developing a sense of individual autonomy and responsibility. As one worker recalled:

> Before we restarted the factory, our administrator was responsible for calling our suppliers when we needed additional stock; our accountant made sure that we were paid on time; our salesmen sold our products. And the owner was the brain behind the operation. . . . Now we do everything ourselves. . . . Running your factory is risky; when you do things right everyone wins, but when you do them wrong everyone loses. . . . I would never work for an owner again [*bajo patron*]. For the first time in my life, I feel I am the owner of my life, of my person. . . . Something happened inside of me, it happened here in the factory.

Several workers, including Enrique, who works in a printing press, recognized that he had become, for the first time in his life, committed to the firm and dedicated to its success. Before restarting the press, he said, "I never thought about work once I left the plant. But now when I go home, I spend my time worrying [about it]. As an owner, you have to think constantly about what I said earlier—marketing, sales, quality, efficiency, saving money, and so on." Enrique and the other workers interviewed acknowledged their lives were more stressful now than when they were salaried employees, but they agreed that they would never go back to working for a boss (*bajo patrón*), even if they were paid a higher salary than what they currently earned.

The workers' commitment to factory life encouraged them to become interested in public affairs as well. Luis, a worker in a food-processing plant, described the relation between the two realms:

> Due to the strike in the countryside, the shipment of peanuts that we ordered from Santa Fe—it was a large order—did not arrive on time; then the price of peanuts went up. We were screwed twice over. We held an assembly and agreed that we would assume the losses ourselves rather than to pass them on to our clients. We had signed a contract with them; we wanted them to know that our word was as good as gold. . . . We are constantly facing problems, sometimes because our supplier runs out of stock, other times because unemployed strikers are blocking the roads and the shipment does not arrive on time. All of these factors lead you to become interested in what is going on in the country and to understand the real reason for these problems.

Luis's interest in public affairs stemmed from the problems he faced in the factory as a result of them. He was encouraged to understand the plight of those groups that had been excluded from public life and were protesting—unemployed strikers, shantytown dwellers, urban scavengers (*cartoneros*). In the case of some workers, the connection between factory life and public affairs was mediated through civic-mindedness, as indicated by the remarks made by Sebastian, a textile worker:

> I was the type who went from home to work, and then back home. If you fell and were lying flat on your face, I would not stop to lend you a hand; let's be honest, most of us are this way. . . . Let me give you a stupid example of what happened to me just the other day. I was on a bus, and this old guy sitting began fondling [*manoseando*] this chick. I went crazy and started yelling, cursing [*puteándo*] at him. . . . Everyone else looked away, did nothing. . . . After working so many years under a boss, I had become an automaton, but now I see things differently.

Self-management in the factory had encouraged some workers to transform themselves into public-minded citizens.

Recuperated factory workers redefined the meaning of productive labor in ways that remain puzzling to small businessmen. During the early years of the factory movement, most workers spent a portion of the workweek in public protests supporting other factories, meeting with commercial judges in their court chambers, and lobbying politicians in their legislative offices. A study of 150 workers from 17 factories across the city of Buenos Aires indicates that

80 percent of them had taken part in one or more acts of public protest before 2004; their level of activism dropped by 30 points after that because the level of conflict had declined as well (Rebón 2007, 101–6). In each factory, workers debated whether public protests and other forms of political action should be recognized as productive labor and remunerated in the same way. Dozens of factories eventually voted in support of this proposal (Dávalo and Perelman 2003, 185–218). In the majority of recuperated factories in Buenos Aires, each worker—from the maintenance person who sweeps the floor all the way up to the administrator who balances the books—earns roughly the same amount. Seventy-five percent of the factories have an egalitarian salary structure; in the other 25 percent, the difference between the highest and lowest paid worker varies slightly, with the single largest source of variation based on whether the worker had participated in restarting the firm (Fajn et al. 2003, 162).

Worker-owned factories have been somewhat successful in reintegrating citizens into economic and public life, and they have accomplished this without much support from the Argentine government. Factory workers and small businessmen concur that the Peronist state-party machinery only funds those welfare programs that it can use to establish patronage ties with the citizenry. Where the two groups part ways is in their response to unemployment, patronage, and other related problems. Workers have relied on communitarian practices that form part of the social economy; businessmen continue to use orthodox market-based methods. The former have been far more successful than the latter in their efforts to improve public life in the region.

Self-Governance in the Factory

Factory workers developed their own structure of governance based on the notion of self-management in ways that small businessmen consider inefficient and an obstacle to commercial life. When the firms were privately owned, authority and power was embodied in the owner; it was also hierarchical and distributed unevenly, with managers at the top making all the decisions and workers at the bottom expected to follow orders. After the factories were recuperated, this Fordist-Taylorist model of production was abolished, and workers became responsible for managing their own factories. From then on, each worker considered himself to be free and equal to all his coworkers, compelling all of them to resolve their differences in public discussions during factory assemblies in a collegial manner based on the majority-rule principle.

Inside the factory, workers established a two-tiered system of governance with an executive council and a legislative assembly. Councils were responsible for establishing general policies, including defining investment priorities and representing the firm in court hearings and in negotiations with politicians and state officials; they usually meet weekly (depending on the situation of each plant). Council members serve for three-year terms and are elected by all the workers (except aspirants).[13] Legislative assemblies, in contrast, attend to everyday problems, such as production schedules and personnel matters (hiring, terminations). Meetings occur twice a month for several hours each time; all the workers (except aspirants) are required to attend (Rebón 2007, 150). A study of 32 factories (5 in the Federal District; 27 in provinces) indicates that 75 percent of the 214 workers interviewed participated regularly in discussions during these assemblies; the remaining 25 percent rarely participated in them (Gracia and Cavaliere 2007, 156, 175).

Several businessmen interviewed were critical of the factories' governance structure and self-management. Leandro, who owns a small metallurgical plant and has been doing business with a worker-owned factory within the same sector, summarized the problem: "Every time they have to make a decision, they call a meeting, even if it is in the middle of the day. They halt production and fifty or more workers will take an hour or so to discuss and make a decision. Meanwhile, outside the factory's main gate, there is a caravan of loaded trucks two blocks long waiting to enter and unload the metal spools. As an entrepreneur, I do not understand how they can tolerate this type of thing." One of the metalworkers interviewed from this worker-run plant admitted that they had problems with scheduling and coordinating factory meetings with deliveries from their suppliers. He went on to note that self-management extracted a certain price (he used the word "tax") but that they were willing to pay it to ensure continued self-rule.

Institutional Relations with the Community

In addition to providing workers with employment, recuperated factories enabled marginalized citizens to become reincorporated into public life. The factories implemented a series of programs that small businessmen claim are the sole responsibility of the state and have no place in economic life. As part of their campaign to repair the social fabric of community life, dozens of factories established high schools and outreach programs in their plants. In the city of Buenos Aires, roughly eight hundred "high risk" students are currently enrolled in factory-based high schools in IMPA (Industria Metalúrgica y Plástica de Argentina, a metallurgical plant), Maderera de Cordoba (a lumber yard), and Cooperativa Patricios (a printing shop and bindery) (Tasat 2006).[14] In addition to taking the same courses as their counterparts who are enrolled in public high school (such as Spanish, history, mathematics), students in factory-operated schools also study subjects like the "history of popular and community struggles in Argentina" and are encouraged by their teachers to become neighborhood activists (Hauser 2004).

Yaguane, South America's largest slaughterhouse (employing five hundred workers), is located in Virrey del Pino in a remote area of La Matanza, the province's poorest district. Yaguane's director, Rodolfo, took me to visit the plant library, which is open weekdays from 9 a.m. to 7 p.m. and is financed by the meat workers themselves.[15] In addition to providing breakfast (mate tea, bread) to more than two hundred children, the center operates an after-school program for grade school students, providing them with afternoon snacks and tutoring in a variety of subjects (math, English, computers). Yaguane's workers also donate cheap cuts of meat to scores of community kitchens in the area.

In another example, located in the town of Saavedra, Pigue's textile workers signed an agreement in 2006 with the director of a nearby medium-security penitentiary to teach inmates to manufacture sportswear. The workers allowed the inmates to use one of their own industrial sewing machines; by the end of the first year, the inmates had produced and sold twenty-five thousand sneakers and sixteen hundred jogging suits. They saved most of the money they made and used it to ease their transition from the penitentiary back into the community; on their release from the penitentiary, many of these inmates were hired by Pigue (Galvan 2006).

Learning from Entrepreneurs

Workers in recuperated factories acknowledged receiving technical assistance and advice from businessmen with whom they had established commercial relations. Some of the most efficient and productive worker-owned factories in Buenos Aires had become so because of the support they had received from businessmen. Ricardo of Ghelco, a food-processing plant, explained to me how, after they restarted their firm, the members of the executive council visited their clients, including their two most important buyers, Nestle and Bonafide, to persuade them to continue to do business with them. The workers explained that they could manufacturer the same quality products as before, only at a lower price since they no longer had to pay the owner a large portion of the profit. Nestle sent a team of inspectors to the firm to evaluate the quality of their ingredients—powdered chocolate, almond mix, and so on. To continue to do business with them, Nestle, according to Ricardo, "required us to purchase a machine that detects metal particles and other impurities in the mix. We discussed it in the assembly, and decided to buy it although it was very expensive, even though Nestle did not give us any guarantee that they would remain our customers. . . . Some of their technicians came to the plant and helped us, because we had proved to them that we wanted to retain them as clients. There was goodwill on both of our parts."

In addition to collaborating with capitalist firms, some worker-owned factories decided to subcontract professionals. In the words of Samuel, a metallurgical worker: "We hired an accountant for a week who explained to us how to keep our books. In addition, some of our own clients, by demanding that we provide them receipts of all our financial transactions, compelled us to maintain careful records of all our sales and purchases, and this served to also improve our administrative division." Factory workers remained committed to self-management and other practices rooted in social economy but were not, in principle, as these examples indicate, opposed to making their firms efficient and productive.

MARKET ECONOMY AND CAPITALIST PRACTICES IN PRIVATELY OWNED FIRMS

Small businessmen who have commercial relations with worker-owned factories are uniquely qualified to evaluate them. They have done so in strikingly positive terms. However, their views and judgments rarely appear in public discussions, making it difficult for other citizens, including other businessmen, to overcome their long-standing prejudices.[16] Nearly all the members of the business community were, in principle, against the creation of recuperated factories because, according to them, they were in violation of property rights; however, they were also critical of ex-owners for having mismanaged them and abandoned their workers. When I asked Alberto, salesman for Resmacon, principal supplier of paper to Chilavert, a worker-owned printing press, whether he was in support of or against what the workers had done in this factory, he replied:

> I am neither in favor nor against them. Let's see if I can explain myself. I disagree with the workers; they should not have taken over the factory. But at the same time I am not in favor of the [ex-] owner. He did everything wrong; he threw the factory overboard, and then forced the workers to swim on their own. . . . I never met him, but I imagine

that he built this factory through hard work, by saving and investing his money. . . . If you are asking me what I would have done had I been an employee of this factory, I can tell you that I would have also recuperated it. The owner behaved like a rat, but there is no denying that these factories are a "freakish accident of nature" [*un aborto raro de la naturaleza*].

Most of the other businesspeople interviewed expressed a similar ambivalence toward the factories; however, they were also critical of the ex-owners.

All the businesspeople interviewed were extremely uneasy about doing business with worker-owned factories because, in juridical terms, their status remains unclear in at least two ways: ex-owners continue to claim that their property rights have been violated and these factories belong to them; and as worker cooperatives, it is difficult, if not impossible, to know exactly in the event of insolvency or bankruptcy who is legally responsible for the factory and repaying its creditors. As one businessperson said: "Our firm is scared of doing business with the cooperatives. . . . If there is a problem with a joint stock or a limited responsibility company, the owners are responsible for compensating creditors. However, in the case of cooperatives, if something goes wrong, things are not so simple. . . . They function like ants; all of the workers carry the same load. . . . If I go to Cacho, he will refer me to Tito; when I talk to Tito, he will send me to talk to Jorge, who will point to Clemente and so on." Recuperated factories are considered, for juridical and financial purposes, cooperatives. However, they do not meet all their legal and administrative requirements, and although commercial courts have been trying to resolve this problem, they have not yet done so. The lack of clear juridical status for worker-owned factories and the problems of property rights that this generates is perhaps the greatest obstacle that capitalist-owned firms face in dealing with them.

Social Inequalities, Personal Networks, and Corporate Groups

In contemporary Argentina, as in most other South American countries, the social distance between small businessmen and factory workers is so great that they rarely have any opportunity to develop personal ties with each other in public life. This is the main reason, as most entrepreneurs told me, that it is nearly impossible for workers to secure credit from bankers, discounted prices from suppliers, and large orders from customers. The entire chain of production seems to be conditioned by social relations, and these are strictly stratified by class, education, ethnicity, and so on. Business life in Argentina is intensely personal and very informal, as a businessman named Leandro explained:

> In the metallurgical sector, we do all our business through personal ties; this is the reason that we spend so much time socializing with each other. Most of the deals are done over breakfast, lunch, and dinner, at a bar or café, during a party, or at a private club. . . . There are enormous class differences between us and the workers of Constituyentes; we have little in common. People come together when there is an affinity between them, when they have things in common. . . . I am now talking only about the personal, human aspects of business life; none of this appears in any price list or in any accounting sheet; believe it or not, this is the key factor. One thing is to sit down to discuss matters with a business associate or a client, and quite another to discuss things with a worker from Constituyentes or any other plant. In addition to dressing differently, talking differently, and having different tastes, there is also the fact that we live in different worlds—the places that I go to are not the places that any of them would go; we even take vacations in different places. The workers of Constituyentes talk with other metallurgical workers from other plants; all of them lack contacts and resources, and this is the reason that they rarely accomplish anything.

Most businessmen acknowledged the closed and corporate character of business life. They also recognized that members do what they can to protect each other and defend their corporate interests.

Marcela, the chief salesperson and a low-level executive of Mayorista (one of Buenos Aires's leading food wholesalers, a supplier to the city's most exclusive hotels including the Sheraton and Alvear Palace), clarified the enormous influence that the press had on business practices and maintaining the corporate unity of small businessmen. As the main purveyor to the Bauen, a three-star recuperated hotel in Buenos Aires, Marcela was especially vulnerable to the "climate of opinion" *La Nación* created against the hotel:

> Each time the Bauen made headlines—because of a street march or because the judge had threatened them with eviction—my boss would get very nervous; he would call me into his office and ask me about the state of their [the hotel's] account. Clients and colleagues from other companies also called and warned me that I . . . should stop doing business with Bauen. They told me that the hotel was losing money, that its staff was incompetent, and that in the end they were going to rob me. . . . In our line of business, everyone knows each other and we take care of our own.

Leandro provided a strikingly similar account:

Every time that the newspapers published an article announcing that such and such a judge was about to evict the workers from Constituyentes, I would be a bundle nerves for the rest of the day and remained awake the entire night. I had a million dollars worth in metal spools in the plant waiting to get processed. . . . In addition, Mr. W [the previous owner] and all his associates—in this business, everyone knows each other from way back, spread all sorts of ugly rumors to discourage all of us from doing business with his ex-workers.

Now that so many firms had declared bankruptcy, conservative newspapers played a key role in preserving the closed and corporate character of business life among small and medium-sized firms.

Crossing the Divide: Personal Ties between Businesspeople and Workers

Despite the personal distance and social barriers that kept businesspeople and workers from having contact with each other, several owners, motivated in large part by entrepreneurial and professional reasons, decided to cross the divide. When Leandro decided to break ranks with the other metallurgical firms in Buenos Aires and establish contact with Constituyentes' workers, several influential owners criticized him publicly and threatened to organize a boycott against his firm. His defiance of them was motivated in large part by economic and entrepreneurial considerations. He recalled:

I knew that the quality of their machinery, it remains one of the best, and I knew that the workers were experienced and capable, simply from the fact that the pipes they produced were of very high quality. So I cooled my head [*enfrié mi bocho*]; as a businessman you have to learn to live with risks. Constituyentes continued to be front-page news, but I decided to continue to do business with them. Instead of going home and having a heart attack, I began visiting the plant more or less once a week, and over time I became acquainted with many of the workers, who taught me a great deal about the production process and, even more importantly, about each other, their strength and weaknesses as workers. From them on, I knew whom I could work with and trust, and whom to avoid.

Marcela of Mayorista provided a similar account, although her initial encounter with the president and other members of the Hotel Bauen's executive council was difficult and could have backfired. She recalled:

[The Hotel] Bauen continued to make headlines, and I continued to get calls from my managers. Until one day I got fed up with them. Bauen by then was one of my best clients, but management was constantly questioning my professional judgment. . . . I also wanted them to assume part of the responsibility for Bauen's account; if we were making money from it, then the managers had to deal with the workers the same way that they treat our other clients. . . . I needed an insurance policy, just in case. So I organized a meeting between Bauen and all of us. Bauen's director at the time—I do not recall her name—was aggressive and unprepared. She assumed that because we were from a major company, we were going to attack her and make unreasonable demands. She questioned our motives, and told us: "Go ahead, disconnect our water and electrical service." We explained that the purpose of the meeting was to become acquainted with each other. . . . Since then, my managers have never called me again about Hotel Bauen's account, although it continues to appear periodically in the press. . . . You know, business relations, like companies, are made up of people.

In this example, it was the Hotel Bauen's president who, unaccustomed to dealing with businesspeople, recoiled and nearly broke off negotiations, which would have put at risk the future of the hotel. The lack of social relations between businesspeople and workers makes it difficult for them to transact business; as they form relationships, business transactions are more likely to work out.

Idiom of Business Life versus Practices of Social Reciprocity

The businesspeople interviewed all used the language of commercial life to describe their dealings with worker-owned factories. However, whenever I asked them to clarify or elaborate on a point they had made, they often shifted registers and would start speaking in the idiom of social reciprocity. When I asked Marcela, the low-level executive and chief salesperson for Mayorista, whether her firm granted any special considerations because of their cooperative character to the Hotel Bauen, a worker-owned hotel, she replied: "This issue has never entered our discussions or influenced any of our transactions with Bauen. . . . Our sole concern is financial. You buy, I sell; you pay me, I turn over the merchandise. Simple enough. The friendship that developed between Mayorista.com and Bauen is based on commercial considerations, nothing else. If at any moment there are problems between us, then our friendship will end. This is how we operate with everyone." Her description is accurate enough, but

it is also incomplete: it does not include any of the small and large acts of reciprocity that form part of business relations between most of the worker-owned
factories and small capitalist firms that I studied. Midway into our interview,
Marcela remarked:

> There is a reciprocity between us that I do not have with the Sheraton,
> Alvear, or the other big hotels; when they place an order, they insert all
> the information—brand, quantity, price, and so on into a [computer]
> program that tells them from whom to buy. It is all robotized; this
> is the way they do business. With Bauen, things are different. . . .
> During the problem [the general strike] with the countryside, all my
> customers were desperate to obtain cooking oil, rice, milk, flour, and
> other products. I always made sure that Bauen, which is one of my best
> customers, was supplied. . . . When they started, no one would sell to
> them; I broke ranks and decided to do so. Now, whenever they need
> supplies, I am the first person that they call. If we agree on a price, then
> we close on the deal. If not, they try elsewhere.

Throughout most of the interview, Marcela used the idiom of markets and business to make sense of her relations with customers, but she used social terms
when discussing her ties to Bauen.

The following two examples underscore other aspects of social life between
the recuperated factories and capitalist firms. Enrique, salesman and co-owner
of Sanaculito de Rana, which sells pharmaceutical and medical products to
Clínica Fenix (which was restarted by its staff), discussed at great length the
nature of business relations with his clients. Every once in a while, he would
lapse into a social account of their ties. He recalled:

> Last year when we were having problems, nearly all our clients aban-
> doned us. After we were able to pull out of the crisis, they returned:
> our prices and products are better. But this time around I refused to
> offer them discounted prices and special payment plans as in the past.
> Some of them severed ties; those who stayed became angry and often
> bad-mouthed me [me putearon]. But I explained to them: you abandoned
> us when we were having problems, so now you have to take your place
> at the end of the line. . . . The Clínica Fenix stayed with us throughout
> the crisis, and although I am still not willing to grant them any credit
> or accept their checks, I always offer them discounted prices.

A shrewd and hardened businessman, Enrique combined market and social
principles in his dealings with Clínica Fenix. Leandro, co-owner of a metallur-

gical plant, described his dealings with a worker-owned factory in social terms as well. "I give Constituyentes roughly fifty thousand pesos worth of business each week," he recalled. "So when they ask me to reserve for them x amount of metal spools from my stock, I go out of my way for them. I do not do this for my other clients, unless they are longtime customers and have treated me fairly. These small gestures are what keep our relationship going." Although it is true that Leandro grants, as a matter of routine practice, preferential treatment to his most loyal customers, it is important to note that all of them are privately owned firms rather than worker-owned factories. Making Constituyentes a preferred customer enabled this factory to survive despite the informal boycott that other metallurgical plants had organized against it.

Collaborations, Criticisms, and Skepticism

Several businesspeople have pressured worker-owned firms to become efficient and rationalize their production processes, due partly to the fact these capitalist-owned firms were losing money. Instead of severing ties, they agreed to continue working with recuperated factories on the condition that they modernize themselves. In one example:

> Before they updated their system, one person would receive the merchandise at the entrance of the factory; he would often forget to pass on the receipt with a list of all the materials that had arrived to the person in charge of cutting and processing them. This caused us enormous delays; we were losing money. So in order to avoid these problems, they agreed to purchase a computer program that keeps track of the administrative and accounting aspects of production. It took them four months to learn this new system. Now they are happy with it and it has given good results.

Despite the willingness of workers in recuperated factories to modernize production and learn new administrative and accounting techniques, most businesspeople remained convinced that the workers who were responsible for these factories lacked the entrepreneurial vision to ensure their success over the long run. One businessman recalled: "They could grow and expand their firm, but because they remained concerned only with the day-to-day operations, they still do not understand the larger picture. As far as I can tell, they still have the mentality of a worker. They do not realize that they are the owners of this firm. . . . If they were ambitious and began to think big, things could change. . . . But this is not going to happen. . . . Four years after restarting the factory, they continue acting as employees." Many of the workers still found it difficult to take reasonable risks and look beyond the immediate present.

In the course of transacting business in daily life, factory workers and businesspeople have influenced each others' practices. Although there is no denying that everyday practices in the social and market-centered economy are radically different, Buenos Aires's workers and businesspeople have transformed each others' commercial practices, fusing and combining key elements (including property rights, ownership, and governance of firms, access to credit and loans, hiring policies, links to community, and so on) from the social economy and market economy in ways that go beyond Castañeda's populism versus pragmatism, with workers in recuperated factories embodying the former and businesspeople in small firms embodying the latter.

Their contact with businesspeople compelled worker-owned factories to become efficient and to rationalize their system of production and administration, enabling them to survive in the formal capitalist economy. Their contact with workers compelled businesspeople to explore an alternative model of public life based on a "gaucho" version of "flexible specialization," which seeks to reconcile social equality, economic development, and regional integration (Hollingsworth and Boyer 1997).[17] How these everyday practices and interaction between workers and businesspeople shaped, and have been shaped in turn, by high politics and public policies of President Kirchner and Fernández de Kirchner's governments and the various political parties has not been studied. Doing so might require that we once again pause and reconsider the populist-pragmatic model that has been used to make sense of the demise of neoliberalism and triumph of progressive politics and forms of life across the region.

NOTES

1. All of the interviews for this chapter were recorded and transcribed between January and November 2008.

2. "Recuperated factories" are factories that were occupied, reopened, and run by their workers after being closed down in bankruptcy proceedings. The terms "recuperated factories" and "worker-run factories" are used interchangeably throughout this chapter.

3. In contrast to other Third World countries, Argentina had low unemployment (6 percent) and 90 percent of its workforce was in the formal sector.

4. Jose Abelli of Movimiento Nacional de Empresas Recuperadas (MNER) presented this figure at a conference held at the University of Buenos Aires (Abelli 2007). Four years earlier,

the Ministry of Labor estimated there were fifteen thousand workers. This suggests that Abelli's figure is too conservative.

5. This description applies to the rank and file; the leaders have a history of militancy.

6. See Fassi and Gebherdt 2000 for a technical discussion of the New Law.

7. After the workers had pressured the government for more than a decade, President Fernández de Kirchner's government recently introduced a bill in congress in support of the law. This reaffirms my claim that changes in the social economy lead (and are far ahead of) government policies designed to support its members.

8. The most active were the Workers' Party (the PO), Socialist Worker's Party (the PST), and the United Left (the IU).

9. The film *The Take*, directed and produced by Avi Lewis and Naomi Klein, which attracted much international attention, greatly exaggerates the importance of leftist groups in the factory movement. For a scholarly article that does this, see Ranis 2005.

10. See the following editorials in *La Nación*: "Usurpaciones protegidas" (May 24, 2004); "El dilema de las fábricas recuperadas" (March 4, 2004); "La propiedad privada en peligro" (September 23, 2005); "¿Nos alcanzará la epidemia de la acción directa?" (June 12, 2005); and "Ocupación de fábricas" (September 11, 2008).

11. Some workers admitted to experiencing prolonged periods of depression, engaging in excessive drinking and succumbing to bouts of family violence.

12. *Negritos* is a sociocultural (not racial) term. It was introduced into public life in the postwar period when black-haired, dark-skinned, poor immigrants from the provinces migrated to Buenos Aires in search of opportunities. See Ratier 1971.

13. Personal interview with Luis Caro, president of the Movimiento Nacional de Fábricas Recuperadas (MNFR), and with Eduardo Murua, president of Movimiento Nacional de Empresas Recuperadas (MNER). Also see Fajn et al. 2003, 48.

14. State officials refer to these students as "intersectoral" because they have "fallen through the cracks" of the educational system.

15. Yaguane's plant, a four-story building, extends twenty-three-thousand square meters and sits in the middle of an open field in a remote part of La Matanza. This slaughterhouse can process seven thousand cows per week.

16. I interviewed a dozen members of the business community but included only the responses of those who had commercial relations with one or another recuperated factory. I excluded the rest because, as I advanced in the project, I realized that the responses of many businesspeople were based on stereotyped images and orthodoxies published in *La Nación* and other conservative dailies.

17. "Flexible specialization" changed public life in northwestern Italy, making it civic and synergistic. This "Third Italy" is often compared and contrasted to the "First Italy" (Fordist/corporativist: Turin, Milan, Genoa) and the "Second Italy" (underdeveloped/clientelist: Sicily, Calabria, Campania) (Hollingsworth and Boyer 1997).

REFERENCES

Abelli, J. 2007. "Programa Facultad Abierta." Presented at a conference at Universidad de Buenos Aires. July 19.

Blanco, Alejandro. 2002. "Fábricas recuperadas: Otra cara de la resistencia civil." *La insignia*. December 14.

Bourdieu, Pierre. 1998. *Acts of Resistance*. Cambridge: Polity Press.

Castañeda, J. 2006. "Latin America's Left Turn." *Foreign Policy* 85 (3): 28–43.

Castel, Robert. 2002. *From Manual Workers to Wage Laborers*. Translated by Richard Boyd. Rutgers: Transaction Publishers.

Chayanov, A. V. 1966. *Theory of Peasant Economy*. Madison: University of Wisconsin.

"Crear el espacio para las nuevas generaciones." 2007. *Nudos* 1, no. 12 (July): 4–6.

Dávalos, Patricia, and Laura Perelman. 2003. "Empresas recuperadas y trayectoria sindical: La experiencia de UOM Quilmes." In *Fábricas y empresas recuperadas*, edited by G. Fajn, Patricia Dávalos, Laura Perelman, and Angel Petriella. Buenos Aires: Centro Cultural de la Cooperación.

Donato, Vicente. 2005. *Observatorio pyme regional conurbano bonarense, 2004*. Buenos Aires: Universidad Nacional de la Matanza.

"Fábricas recuperadas y también legales." 2011. *Página/12*. June, p. 2.

Fajn, G., Patricia Dávalos, Laura Perelman, and Angel Petriella, eds. 2003. *Fábricas y empresas recuperadas: Protesta social, autogestión y rupturas en la subjetividad*. Buenos Aires: Centro Cultural de la Cooperación.

Fassi, Santiago, and Marcelo Gebherdt. 2000. *Consurso y Quiebra (ley comentada)*. Buenos Aires: Editorial Astrea.

Galván, Carlos. 2006. "Grupo de presos hará ropa deportiva con máquinas de fábrica recuperda." *Clarín*. November 14.

Gracia, Amalia, and Sandra Cavaliere. 2007. "Repertorios en fábrica: La experiencia de recuperación fabril en Argentina, 2000–2006." *Estudios sociológicos* 25, no. 1 (January–March): 155–86.

Hauser, Irina. 2004. "El saber, otra empresa recuperada." *Página/12*. March 23, p. 4.

Heller, Pablo. 2005. *Fábricas ocupadas: Argentina, 2000–2004*. Buenos Aires: Ediciones Rumbos.

Hirschman, Albert. 1991. *The Rhetoric of Reaction*. Cambridge: Harvard University Press.

Hollingsworth, J. Rogers, and Robert Boyer. 1997. *Contemporary Capitalism: The Embeddedness of Institutions*. Cambridge: Cambridge University Press.

Instituto Nacional de Estadísticas y Censos. 2002. *Encuesta Permanente de Hogares*. Buenos Aires: Instituto Nacional de Estadísticas y Censos.

Instituto Nacional de Estadísticas y Censos. 2003. *Encuesta Permanente de Hogares*. Buenos Aires: Instituto Nacional de Estadísticas y Censos.

Instituto Nacional de Estadísticas y Censos. 2004. *Encuesta Permanente de Hogares*. Buenos Aires: Instituto Nacional de Estadísticas y Censos.

Instituto Nacional de Estadísticas y Censos. 2005. *Encuesta Permanente de Hogares*. Buenos Aires: Instituto Nacional de Estadísticas y Censos.

James, Daniel. 1988. *Resistance and Integration: Peronism and the Argentine Working Class.* Cambridge: Cambridge University Press.

Kulfas, Matías. 2003. "El contexto económico: Destrucción del aparato productivo y reestructuración regresiva." In *Empresas Recuperadas, Ciudad de Buenos Aires,* edited by Secretaría de Desarollo Económico, 23–46. Buenos Aires: Gobierno de la Ciudad.

La Vaca. 2007. *Sin Patrón: Stories from Argentina's Worker-Run Factories.* Buenos Aires: Haymarket Books.

Lobato, Mirta Zaida. 2001. *La vida en la fábricas: Trabajo, protesta y política en una comunidad obrera.* Buenos Aires: Prometeo.

Lozano, Claudio. 2005. *Los problemas de la distribución del ingreso y del crecimiento económico en la Argentina actual.* Buenos Aires: CTA, Instituto de estudio y formación.

Magnani, Esteban. 2003. *El cambio silencioso: Empresa y fábricas recuperadas por los trabajadores en Argentina.* Buenos Aires: Promoteo.

Merklen, Denis. 2005. *Pobres ciudadanos: Las clases populares en la era democrática.* Buenos Aires: Editorial Gorla.

Moreno, Graciela. 2009. "El gobierno nacional asumió compromiso." *Veintitrés* 40 (June).

Palomar, Jorge. 2002. "Capital Humano." *La Nación.* June 30, p. 6.

Pitkin, Hanna Fenichel. 1998. *The Attack on the Blob: Hannah Arendt's Concept of the Social.* Chicago: University of Chicago Press.

Ranis, Peter. 2005. "Argentina's Worker-Occupied Factories and Enterprises." *Socialism and Democracy* 19, no. 3 (November): 1–23.

Ratier, Hugo. 1971. *El cabecita negra.* Buenos Aires: Centro Editorial de America Latina.

Rato, María. 2009. "En los últimos meses surgieron mas fábricas recuperadas." *La Nación.* June 13.

Rebón, Julián. 2007. *La empresa de la autonomía: Trabajadores recuperando la producción.* Buenos Aires: Coedición Colectivo Ediciones/Picaso.

Rodríguez, Maria A. 2002. "Argentina: May 2002 Bankruptcy Law Changes." IMF Working Paper.

Roitter, Mario. 2008. "New Experiences in the Social Economy: The Case of Recuperated Companies in Argentina." Paper presented at the Third Sector and Sustainable Social Change: European Research Network conference, Barcelona, July.

Tasat, M. 2006. "Entrevista: Juan Pablo Nardullis." *Mundo docente* (November): 4–6.

Vales, Laura. 2008. "Un caso testigo para las recuperadas." *Página/12.* November 3, p. 7.

Vidal, Armando, and Carlo Eichelbaum. 2002. "Luego de un debate tenso, se aprobó la Ley de Quiebras." *Clarin.* May 15.

World Bank. 2002. "Argentina, Insolvency, and Creditors' Rights System." World Bank Technical Paper.

World Bank. 2007. "Latin American Insolvency Systems: A Comparative Assessment." World Bank Technical Paper.

Zaffaroni, Raul E., ed. 2003. "El derecho penal y la criminalización de la protesta social." In *Situación de los derechos humanos en Argentina: Informe del 2002-2003.* Buenos Aires: Comisión de Investigación Jurídica.

6

BOTH SIDES NOW

THE RISE OF MIGRANT ACTIVISM AND CO-INVESTMENT IN PUBLIC WORKS IN ZACATECAS, MEXICO

Heather Williams and Fernando Robledo Martínez

Figure 6.1. Migrants back in Mexico in the stadium they built via the three-for-one program. Photo © Alex Rivera.

Driving through the Mexican state of Zacatecas, one sees an undeniable contrast between past and present and between wealth and poverty. A few hardy trees, barren of leaves most of the year, lie on the fringe of arid, hard-scrabble red-clay soil expanses. Crops of black beans, prickly-pear cactus, and white corn thrive only where rains are plentiful or water can be had from the few modest rivers that water this north-central state, eight hours from Mexico City and thirty-two hours from the U.S.–Mexico border. The cities, however, suggest that wealth in Zacatecas has come from something other than what meets the eye. In the capital city, Zacatecas, as well as in the fading small towns of Fresnillo, Jerez, and Sombrerete, there are sumptuous churches hewn of rose sandstone, grand theaters in baroque and neoclassical styles decorated in marble with crystal accents, elaborate central plazas with statues and monuments, and mansions with balconies made of hand-wrought iron. Cemeteries speak of the once-rich dead. Mausoleums as grand as small museums bear the names of the state's former elite: Bañuelos, Díaz, and Tolosa.

This is the wealth that silver built: some one and a half billion ounces of silver were extracted from the region's hills over three hundred years of colonial activity; along with a few other key mines in the New World in Bolivia and Peru, the precious lode in these hills fueled Europe's early industrialization. Even after the exit of the Spanish, the wealth of Zacatecas came from what was underneath its arid surface. With the exhaustion of its richest reserves, Zacatecas, much like Potosí, its colonial counterpart in South America, fell from wealth to poverty in the twentieth century. As chronicled by Immanuel Wallerstein (1980), the eclipse of these once vital mining centers was part of an inevitable arc and decline determined by early global capitalism. The extraction of wealth from this area was part of a development process that sent wealth outward and left an economy dependent on external markets and exogenous sources of finance.

It is revealing that as of the end of the twentieth century, the built landscape of Zacatecas saw new growth and dynamism related to market exchanges not entirely within its geographic boundaries. Alongside the classic *cantera* buildings of the mining era, there are new structures in place: elegant homes with double-paned glass windows and stucco exteriors, satellite dishes, and tiled details in the walls and porticos. Towns long neglected by an indifferent federal government in Mexico City suddenly, by the late 1990s, were no longer the desolate *ranchos* that they were even twenty years earlier. Towns that had been nearly unreachable in the rainy season have new access via paved roads and graded avenues. The bridges have been rebuilt. Schools sport new computer labs and bathrooms. Drinking water systems are in working order. The church facades are pristine once again. Central plazas are replete again with flowers and stone detailing. And now, even in some of the smallest towns, there are sports parks and *lienzos charros* (rings for a stylized rodeo art).

Many of the new public works projects in rural areas have come not from any single personal fortune or mineral bonanza but instead from a public-private partnership that matches contributions from migrants for public works in their hometowns with contributions from the federal, state, and municipal governments—and in some special cases with grants from transnational private sector corporations. The Programa Iniciativa Ciudadana has expanded from a one-to-one state-level program in Zacatecas involving a few thousand dollars in the 1980s to a national program that enables communities to access three-for-one matches. The Mexican state of Zacatecas counts the support of more than 250 registered hometown associations, or *clubes de migrantes*, in the United States that have sent donations to their Zacatecan communities of origins. Nationally, since 1999, combined investments from over five thousand projects have funneled more than 250 million dollars for projects all over Mexico (Instituto Estatal de Migración 2008 and Secretaría de Desarrollo Social 2008a).

Although the sums involved in the program are small relative to the Zacatecas state gross domestic product, these projects have had an outsized impact on the state's rural communities, accounting in some municipalities for as much as 30 percent of public works budgets (Delgado 2003 and Secretaría de Desarrollo Social 2008b). In political terms, the Iniciativa Ciudadana program unquestionably represents a victory of transnational civic organization and a deepening of democracy. Utilizing the triple standards for deepening democracy from the Enduring Reform comparative study design, we feel confident in stating that this program overall has functioned to allow Zacatecans living abroad and Zacatecan counterparts at home to: (a) participate in deliberation and decision making; (b) control resources that are central to poor people's daily lives; and (c) promote self-reliance and develop social capital.

In simplest terms, the Iniciativa Ciudadana is a matching-grant program that funds infrastructure and job-creating business start-ups in rural Mexico by pairing donations from Mexicans living abroad with equivalent contributions from the federal, state, and municipal government. In an experimental phase of the program, the so-called four-for-one program, migrants' pooled donations were matched by contributions from private industry donors such as Western Union and also from the three levels of government. In the latter program, funds were channeled toward business start-ups that were to generate jobs for Zacatecans and stimulate growth in hometowns, with the idea that remittances could be used to keep Zacatecans from being forced to leave their hometowns to migrate elsewhere for work.

The infrastructure program, first Zacatecan and now administered federally through the Secretariat of Social Development (Secretaría de Desarrollo Social, SEDESOL), has funded the construction of roads, bridges, water treatment facilities, schools, university extension buildings, community centers, sports parks, and health posts. The four-for-one business start-up program has funded, among other projects: a greenhouse complex in the municipality of Jerez; a prickly-pear (*nopal*) cactus production plant in the county of Nochistlán; and an ecoresort and commercial space for local business in Valparaiso county. The exponential growth of matching-grant investment in public works since the late 1980s in Zacatecas (and now in at least twenty other Mexican states) is a phenomenon that few would have predicted at the outset. Unlike many top-down initiatives that rise and fall with governors and presidents who routinely dismantle their predecessors' social programs and build new ones with their own trademarks, the basic design of the program has persisted through changes in administration and changes in governing party. This is particularly notable because our interviews and research in Zacatecas show that migrant leaders who organized support for the program faced much well-founded skepticism among other migrants about the capacity or willingness of Mexican government agencies to administer project funds properly and maintain the program over time. Many migrants returning to Mexico, for example, face harassment and extortion by police, and migrants' families often still have funds skimmed from remittances by banks and wire services.[1]

The Iniciativa Ciudadana program has overcome these problems of institutional discontinuity and graft by offering unprecedented guarantees of transparency to migrant donors in the form of program rules that mandate citizen oversight of spending and construction. In this sense, the program constitutes a social reform that is genuinely shaped by civil society. Among the enduring reforms described throughout this book, the Iniciativa Ciudadana program undoubtedly enjoys relatively high expressed approval from members of the business community. Some businesspeople with industries in Zacatecas interviewed for this chapter expressed a bit of skepticism privately about the long-term viability of several of the public works or job-creating projects executed by migrant activists; others grumbled quietly about what they believed to be partisan meddling by migrant leaders representing federations of hometown clubs of migrants in the United States. Nonetheless, businesspeople were careful in indicating their own solidarity and support for migrants as well as their desire for migrant development to improve the general economy of Zacatecas as a whole.

At first glance, this might seem unsurprising when one considers that several of the most prominent representatives of migrants—particularly those heading such powerful groups as the Southern California, Orange County, and Fort Worth, Texas, federations of hometown clubs—have often been self-made businesspeople themselves. Nearly all were from humble backgrounds in rural regions, emerging as leaders because of the success of small and medium-sized businesses they had built in the United States. In addition, the mission of the four-for-one program—job creation through entrepreneurial start-ups—is consistent with a business point of view on development that posits poverty and unemployment as resulting from a lack of capital for private investment. These obvious affinities, however, belie a much more complex relationship of the matching-grant programs to the private sector and close-knit political elites in Zacatecas. Secular private-sector giving in Mexico is notoriously thin (Layton 2009); such activism as migrant hometown development that targets structural inequities and puts a spotlight on long-neglected schools, roads, potable water systems, and basic sanitation indicates a long history of corrupt public admin-istration in the state.

The Iniciativa Ciudadana program, with its multiple civic oversight mech-anisms, in contrast with old-style cronyism (in which state elites used social programs to direct resources to friends in the private sector), has not been a source of direct or indirect profit for migrant activists. With almost no excep-tions, migrant leaders and hometown clubs have put in vastly more resources to the building of works than they have enjoyed as users of public services or as entrepreneurs setting up job-creating projects. In addition, the thousands of volunteer hours spent in fund-raising and project design and oversight have taken much time from profit-generating activities that activists would other-wise engage in; migrant activists cite this factor most often in resigning posts as leaders of hometown associations after periods of intense fund-raising and project oversight.

This chapter argues that matching-grant programs have served as a forum in which civil society actors have challenged state power over public works; these programs have provided a touchstone for important debates over the rights and responsibilities of migrants who seek to maintain membership in Zacatecan politics and civic affairs. There are two salient issues: First, migrant leaders' views about home state and hometown affairs and their actions toward philanthropic initiatives are formed in a complex, binational social field. Migrant activists often operate with multivalent identities that entail simul-taneous loyalties to church, community, state, and country, and carry with them their past experience as *campesinos* (rural laborers). In this sense, the three-for-one program simultaneously serves multiple utilities: for the most ambitious migrant leaders, particularly federation-level activists, matching-grant activism undoubtedly serves as a component of an individual struggle for upward social mobility in Zacatecan society; for many club leaders and activists working more directly for their hometowns, it is a powerful means of dealing with the alienation of migrant life, of separation from hometown and from extended family.

Second, a language of business has infused political contention over these philanthropic programs and is used by actors who may disagree with one another sharply on procedural and substantive issues in the program. Intriguingly, migrant activists whom we interviewed who also happened to be business owners themselves, or who had worked in the U.S. private sector, repeatedly framed their criticisms of the program and of their discussion of the state's development gaps in light of their experience starting small businesses or farm enterprises from scratch. This business experience served at points as a field of resistance to what these activists saw as an entrenched and self-dealing business and political elite at home. By using their backgrounds as self-taught *empresarios* or local political activists in the United States, they emphasized the legitimacy of their involvement in hometown and home state affairs from abroad. Framing themselves as tribute payers and job creators rather than as party clients and dependents of the state, their status as businesspeople or successful community and municipal organizers then comes to function rhetorically as a legitimizing factor in pressing their points of view about how investment in public works should be structured.

We include a general chronology of migrant participation in home state affairs in Zacatecas, showing how voluntary investment in public works and matching-grant programs provided a platform for migrants to contest state government's top-down control projects and forced it to implement civic oversight mechanisms on public works. This contestation in turn bolstered migrant leaders' demands for involvement in home state politics and elections, including a law that finally enabled Zacatecan migrants living abroad to run in municipal and state legislative elections. The views are discussed of Zacatecan and migrant businesspeople toward two phases of the Iniciativa Ciudadana program: the three-for-one program (an initiative intended for public works) and the Proyectos Productivos program (a more complex initiative that was intended to generate new economic growth in undercapitalized regions and sectors of the state).[2] This latest, experimental phase of the program carries with it the thorniest questions about public and private benefit; at the same time, it carries the hopes of migrant leaders in severing a pattern of dependency that continues to send Zacatecans away from home. This phase is the touch point for some disagreement about the internal mechanisms of the program and may indicate something about its future direction.

WHY RISK THE MONEY? THE PUZZLE OF MIGRANT PUBLIC INVESTMENT

It is no small paradox that Mexican migrants collaborate with the government in building public works in their hometowns. In our interviews, migrants often stressed that one of the reasons they were compelled to leave their communities was endemic corruption at county and state levels. The modest budgets that were allocated for rural schools and roads throughout the twentieth century often never arrived to their ranchos and *aldeas* at all. One migrant interviewee spoke of the roads leading to her small town that remained ungraded for years despite promises and apparent funds to pave the eleven kilometers between her community and the main highway. "The worst," she recalled, "was that an ambulance couldn't get through in the rainy season. And then of course, the ambulance was in sorry shape. It was a really big problem."

Another interviewee raised in the countryside remarked that public officials only seemed visible during election years, and then, just before balloting, would announce magnanimously that the ruling party's campesino organization had arranged for a forgiveness of debts to the Banrural (the government rural bank for small farmers on land reform plots). "We were serfs, not citizens," he said, pointing out that between elections, the same officials would turn a blind eye to profiteering by local *caciques* (rural bosses), who readily extorted profit from small producers by monopolizing grain transport and storage, forcing farmers in remote communities to sell their harvests at below-market prices established by the government grain-buying agency. Yet another interviewee spoke of the problems of maintaining property rights while abroad and of keeping money from being stolen when returning each December. "Police always stopped us on the highway to ask for bribes," he said. "Sometimes several times. You didn't want to bring cash, but then in those days if you didn't have someone you trusted [*alguien de confianza*] to take it down, you got bad terms from Western Union. And then when they [family members] went to get the money [several hours away from home], they [the Elektra department stores who dispensed wired funds] sometimes wouldn't have the cash and would say 'come back tomorrow.' Or would you like this nice blender instead of money?"

Other respondents recalled that political factors also stymied prospects of economic mobility in the Zacatecas of their youth. Schools in the countryside often had little more than dirt floors and thatch roofs, with no books, no paper, no pencils or crayons. Older informants recalled that teachers often went absent, and high school remained an impossibility for many, with even public schools costing money for uniforms and tuition, and most schools being located hours from home. Beyond that, migrants mentioned that business, managerial, and bureaucratic professions remained closed to all but a number of connected families. For others, there was subsistence farming, minimum-wage work, or migration. A former migrant in Zacatecas, now in his forties, recalled that when he was a teenager, if one weren't from an elite family, "girls didn't even talk to you unless you had papers to migrate [legally]." Given poverty, corruption, and dead-end economies for those without connections, it remains notable that thousands of Zacatecans who left the state should find themselves within a generation's time or less turning back toward their hometowns to partner with the government on projects that in many cases rightly should have been built decades ago.

Properly speaking, the roots of Iniciativa Ciudadana as a bottom-up social and political reform emerged out of the norms and practices of transnational communities who had to compensate on a daily basis for a lack of institutional support for basic needs. Echoing the findings of a wealth of studies on transnational lives and migrant practices, Zacatecan migrant activists in interviews attested to the importance of kinship and hometown ties in the migration process. Cousins, friends, in-laws, and fictive kin (godparents and co-parents) were often bridges to jobs and housing or sources of critical advice and support in times of need. Weddings, burials, *quinceañeras*, and hospital stays were often funded through solidary financing and loans secured and paid by honor and sealed with one's word.

Building on Larissa Lomnitz's classic discussion of *confianza*—defined as a condition when a person "trusts the other to have the ability, the desire, and the good disposition to initiate a personal relationship of reciprocity exchange, or when his own familiarity with the other would encourage him to make the first approach himself" (Lomnitz 1977, quoted in Vélez-Ibañez 2010, 45)—Carlos Vélez-Ibañez has argued in an updated study of transnational economic practices that sophisticated rotating credit associations operating largely on the basis of mutual trust of participants are not exceptional but modal. His data indicated that rotating savings and credit associations (ROSCAs) operated in 130 urban, suburban, and rural municipalities in the United States and Mexico, varying from highly informal round-robin lotteries and rotating funds to legally constituted small credit societies. As with ROSCAs, hometown clubs and networks have served as systems that have enabled migrants to deal in a dignified way with untenable hardships: parents or siblings who needed to be buried at home in a parish graveyard; a relative who needed to post bail; a child who needed to be enrolled in school; a problem cousin who needed to move out of a family's living room and into a job.

Notably, several of the migrant activists interviewed indicated that in the years after their initial migration, when hometown and kinship ties were less necessary for survival, they found themselves so busy with work that hometown ties waned. One migrant, who would later emerge as a Zacatecan club federation leader and eventually would move back to Mexico and become a visible presence in Zacatecan politics, described his reinsertion into hometown networks two decades after leaving his hometown as a teenager to join his father in Southern California:

> It must have been the late 1980s, and we decided to have a Thanks-giving reunion for our town. We got word out and were amazed. Seven hundred people showed up! The police even came and wanted to shut us down—it was that big a crowd. We were so blown away, discovering all these old ties, exchanging addresses and telephone numbers as fast as we could. There were people who had gotten word and had come all the way from Colorado, Texas, and Northern California. I'll always especially remember my father at that party, choked up, seeing people he hadn't seen in twenty years.

The gathering of migrants from his hometown in western Zacatecas precipi-tated a flurry of networking among neighboring ranchos in the same county, he recalled. Much in keeping with David Fitzgerald's (2009, 70–102) account of the Catholic Church's strategy to staunch the dissolution of parishes through emigration, the home county priest traveled to the United States to reconnect with local residents who had migrated and to ask for their help in repairing the church floor. Migrant energies readily produced a raffle that included among the prizes (rather astonishingly, according to the interviewee) several valuable bulls. The fifteen thousand dollars raised bought a floor of fine marble, not merely the concrete originally envisioned for this formerly humble parish.

This interviewee and several others stressed that the hundreds of hours spent raising funds for hometown projects were worth it for the sociability of hometown ties as well as a sense that they had a newfound power to raise money and spend it well collectively. Notably, a number of men kidded in one interview that hometown club activity planning gave them an excuse to be away from their wives; meanwhile, in another interview, a group of women winked and said that the communal cooking and baking for events got them away from their husbands. Joking aside, however, the success of any club in raising funds also put them on the radar of aggregating organizations—such as the state-level federations. In the case of the aforementioned migrants who raised money for their parish, the hometown clubs were contacted almost immediately after their fund-raising raffle for their parish by emissaries of the Zacatecan governor and the Southern California federation of clubs, who asked them to join the Southern California Federation of Zacatecan Home Town Clubs and propose more projects.

SCALING UP AND INSTITUTIONALIZING PROJECTS

The experience of the migrants who funded the refurbishment of their church floor, and would go on to build over a dozen more projects in their home county in following decade (including roads, electrification, sidewalks, potable water systems, school improvements, and bridges) was echoed throughout Zacatecas in approximately three-quarters of the state's counties. Given the program's success and international visibility, many people and institutions claim credit for what became the Iniciativa Ciudadana program. Members of the Institutional Revolutionary Party point out, correctly, that in 1988, Zacatecan governor Genaro Borrego Estrada (1986–92) negotiated the first one-to-one matching-grant project with members of a Los Angeles–based federation of migrants. This program, little noticed at the time, would increase resources for parish-based projects and create a record of public-private cooperation on rural projects in the state.

Governor Borrego's public recognition was an important break with a more general government treatment of migrants and the issue of transborder labor markets. Several migrants mentioned the importance of confianza and person-to-person contact with Borrego or his successors in undertaking investment partnerships. The fact that the migrant groups were recognized at all by state leadership was novel and significant: federal officialdom throughout much of the twentieth century publicly dismissed migrants as people who had abandoned Mexico for lack of patriotism, evading the issue of laborers without work or small farmers without credit or markets in a state-dominated economy. In unofficial terms, they were disdained by ruling elites and even the middle classes in an infamously unequal economy as low-born individuals whose absence cost the country little. Song lyrics by the fiercely pro-migrant *norteño* band Los Tigres del Norte put it this way: "No son los doctores y los ingenieros que cruzan mojados para pro-gre-sar" (It's not the doctors and engineers who cross with wet backs to move up). Mexicans who could afford college educations, decent houses, and whose social connections would guarantee them capital, good land, or employment had little reason to leave. Landless and land-poor workers, the indigenous, and the urban unemployed, on the other hand, were those whose circumstances most often compelled them to travel north for work. For as long as this political framework dominated official thinking on migration, migrant remittances for public works were simply seen, if they were noted at all, as a product of migrant *arraigo* (emotional and social rootedness to home) but certainly not pertinent to questions of development or democracy.

Ironically enough, the emergence of the two-for-one program in 1992, and later the three-for-one program in 1998, as a migrant-led force in Mexico owed a great deal to elites who mistakenly assumed that migrants' support could be won cheaply when necessary and that they could be easily organized from above in times of political need. The 1988 elections proved to be such a juncture. In that presidential contest, PRI candidate Carlos Salinas de Gortari prevailed (with considerable doubt about the integrity of the election), but the ruling party was highly aware of anger and dissent among Mexicans abroad over reports of fraud and ballot tampering. PRI officials duly noted the visits of opposition candidates Cuauhtémoc Cárdenas and Manuel Clouthier to Los Angeles, Dallas, and Houston, where large crowds gathered to cheer their campaigns and later to protest the PRI's claim to victory.

To address this dissent, the Salinas administration directed the Mexican foreign ministry to begin organizing migrants through its consulates. According to Matt Bakker and Michael Peter Smith (2008), attempts to organize migrants according to the regions where they resided in the United States foundered because most migrants tend to identify more closely with their states and villages of origin than with Mexico as a whole or with the places where they lived in the United States. The Mexican government altered the organizational thrust to focus on state-level organization. As a result, under the Program for Mexican Communities Abroad, which developed a network of twenty-three state-level offices attending to Mexicans living in the United States, the consulate and state governments took on the role of finding and also forming migrant associations and federations (Bakker and Smith 2003).

Thus migrants themselves indicated to the Mexican state what type of organizations suited them. The Southern California Zacatecan Federation came to be a prototype for other umbrella organizations of migrants in other cities corresponding to Zacatecas and other states.[3] In the years to come, Governor Borrego's courtship of his states' migrants would be followed by similar actions on the part of other governors and federal officials. Small acts of public good then generated sufficient trust to begin early steps on small collaborations with the government. This is notable because migrants widely regarded the state in general as corrupt and ineffective.

By the 1990s, these minor collaborations were simultaneously altering the incentives for migrants in the United States to participate in home state affairs.

Increasingly, the doings of migrant federations, soccer clubs, and community clubs often made the front pages of local papers in Zacatecas, such as *Imagen* and *El sol de Zacatecas*. By the late 1990s, the Southern California Federation of Home Town Associations of Zacatecas had become sufficiently visible that candidates for state and federal office in Zacatecas were seeking press with migrant leaders, who in turn were assumed to be amenable to endorsing nominees of the PRI. According to one former president of the Southern California Federation of Zacatecanos, promises of money for migrant projects had become prevalent by the mid-1990s, and PRI officials openly took an interest in the federation officer elections of 1996. Before that election, he recalled, offices in the federation were often avoided by members because it was seen as little more than civic duty with minimal prestige. However, as the PRI became more interested in the federation and more willing to promise resources in exchange for public loyalty, he said, the offices became highly contested (Gómez 2003).

What ruling party elites did not anticipate was a migrant bloc that would readily accept government promises of hometown investment, and then make use of this rising visibility to weigh in on political affairs in Zacatecas. Whereas old-style PRI party elites saw their support of migrant organizations and their projects as a reward for migrant political loyalty, migrants instead saw *their* contributions as actions that deserved further reward from the government. The fact that a significant number of the migrant leaders ran successful small businesses and had sources of financing outside the Zacatecan state made their organizations increasingly difficult to capture politically. Here, business language served migrant leaders as a rhetorical tool because they could make credible claims to being self-made successes rather than crony clients of a corrupt state. Businesses themselves served migrant organizations because working capital gave migrants greater autonomy and freedom of maneuver from state elites and political parties.

The relationship between public works investment and electoral politics intensified with the emergence of multiparty competition in Zacatecas and Mexico at large. In Zacatecas, a contentious election in 1998 brought the first opposition party governor to power, and this very governor, Ricardo Monreal, owed migrant groups some credit for his victory. Prominent groups had formed inside federations in the United States and had backed him in word and press appearances during the campaign. What remained unresolved was who between migrants or the government had the upper hand in a matching-grant program. Monreal, grateful to migrant activists for their support, immediately assented to their demands for more investment (and thus more home state prominence) by expanding the state program from a two-for-one match to a three-for-one match in which the state government would provide two dollars of the match and the *municipi* government would provide one.

Monreal, who by this time was coyly harboring presidential aspirations, was not eager to see Zacatecan migrant leaders' next move: lobbying the federal government for an all-Mexico three-for-one program (Gómez 2003). Nor was he happy with federation leaders. Not long into Monreal's term as governor, they had begun to berate the governor and a number of county presidents who allegedly were sabotaging projects financed by migrants who favored political parties other than their own (Garcia Zamora 2003). Migrant leaders such as Guadalupe Gómez, Efraín Jiménez, Rafael Barrajas, and Martín Carvajal—notably, all self-made businesspeople with enterprises in the United States—became very vocal in their denunciations of political manipulation, fraud, and corruption on public works that member clubs from their federations were sponsoring. They also denounced the federal SEDESOL for program rules that excluded projects related to church restoration and *charro* (cowboy) festivals. Their remarks became fare for an increasingly combative and competitive press in Zacatecas, garnering *j'accuse* headlines in such papers as *Imágen, El sol de Zacatecas* as well as the leftist *La Jornada*'s new Zacatecas edition. Migrant leaders' preferences prevailed in nearly every instance, with federal officials eventually relenting on churches and charro rings, and state and municipal governments relenting on many individual case-related demands for better information and communication with migrant donors and oversight committees.

These tensions were also reflected in the budgets of the three-for-one program. As the following figure on matching-grant budgets shows, in years when political successions were uncertain, or when there were tensions between migrants and state officials over attempts to funnel political advantage from the program, investments dropped measurably. This was the case in 1997 in the final year of Governor Arturo Romo's administration and again in 2003 and 2004, when investments dropped in the wake of battles that divided the powerful Los Angeles Federation of Hometown Associations. In that period, migrant leaders publicly lambasted the machinations of a gubernatorial appointee, Manuel de la Cruz, who was charged with overseeing migrant activities in Los Angeles. De la Cruz was accused of having orchestrated a split in the Los Angeles federation in order to create a new, and presumably more pliable, Zacatecan federation in Orange County (Quiñones 2002).

Amid this political contention, the three-for-one program became a basis for migrant claims to power and voice in home state affairs, and their primary legitimizing argument in denouncing officials in Zacatecas became their stated commitment to transparency and above-board management of public works

Figure 6.2. Migrant investment in matching-grant programs, by year.

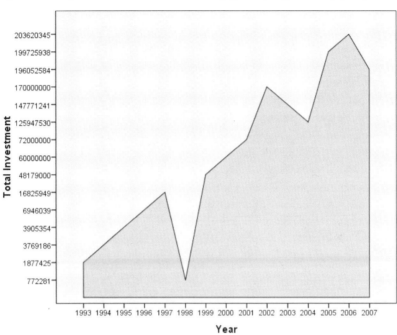

Source: Fernandez de Castro et al. 2006; and SEDESOL 2008a and 2008b.

projects, most often referencing their association with business as proof of their autonomy from political parties and the state. Rank-and-file members of hometown associations remarked in several instances in interviews for this project that they and many people they knew in the federation preferred to stay out of politics. However, the same rank-and-file members indicated that the federation leaders' technical expertise and visibility protected migrant projects from corruption and party manipulation in Zacatecas. Members of hometown associations from Nochistlán and El Cargadero reported in interviews in 2003 and 2006 that problems with uncompetitive bids going out to expensive contractors as identified by binational oversight committees (*comités de obra*) were resolved quickly with the intervention of migrant leaders. Interviewees affirmed that they believed the problems were resolved more quickly because of this public pressure than they otherwise would have been. Many of these migrant leaders, unlike rank-and-file members, were far more likely to harbor aspirations for political power, either in Zacatecas or in California.

This political underpinning to migrant investment in public works at the federation level was also accompanied by increasing talk among migrants about their rights to vote and run for office in Mexico. Organized campaigns for the *voto en el exterior* (absentee ballot) were spearheaded by the Organización de Mexicanos en el Exterior, whose leaders in turn were well connected in several state migrant federations in Chicago, Houston, and Los Angeles. Lobbying of the three major Mexican political parties and pressure on the Mexican congress by migrant leaders resulted in measures in 1996 and later in 2005 that opened narrow but real doors to Mexican migrant suffrage. The 1996 legislation permitted migrants to vote in polling stations near the northern border of Mexico in so-called *casillas especiales*. This bill appeared to open up the legal possibility for absentee balloting, though enabling legislation was blocked in the late 1990s. Mexicans who could not cross the border therefore were unable to vote in the pivotal 2000 federal elections. This was hardly an accident; the PRI's role in stalling absentee voting was not lost on many. The eventual winner of that race, Vicente Fox of the opposition National Action Party, was also the favorite of some 80 percent of Mexican-born migrants in the United States.

In Zacatecas, this came to a head in the 2001 state elections for county presidents (*presidentes municipales*) and for seats on the state legislature. A much publicized race in the county of Jerez featured two wealthy migrant candidates, Andres Bermúdez and Salvador Espinosa Escobedo. These self-made millionaires and entrepreneurs who had made much of their humble ranch backgrounds readily referred to themselves as *mojados* ("wetbacks"). They both pledged that they would "make Jerez more like America" and promised to use their business expertise to bring an end to political corruption and impunity (Ronfeld 2001 and Thompson 2004). After the victory of Bermúdez, the state PRI took the case to court and annulled the election on the grounds that Bermúdez had violated electoral laws specifying that only residents could stand for office.[4] The case then became a cause célèbre, prompting the formation of a bloc of migrant leaders and sympathetic allies in Zacatecas who would lobby successfully for the 2003 passage of a bill entitled the Burmúdez Law, and later the Migrant Law.[5] This law permits migrants to stand for state office and also directs the state to facilitate the absentee vote of Zacatecans abroad. It enabled the election of two migrant mayors and two migrants to the legislature in the 2004 state elections in Zacatecas. One of the mayors later resigned his post to run successfully for the federal legislature in 2006.

This increasing politicization of migrant affairs did not sit well with many rank-and-file members of hometown associations who lobbied internally in federations in Chicago, Los Angeles, and Texas for leaders to separate investment in public works from partisan battles. Sam Quiñones (2002) reported that federations in Southern California had become polarized over the question of whether and how politics should play a role in federation affairs. Off-the-record remarks by federation members and civil servants in the Zacatecan state government indicated that these tensions led to a swing in rank-and-file sympathies to the candidacy of less politicized migrant leaders.[6] After the succession of new Zacatecan governor Amalia García to power in 2004 (the period of governance was September 2004 through 2010), tensions had reportedly ebbed, and interviews in 2008 with former state party militants with the PRD and PRI as well as with migrants suggested that both migrant leaders and state officials had stepped back somewhat in attempts to utilize the three-for-one program for electoral or political ends. What had replaced the tensions of the Monreal years (1998–2004) was a rough-and-ready compromise by which migrant leaders had stepped back to some degree from open condemnation of high-ranking members of the Zacatecan state government, and the state government had taken steps to further institutionalize and routinize oversight practices that protected hometown associations' contributions from graft.

FROM PUBLIC WORKS TO JOB CREATION AND THE RESPONSES OF BUSINESSPEOPLE

Two and half decades after the beginnings of state-migrant cooperation on public works, and more than a decade after its institutionalization at federal levels, the question of what will happen to this enduring reform has much to do with the capacity and the inclination of migrant leaders and partisan state officials to assimilate lessons learned and formulate joint responses to increasingly complex problems. In many areas, the low-lying fruits of roads and electrification and connecting bridges to small ranchos have been completed successfully. Many of these projects, however, serve communities that sit half empty, with most residents having already emigrated to the United States. Going further with state-migrant cooperation would mean addressing questions of unemployment, thin banking services, health care, and education.

Partisan loyalties certainly create divisions among migrants and between various migrant groups and intermittent rivals in succeeding gubernatorial administrations. However, all of our interviewees inside and outside the business community pointed to high poverty rates and unemployment as the state's most pressing problem. Migrant activists emphasize repeatedly that these very forces compelled them to leave, and they maintain that a deepening of state-migrant cooperation could provide a road forward in capital formation and job creation. Businessmen in Zacatecas, on the other hand, chose their words carefully, lauding migrant activism for having rebuilt rural communities and in making local government more accountable on such projects. But all expressed great skepticism about the ability of matching-grant programs to create inroads for industrial development.

Two in-depth interviews with Zacatecan business owners who were also very familiar with matching-grant programs indicated that although the method for implementing public works projects in underserved rural villages was adequate, stimulating job growth through seed money for fairly small businesses was unlikely to do much beyond create a handful of jobs. One midsize manufacturer with a Zacatecas-based manufacturing business declared, for example, that public money would be better spent creating public-private trusts or utilities that would finance the building of enterprise zones, industrial parks, or business clusters that in turn would attract wholesale buyers and enable entrepreneurs to buy inputs at lower prices. The same interviewee also pointed out the importance of creating binational business chambers of commerce that would negotiate with the state government on business matters separately from migrant hometown associations and federations. "What is required," he commented, "is a business vision. That means that the project will be planned so that it will be successful. . . . We businessmen know that to be able to consolidate a business, we have to work hard day by day. A business is built every day. [With the four-for-one business investment program] there is a lack of consolidated groups, highly disciplined, highly involved. I don't doubt the money is well used, but money is used in a dispersed way."

Another Zacatecan businessperson familiar with the program lamented that the experimental Proyectos Productivos four-for-one program had poured money into production facilities that had never been completed, or which had yielded a product without a market outlet. He indicated that he had even been in a forum with migrant leaders discussing job-creating projects for Zacatecas, and that migrant activists had been resistant to the idea of creating what he called "business incubator" groups that would pair university business school faculty with prospective co-investment teams to devise business plans and cost out each phase of a proposed job creation project. Migrant businessmen countered that they did not oppose business planning groups as such, but that instead more government resources needed to be applied to placing Zacatecan products in retail markets abroad. One migrant businessman cited the example of a high-end craft mescal that had been developed with migrant investment but that had foundered because of the difficulties of capitalizing distribution and competing with much larger and more powerful Mexican conglomerates for shelf space.

A unique perspective emerged from another interviewee who had alternately worked in Zacatecan private sector industry and in an area of government administration. In general, he was positive about the program and the political weight that migrants had acquired through participation in the program, remarking that matching-grant programs "have been a tool enabling Zacatecan leaders living in the United States who are interested in home state politics to get involved here but also a mechanism in building cohesive networks of Zacatecans abroad." This individual maintained that although the three-for-one program had been an important instrument in promoting regional and community development, he felt that job-creating projects presented much greater challenges for enduring success. "Many of the job-creating projects under this program are not successful," he said, noting that the method for selecting projects was problematic. The struggle to control the direction of funds also made it difficult to offer counsel on projects. "We're looking to have professional capability," he said, "but as of now, the main obstacles are the same actors involved in the program and they are indisposed to accept advice." At the same time, he believed that increasing involvement of migrant leaders in public administration and business would be very positive, cutting into what he saw as rigid, ingrown ways of doing things. "It would make the state more cosmopolitan," he explained, "bringing people here who got tired of living elsewhere . . . and who saw how you could take the assets we have here in Zacatecas and find innovative uses for them."

Most important, this individual felt that if the program were to go more in the direction of financing job-creating projects, it would need to take on a distinctly business-oriented character. This would mean, for example, using different criteria for selecting projects and for overseeing them. Whereas with hometown projects, he noted, few community members objected to works such as street paving or health clinics or potable water systems; but it was not so clear what business priorities there were in migrants' home communities. To achieve better project selection, this individual argued that a highly elaborated planning process needed to be in place and those migrant activists had to buy into the idea of getting some direction from the state or from Zacatecan civil society.

Those who spanned the world of business and civic activism as transnational entrepreneurs with small and midsize ventures in the United States and in Zacatecas felt differently; they resented the idea that they and their counterparts lacked business acumen. One migrant activist who had served in leadership positions in Zacatecan migrant federations in Texas and also had built businesses on both sides of the border emphasized the crushing weight of corruption on the state. He stated that at the beginning, when the three-for-one program began, he and others had raised funds reluctantly because they so distrusted the state government. He painted the success of matching-grant programs as the fruit of a long struggle against state graft and the worst impulses of government bureaucrats. "After all these years," he said, "we have learned to take care of our investment and to generate rules that force us to take good care of our resources. That was the change from negative to positive. That's why the program has grown and become strong. That's why we now have better performance, more commitment, and better policies toward migrants from all levels of government."

This individual, in contrast to the former two interviewees, stated unequivocally that the long-term goal for social remittances should be channeled toward the creation of businesses that would generate employment opportunities and reduce migration. To achieve this, he argued that matching grants should be directed toward financing agriculture, small construction industries, and value-added enterprises. With regard to developing the conditions for business success, he felt that education, rather than state tutelage, was key in binational development projects "Society should not wait for the government to do everything," he stated. "All of us are the government. Society *is* the government." In contrast to the former respondents' ideas about planning groups, this interviewee said that imaginative commerce ideas were likely to come from exchange programs of university students from Zacatecas and the United States. Bilingual education, he felt, should be standard for children of Zacatecans on both sides of the border.

Yet another interviewee, a businessman in California and a state legislator representing migrant voters in the Zacatecas legislature, stated that his activities in the program began by collecting donations from fellow migrants from his hometown for church improvements. They started to participate in projects not oriented toward improving churches. After the projects became secular, this individual noted that divisions were much more likely to emerge in organizations and fall on party lines. He became so fatigued by splits that occurred in his federation during the Monreal years that he retired from investment in public works to work on his business. With the changes under Governor García, however, he saw new openness and became involved in politics and investment in public works again. With regard to the question of using matching-grant funds for public works versus job-creating projects, this interviewee believed that there was a dilemma: whereas the public works projects clearly benefited everyone and elicited fewer accusations of political favoritism, job-creating projects would have a more lasting benefit. The issue of investing in jobs without creating schisms had not been fully resolved, he said. "People were taking good care of the money for the programs to be invested in social projects. Then if somebody wanted to invest in a tortilla dispensary, or a project for his family, they were going to be given $4,000. Then the question was, why should somebody benefit from this resource? People would get jealous and uncomfortable."

The interviewee wondered openly about how civil society, particularly binational oversight committees with members in the United States, would continue to monitor investments over time. Solutions to these problems, he argued, could only be solved by deepening democracy. "Sectors of society must collaborate to solve problems by means of proposals and open forums," he maintained, arguing that these growing pains were a part of the rising democracy in Mexico: "It's an opportunity for people to go beyond ideology and to evaluate the benefits of different courses of action."

BINATIONAL CITIZENS, MONEY, AND STATE ACCOUNTABILITY

Much has been written about the Iniciativa Ciudadana program and about the phenomenon of migrant organizing, much of it focusing on the relative presence or absence of economic development potential embodied by the flow of so-called collective remittances. What is less well explored is the role of the three-for-one program in shaping politics and political expectations about the relationship between the state and the private sector. Matching-grant programs, though of limited economic scope, are unarguably an important arena for institutionalized, rule-bound struggles over policy and politics between state and sectors of transnational civil society. Migrant investment in public works also functions as a component of a struggle for upward social mobility of prominent migrant civic leaders and volunteers with multivalent identities, who readily celebrate their labor and campesino roots, their belonging in home parishes, *and* their status as survivors in a grueling process of migration and adaptation to a new country with little but their wits and their community ties to back them. Prominent Zacatecanos who have become involved in cross-border politics or civic affairs are often successful entrepreneurs, but they tend to define themselves not as businessmen first but instead as binational citizens who happen to work in business, who act in multiple spheres, including politics, culture, and civic life.

These multivalent public identities have been instrumental in expanding the role of migrant leaders and federations inside state politics in Zacatecas;

they are portrayed as loyal sons and daughters of Mexico and as self-made persons abroad. A rhetoric of antipolitics and of outsider status ironically boosted the role of migrant activists inside state and municipal affairs and at times threatened the survival of the Iniciativa Ciudadana program when partisan schisms caused divisions inside the ranks of migrant clubs and federations in the late 1990s and early 2000s. With novel arrangements having softened these differences in recent years, important questions remain as to whether a matching-grant program that was originally designed to install parish improvements, and later public infrastructure, can actually create jobs inside Zacatecas and eliminate the need of Zacatecans to emigrate. This new mission, obviously much more complex and politically fraught than any before it, is shaped by a distinct sector of binational citizens; the outcome of migrant-sponsored job-creating programs, in turn, will also affect the role of binational Zacatecans in the years to come.

NOTES

1. Mounting evidence also indicates a vexing regressiveness in patterns of bribery: studies by Transparency International (2008) and Fried, Lagunes, and Venkataramani (2010) showed that corruption in the form of solicitation of bribes by police and government officials affected lower-income citizens far more than affluent citizens. Transparency International's (2008) survey data showed that minimum-wage workers paid on average 14 percent of their income in bribes; in the study of traffic and bribes by Fried, Lagunes, and Venkataramani (2010, 84), lower-class drivers were 40 percent more likely to be stopped for infractions than upper-class drivers.

2. The nomenclature of this program has changed over time. The Proyectos Productivos program, specifically meant for investment in job-creating ventures, was referred to for some time as the four-for-one project in a period in which Western Union was putting in funds for an additional dollar match. The program did not generate the commerce projected, however, and as of 2010 it was reduced to a two-for-one match.

3. Why Zacatecas should have emerged at the forefront of transnational state-society linkage is an important question. Some point to sheer numbers. Using census data, Amador Sanchez (2005) argued that Zacatecas was literally split in two: for the 1.4 million Zacatecans residing in the state, there were 1.5 million in the United States. While only 550 thousand of those in the United States are Zacatecan-born, nonetheless, the sense of half the region's families being elsewhere is palpable in the state. Zacatecas may also be characterized by a more fully "binational" condition than other states because of its curiously high levels of remittances relative to the duration of its migrants' residence in the United States. Zacatecas has a century-long pattern of migration to the United States, much older than that of now high-sending states such as Chiapas, Puebla, or Veracruz, and its migrants typically have

lived in the United States longer than migrants from newer high-sending states. Statistically, studies have shown that newer migrants send home larger remittances than migrants with more time abroad (Suro et al. 2003), but Zacatecans do not conform to this pattern. Despite being seasoned migrants, a majority with legal papers and/or U.S. citizenship, Zacatecans remit more money per capita—about 340 dollars per year—than citizens of any other state in Mexico (Instituto Estatal de Migración 2008). This meant that many Zacatecan families had legal means of moving back and forth from Mexico, and that many had equity, savings, and businesses in the United States. This relative stability of at least a sector of state migrants meant that leaders with fund-raising and administrative capacities were likely to emerge from migrant social networks. Also, the number of migrants as a percentage of the total state population is one of the highest in Mexico, as are remittances as a percentage of gross state income—just under 10 percent (Banco de Mexico 2007). Migrant respondents also attributed the activism of Zacatecans to its social conservatism and the devotion of Zacatecans to Catholic parishes at home.

4. Bermúdez is often referred to as the Tomato King—a reference to his farm empire in Winters, California.

5. The change in the name migrant advocates used for the bill was due to increasingly flamboyant and self-promoting actions by Bermúdez himself that caused some of his former allies to turn against him.

6. Notably, Katrina Burgess's study of governance of three-for-one projects showed, in fact, that partisan division among the key actors on individual projects, especially those that pitted members of the *comité de obra* against the donors and/or municipal officers, was a factor that negatively affected project outcomes (Burgess 2005).

REFERENCES

Bakker, Matt, and Michael Peter Smith. 2003. "El Rey del Tomate: Migrant Political Transnationalism and Democratization in Mexico." *Migraciones internacionales* 2 (1): 59–83.

Bakker, Matt, and Michael Peter Smith. 2008. *Citizenship across Borders: The Political Transformation of El Migrante.* Ithaca: Cornell University Press.

Banco de Mexico. 2007. *Las remesas familiares en Mexico.* Mexico City: Central Bank of Mexico.

Burgess, Katrina. 2005. "Migrant Philanthropy and Local Governance in Mexico." In *New Patterns for Mexico: Observations on Remittances, Philanthropic Giving, and Equitable Development,* edited by Barbara Merz. Cambridge: Harvard University Press.

Delgado, Felipe. 2003. Interview by Heather Williams. Secretaría de Desarrollo Social. Zacatecas, Mexico. July 8.

Fernandez de Castro, R., R. Garcia Zamora, et al., eds. 2006. *El Programa 3 × 1 para Migrantes.* Zacatecas, Mexico: Universidad Autonoma de Zacatecas.

Fitzgerald, David. 2009. *A Nation of Emigrants: How Mexico Manages Its Migration.* Berkeley: University of California Press.

Fried, Brian, Paul Lagunes, and Atheendar Venkataramani. 2010. "Corruption and Inequality at the Crossroad: A Multimethod Study of Bribery and Discrimination in Latin America." *Latin American Research Review* 45 (1): 76–97.

Garcia Zamora, R. 2003. Interview by Heather Williams. Zacatecas, Mexico. July 11.

Gómez, Guadalupe. 2003. Interview by Heather Williams. Santa Ana, CA. August 14.

Instituto Estatal de Migración. 2008. "El Programa 3 × 1. Zacatecas." Zacatecas, Mexico.

Layton, Michael. 2009. "Philanthropy and the Third Sector in Mexico: The Enabling Environment and Its Limitations." *Norteamérica* 4, no. 1 (January–June): 87–120.

Lomnitz, Larissa. 1977. *Networks and Marginality*. Translated by Cinna Lomnitz. New York: Academic Press.

Quiñones, S. 2002. "Home, Tense Home." *LA Weekly* (Los Angeles). March 8.

Ronfeld, A. 2001. "New Mayor Touts Migrant Worker Roots; Returning Home to Mexico, Former Migrant Workers Hope to Make Their Mark in Politics." *Grand Rapids Press*. July 2.

Secretaría de Desarrollo Social (SEDESOL). 2008a. "El Programa Iniciativa Ciudadana 3 × 1, 2008." Secretariat of Social Development. Mexico City.

Secretaría de Desarrollo Social (SEDESOL). 2008b. Project files by municipality for Iniciativa Ciudadana, Microrregiones, Ramo 20. Opciones Productivas, Proyecto de Empleo Temporal.

Suro, R., S. Bendixen, B. Lindsay Lowell, and Dulce Benevides. 2003. "Billions in Motion: Latino Immigrants, Remittances, and Banking." Pew Hispanic Center, Multilateral Investment Fund.

Thompson, G. 2004. "Migrants Seek Power in Mexico; Candidate Embodies Yearning for Reforms." *New York Times*. October 28, A4.

Transparency International. 2008. Corruption Perception Index.

Vélez-Ibañez, Carlos. 2010. *An Impossible Living in a Transborder World: Culture, Confianza, and Economy of Mexican-Origin Populations*. Tucson: University of Arizona Press.

Wallerstein, Immanuel. 1980. *The Modern World-System*. Vol. 2, *Mercantilism and the Consolidation of the European World-Economy, 1600–1750*. New York: Academic Press.

7

WHEN CULTURAL ACTIVISTS SPEAK A BUSINESS LANGUAGE

SUCCESS ON THE STAGE, APPLAUSE IN THE BOARDROOM, AND THE DIFFICULTIES OF SCALING UP SOCIAL CHANGE IN RIO'S FAVELAS

Jeffrey W. Rubin

Figure 7.1. Teen member of Afro Reggae performance group. Photo © Jeffrey W. Rubin.

WHEN COMMUTERS GET OFF the bus from downtown Rio—after winding through miles of working-class suburbs and industrial zones—a train track divides the bus stop from the entrance to Vigario Geral. Returning from jobs and school carrying shopping bags, purses, and children, the residents of the shantytown make their way up the stairs and over the tracks, passing from the *asfalto* to *não-asfalto*, from the paved to unpaved streets that make Rio a divided city. Some return exhausted, others step gingerly into the war zone they call home. There are so few entrances to Vigario that the drug traffickers, the shopkeepers, and the neighbors—as well as the police when they are there—know who enters and leaves, and undoubtedly where they are going as well. It is the eyes and presence of the Afro Reggae Cultural Group, a hip social movement popularly known as Afro Reggae (AR), that make this a safe crossing for its young members and for visitors like me.

Safety is hard to come by in the shantytowns (favelas) of Rio, and the kids in Afro Reggae know danger up close. Until he joined Afro Reggae in 1997, Jonathan—a handsome, dark-skinned teenager with a wide-toothed grin and boyish lankiness—lived in constant fear that his mother, a drug trafficker, wouldn't come home at night. Trapped between the police and the traffickers, Jonathan's childhood was tied to the drug trade and its violence. Trafficking put food on the table but along with thousands of kids whose parents live in the drug world, Jonathan was left to navigate the threatening streets alone, living in fear that his mother would die.

Most of the people Jonathan knew as a child were dead or risking their lives daily. But when I met him in 2002, instead of dealing drugs, Jonathan had become a skilled acrobat and juggler in the circus training program that Afro Reggae founded with the support of Canada's Cirque du Soleil. Still in school, he navigated the favela with a tight-knit group of Afro Reggae friends. He had performed throughout the city, including guest appearances with Intrépida, one of Brazil's celebrated avant-garde circus groups. All over Rio's slums, amid the gun battles of rival drug gangs and streets overflowing with sewage, teenagers hoping for a different future have been following Jonathan's path. Playing drums, learning improvisational theater, and dancing, they are moving away from trafficking.

A group of young Afro-Brazilians started the Afro Reggae Cultural Group in 1993 after police stormed Vigario Geral and killed twenty-one innocent people, leaving unbearable grief and despair in their wake. This event marked Vigario as a national symbol of urban warfare. The nascent activists had already been sponsoring musical events and publishing an Afro Reggae newsletter, a modest effort to invigorate favela culture with news of national and international trends. After the massacre, local cabdriver José Junior started organizing drumming workshops for kids inside the favela. The musicians who came to Vigario Geral to teach were astonished by the raw talent they encountered and helped local drummers form a band. From that beginning, the Afro Reggae Cultural Group built a movement that today involves more than a thousand young people. Afro Reggae's performance groups travel to favelas throughout

Rio, perform on the city's best stages, and tour internationally to New York's Carnegie Hall and throughout Europe. Professional actors train theater and dance troupes made up of local kids to teach about violence and AIDS, and Afro Reggae leaders coach police on how to diffuse violence. The group opened a new, state-of-the art cultural center in the heart of Vigario Geral in 2010. Every day after school, children come for tutoring, music lessons, and dance classes. The older students often receive a stipend for supervising activities or teaching younger kids.

Afro Reggae (AR) has gained extensive business approval as an enduring reform because it speaks a business language, embraces entrepreneurialism, and successfully controls its image in the media. Businesspeople have become aware of AR through its gala shows, and the information they receive about the group through the media dovetails with familiar portraits of the "divided city," where favelas are zones of crisis and violence, with self-respect and a way out as the best solutions.[1] Businesspeople view Afro Reggae's track record of toughness and pragmatism as spot-on, and they support and praise the organization. At the same time, they know few details about AR's actual activities—from its diverse projects and day-to-day work in favelas to its goals of fighting racial discrimination and preventing police violence. To businesspeople, Afro Reggae runs an efficient operation, nurtures a sense of self-worth, and secures jobs for young people. In so doing, it creates income-generating projects and provides sponsors with high-profile advertising opportunities. Businesspeople and foundations alike have judged this endeavor to be worthy and support it with both praise and funding.

The vision of Afro Reggae that businesspeople accept—the one put forth by the media—is precisely the image that Afro Reggae works hard to disseminate. Indeed, the group's control over the public presentation of its work is one of AR's greatest successes. Afro Reggae controls the way it comes into public view (through spectacular shows in both fashionable areas of the city and favelas), and it monitors and shapes the accounts that are given of its activities in news and cultural reporting. Businesspeople have accepted these accounts without any real knowledge of the favelas where AR works. In the business imagination, these favelas are uniformly ramshackle and poor, crisscrossed by gunfire that can barely be contained. Rio's very real favelas—where more goes on than violence, drug trafficking, suffering, and music—are displaced by AR's representations. Businesspeople add to their uniformly negative view of favelas a rejection of the possibility of effective government action to address the problems there, and they do so in a way that affirms their view that they themselves do not bear responsibility for the situation or its improvement.

Interviews in Rio de Janeiro for the Enduring Reform Project with high-level managers of national and transnational corporations, owners and managers of smaller enterprises, and foundation officials show that in the eyes of business-people, Afro Reggae is a praiseworthy and successful effort to help favela youth, but can do no more than make a small dent in an enormous problem. For these businesspeople, it is the state's responsibility to change the dire situation in the favelas and control the violence that spills over to other parts of the city. But the interviewees stated repeatedly that at all levels the Brazilian government is incapable of addressing this problem, so nothing can be done.

This chapter begins with a description of Afro Reggae from the point of view of its participants, based on interviews and participant observation carried out during Afro Reggae's first decade, in 1997, 2001, and 2002. It then explains, using Enduring Reform interviews carried out in 2008, how businesspeople in Rio first became aware of the group and understand its goals and projects, comparing businesspeople's perceptions with representations disseminated by the media and by AR itself. Next, these representations are contrasted with the complexity of AR's presence in Vigario Geral and the ways the group nego-tiates its own survival and successes on the ground. Part of this balancing act involves embracing a business model, a path that has been pursued by the Afro-Brazilian left in Rio more broadly, as described through interviews with activ-ists. Although embracing a business approach has enabled Afro Reggae to endure and achieve noteworthy successes, it limits the transformative potential of the project, as businesspeople see no pathways for moving from AR's achieve-ments with individual kids to broader processes of policy change or social trans-formation. These limits are examined in the final sections of the chapter.

AFRO REGGAE FROM THE INSIDE

What has made Afro Reggae appealing to favela youth is that it is exciting and cool, offering kids something fun to do. Roseli Moreira, an outspoken young woman who helped form the Afro Reggae theater troupe, used to see her life as a trajectory from home to school. She walked with her head down and spent much of her free time looking out from the doorway of her house. In 2002 she told me, "Today I wear earrings, necklaces, straighten my hair. I walk down the street and talk to anyone." Marcia Florencia, one of Afro Reggae's founders, said that you can instantly tell the difference between kids who are in the group and those who aren't—the Afro Reggae kids look you in the eye.

For José Junior, AR's key visionary and the head of the organization since its formation, Afro Reggae is first about seduction. Building a new world in the favela means attracting kids who are drawn to the money and guns of the traffickers. When Junior describes the kids in Vigario, he reaches back to his own experiences growing up in bad neighborhoods, around prostitutes and drugs, and the many facets of the city he saw as a cabdriver. "The kids here notice the watches and shoes I get from the U.S.," he said. "So I chill with them and talk about things like women and soccer. They're confused, and they think, this guy has everything, and he isn't a criminal." The kids know that in Rio, entry-level drug trafficking pays more than four times the minimum wage, which is all most favela kids get if they're lucky enough to find a job. They know that for dark-skinned teenagers from places like Vigario Geral, most doors will be slammed in their faces before they can apply for a job. So Junior's clothes, his banter and self-assurance, and his world of music and performance pique their interest.

Anderson Sá, for many years the lead singer in Afro Reggae's main band, looked head-on at the stark reality of poverty in the favela when he got kids involved in AR activities. With no money and no options, he explained, kids take the path that promises economic survival. Trafficking even provides a support network in the favela—for example, by getting local families access to doctors and money for medications. Anderson used culture to show kids another path and a different kind of network. He got kids from the most marginalized parts of the favela to come to drumming workshops and to classes in capoeira (a Brazilian mixture of dance and martial arts), and he brought them to Afro Reggae's cultural center in Vigario and to shows downtown. He wanted them to see that culture is a path away from despair and drugs. "It's about bringing kids into our group *and* taking them out of the favela," he said. "Because the favela is a closed world. When you take them out of here, they discover new ones."

Junior warned me about entering Vigario alone. He always had someone meet me at the entrance and accompany me down the narrow streets. But at Afro Reggae's cultural center, even the police had to enter unarmed. Though it was only a short walk from Vigario's main entrance, when I reached the top of the stairs and turned into the bare three-walled room where AR's theater troupe rehearsed, it was clear that a new world was being created right inside the favela. First, the troupe members, ranging in age from eight to eighteen, went over skits about AIDS, drugs, and teen pregnancy. Then, in front of a wall of mirrors, the group improvised: they're born and then dying, individually but connected; they're arguing in small groups, jostling into one another, the arguments escalating and spilling over from one group to the next, out of control; and then they're all on a train, swaying in unison as if that moving train were their whole world. The acting coach was right in there with them, praising their strengths, offering a running critique, supporting individual performers, and getting them all to talk about what they were thinking and doing. When I looked out the open side of the room, I saw the reality I had walked through to get there: muddy streets, stagnant water, wooden shacks, colorful clotheslines, burning garbage. I turned back to find the troupe writing in journals and creating a set of essays and drawings for a collective biography. A fifteen-year-old girl wrote: "I wish I could fly, love, but who will teach me how?" Another boy described the drug traffickers and drew pictures of corpses.

In 2002, the Afro Reggae Cultural Group distributed video cameras to kids in the favela. The handheld cameras were easy to hide in pockets and took the place of the pretend guns they had played with as children. The camera program—meant to give youths a new way to see and document their lives— produced a shocking chronicle of the violence they witness every day. Kids followed behind police as they stormed through the favela, capturing gun battles outside their own windows. New York filmmaker Jeff Zimbalist knew the minute he saw the footage that he had found something remarkable. The youngsters from Afro Reggae became the eyes behind his feature documentary *Favela Rising*. Upon its release in 2005, the hard-hitting account of Afro Reggae and its lead singer won awards at film festivals across the United States and Brazil, including "Film of the Year" from the International Documentary Association. Officials at the Ford Foundation got so excited about the film that they funded an international tour of the Afro Reggae band and the film. The idea was to take the music and the story to places like Mumbai and Soweto, where people face urban devastation similar to that in Rio's favelas, and get people thinking about how they can make change from within.

On a deeper and more personal level than the band and the film, and even the classes, Afro Reggae changes the way kids live their lives. Some, like Paulo, become stars. At age sixteen, after training with Afro Reggae, Paulo was hired by O Rappa, one of Brazil's most popular bands. His premiere concert at the Metropolitana, a posh club in an all-white neighborhood, brought Vigario's dark-skinned teens to a part of the city they had never before entered. Between tours, Paulo began coaching the little kids in Vigario who followed him around banging on strips of metal. He called the new band Afro Lata, the tin can band.

Entering Vigario Geral on a Saturday afternoon, the first thing I heard was the sound of drumbeats. On a concrete stage in a vacant lot turned performance space, kids ages nine to nineteen pounded enormous drums and swiveled their hips in a mix of eroticism and defiance. I couldn't hear myself think, yet Paulo kept everyone in time with intense, clipped instructions. Even five-year-olds beat out rhythms on the ground, and adolescent girls danced for hours to the ear-splitting beat, hoping for a place in the show. Seemingly oblivious to the sound, Junior crisscrossed the lot and adjoining streets, checking in with parents, storekeepers, and community leaders, aware of exactly who was linked to the drug trade and how his presence and conversation staked out a safe space for the youngsters. Sporting a baseball cap and Nike shorts, Junior is a master at building connections and drawing people into his vision of transforming favela life through music.

Most kids in Afro Reggae won't become stars in music groups or even grow up to work as performers. What they have is profound and near to home: their lives change because of what's happening around their dinner tables, the discussions and interactions they experience daily, and the choices they can make. In Roseli's house, for example, evenings changed completely once she and her brothers joined the AR theater troupe. Before that, no one in her family had acted. Dinners had been perfunctory and focused on the nightly telenovelas. But after the young people joined Afro Reggae, the nighttime discussion around the table became animated. They talked politics and ideas, clowned around, and mimicked each other affectionately. They kept the party going till midnight.

Since its early years in the mid-1990s, Afro Reggae has come to be about more than drumming, more than even the music that is its medium. AR shows people who have never set foot inside the favela, as well as the people who live there, what a thriving space of creativity and excitement the favela can be. Many residents already know this, because they have built their neighborhood's streets and shacks with their own hands and found ways to fall in love, raise kids, and work for the future. But awareness of their own self-worth is too often overshadowed by fear and despair. Psychologist Marcia first came to Vigario after the police massacre in 1993 that had killed twenty-one innocents; she found a community too grief-stricken even to speak. Seeing corpses cleared away and family members in shock, Marcia found new ways of responding to misery. "I learned to leave behind my training, with its emphasis on coldness and distance, and get much closer," she recalled. "Not intimacy that confuses roles, but to hold kids in my lap, to take off their clothes and wash them when that's what they needed." Marcia's mixture of political savvy and capacity to heal typify Afro Reggae's style and talent. The group has an uncanny ability to seduce people where they live and bring them to places they have never been, reshaping the life of the city of samba and Carnaval in the process.

Afro Reggae is about unexpected kinds of mixing and choice, about standing up and making noise. For Duda, the impish nineteen-year-old who ran the cultural center in 2002, joining AR was a religious awakening in an unconventional sense. Until he defied his mother and quit his job, Duda was afraid to join Afro Reggae because he was an evangelical and his church rejects Afro-Brazilian spiritual practices. But in the midst of Afro Reggae, where people come together to make music and borrow from all sorts of cultural traditions, he realized that religion was something about which he could learn and make choices. Talking to Duda, I realized that kids in AR are living the globalization of culture, mixing musical and religious styles from Africa, Brazil, the Caribbean, and the United States. Through this, they realize that they have the same rights as the people in "the asphalt" part of Rio and the rest of the world—and that they need to claim these rights. "Before, we knew we had rights, but we didn't fight for them," Roseli told me. "I mean, our right to come and go. The right to go to the movies, to go to college. The right to have dignified work. The right not to be ashamed of the color of our skin. The right to look for work. The right to know that if a policeman wants to beat me, it's not okay. Why should he hit me? I don't have any drugs."

If you ask Junior the secret of Afro Reggae, he will tell you it is language: "It's the language of the street, of police, prostitutes, and workers." He learned these various languages growing up, and he uses them to communicate across Rio's heavily guarded borders. When I met with Junior in his mother's house or in the Afro Reggae offices, both downtown, he carried multiple cell phones and maintained constant radio contact with staff in Vigario and other favelas. In between decisions about concert plans, T-shirt logos, and adolescent crises, Junior talked to businessmen, traffickers, musicians, and mayors with an uncanny ability to get them all on board, one new project after another. Marcia commented on the extraordinary set of skills that participants in AR continue to discover: "At first, people saw a potential in us that we didn't perceive ourselves," she explained. "But they also thought Afro Reggae was just a group that played music, not capable of dealing on an equal footing with the city government or international foundations." As they began to act on a larger stage, leaders of the group realized they had to recognize their own capacity and learn to use it. Soon they were insisting on—and getting—meetings with the mayor and the chief of police to talk about the racism and violence that plagued the favelas.

Relationships with government officials in Rio changed further when Afro Reggae convinced the city and several large corporations to fund a big-name concert once a month, in the city's favelas. The shows are gala events, featuring some of Brazil's most famous stars, local samba clubs, and the Afro Reggae Band. As the concert program picked up steam, it was Afro Reggae that increasingly set the terms. The performances came right to where people lived, even the most distant and isolated neighborhoods, bringing a message of pride and empowerment. "When we go into meetings," Junior observed, "we know that even if they're the ones financing us, they have to do what we want. Otherwise, we'll do it ourselves." He put this lesson into practice in a meeting in Miami with the codirectors and investors of *Favela Rising,* flatly rejecting their plan to donate profits from the film to Afro Reggae as a form of charity. Junior felt that this did not properly reflect AR's contribution to the film. "You put part of yourselves into it," he said to them. "Well, we put ourselves into it too, and we want part of our film to belong to us." Ten minutes later, Afro Reggae owned half of *Favela Rising.*

People say Vigario used to be the Brazilian Bosnia, a war zone. When I asked if violence had diminished as a result of Afro Reggae, I was told, "No, but it's more hidden, during the night and in the hours just before dawn. You don't see it as much." But that wasn't enough for Junior, who wanted to keep the cultural center open during these times and call it a twenty-four-hour creativity room. He said that other social projects in the city were funded eight to six, so to make a difference, Afro Reggae had to be available all the time. Everyone involved in AR grapples with the question of permanence, of having created something great and wondering what will sustain it. Junior worried about what he has called the third generation, the ten- and twelve-year-olds who have always had AR and don't know what it's like to struggle alone in a hostile environment. "When they hear a gun shot, they're scared," he explained. "We weren't scared." Junior's generation had learned on their own how to live with violence and use activism to keep fear at bay. Marcia worried about AR becoming so good at negotiating with people in power that the group ends up seeing things too much from the perspective of the boardroom and perhaps failing to stem the tide of violence before the favelas explode.

Some things are harder to change than others, and it is clear that maintaining a vibrant movement like Afro Reggae amid fear and killing is a constant challenge. After twenty years, the streets of Vigario are still strewn with garbage. As in many of the shantytowns of the globalized world, people have more appliances in their houses than they did in the past, and kids are more educated than their parents. But basic services are still inadequate and violence is pervasive; there are few good jobs. In the favela, some things stay and some things go. NGOs move on. The Peace House that was constructed on the site of the 1993 massacre became a recycling center. The organization Doctors Without Borders, which arrived at the height of the violence, left the favela for newer wars.

Afro Reggae leaders hope the movement is creating some kind of leadership that will continue. "We've gotten a lot further than drumming," Marcia observed. "Our investments are in the young people. They're long-term invest-ments. Tiring ones. The question for us is whether someone else will sustain these ideas, whether they'll be taken up by new people coming on the scene." Leadership takes unexpected forms. Roseli told me a story about a drug traf-ficker who told a ten-year-old to join Afro Reggae. The boy wanted a job dealing drugs, and the trafficker hesitated. "Look," he told the boy, "if I were your age, I wouldn't need this life. Go to Afro Reggae and see what they do. If I had the chance you have, I'd grab onto it with my fingernails and teeth. I wouldn't give it up for anything."

COMING ON THE SCENE THROUGH SHOWS

Businesspeople see Afro Reggae as a movement that uses music-based cultural work to promote the social inclusion of favela residents, particularly children and youth, in Rio de Janeiro. One of the businesswomen interviewed for the Enduring Reform Project, a female executive of a major transnational industrial corporation, was surprised when she learned that Afro Reggae is an NGO. She had associated the group exclusively with a "cultural movement related to music." The statement of a male project manager for a firm special-izing in information management summarizes well the view of interviewees in general: "I know it's a group that looks after disadvantaged children through music and has its own instruments." A high-level manager of a large national corporation put it this way: "I know that they work in disadvantaged commu-nities with music that involves percussion. They traveled the whole world with their work, playing and taking along kids to play. Apart from that, they also do private shows to raise funds for their institution. Now, their own story, how they came to be, I don't really know."

Some of the interviewees gained personal experiences related to Afro Reggae through music. It was at the invitation of a friend who worked with Afro Samba, one of several AR bands, that one of the businesspeople interviewed came into contact with the group, at a performance in a prestigious downtown cultural center. He classified the event as "excellent," not only because he likes samba but also because he understood that it was "rather serious social work with disadvantaged children." He had never talked specifically about the activi-ties of Afro Samba with his colleague but had read in the newspapers that one of the kids who used to be part of the group back then is currently doing his own shows. A social project involving music, with a good samba repertoire and even its own compositions, thus generated respect for Afro Reggae's work.

Two executives interviewed had also seen Afro Reggae musical performances. One of them remembered seeing "kids playing in the streets, probably in the city center." Another said that through indirect contact with one of Afro Reggae's founders, facilitated through a friend, she had seen Afro Reggae Band shows in the late 1990s and early 2000s. This businesswoman had watched these shows in clubs in one of the city's most upscale neighborhoods. She described the shows as events that transmitted a "good energy" and emphasized their importance as a possible path for the integration of residents of the favelas with middle-class people living in the Zona Sul (Southern Zone) of the city. "It was very lively," she recalled. "They had good interaction with the audience. It was funny to see favela residents playing for the Zona Sul crowd. And people from Zona Sul thinking it was great. I used to like it, the atmosphere of the shows was really cool."

This businesswoman underscored that the audience did not go to these shows for the social issues dealt with by Afro Reggae but only for the entertainment: "to enjoy the music" ("a sound that came from Africa," mixing reggae with Brazilian music). Although she noticed that Afro Reggae's social work was always publicized before the shows, this businesswoman did not perceive a direct connection between the shows and the social projects announced by the group. "But you can see it in the people playing," she added. "You can see that they come from poor communities. The publicity campaign says that everything will be invested in workshops to generate more funds to continue with the projects." Back when she still had contact with the group's work (through shows in the upscale neighborhood where she used to live), she recalled that Afro Reggae was very popular at nightclubs in Rio's upper-middle class areas. But this situation changed as the group gradually gained more space in the media and consequently access to bigger, more prestigious, and even international stages.

GAINING SUPPORT THROUGH THE MEDIA

The experiences described by this businesswoman are important in understanding the experiences of other businesspeople who did not have the same contacts. The growing publicity and media support accorded Afro Reggae were the most important factors in the positive image and values attributed to the group by the other interviewees. They all emphasized that they had become aware of Afro Reggae through the media, news articles and press releases, and the publicity for the shows over the past few years, although nobody knew for certain when he or she first started to hear about the group. The space that Afro Reggae had gained in the media, along with shows outside the favelas, had allowed these businesspeople to accord credibility and recognition to AR, even if they did not have any experience or concrete knowledge of the social projects the group developed in the favelas. The male owner of a small commercial business observed that the recurrent media coverage of the group and its work has shown that with time, Afro Reggae managed to synthesize social work and publicity. He identified this as a necessity for reaching the goals that Afro Reggae and similar organizations have.

> I actually have little knowledge of Afro Reggae's concrete activities. But I have obviously heard a lot about them and this is precisely what I know: I heard a lot about them through the media because of their activities, although I'm not exactly sure what they are. The media has talked a lot about them in a particular way for some time. One of the images I have is that the people who play with or develop Afro Reggae knew how to reconcile a difficult issue—that is, doing social work and publicity at the same time.

For the businesspeople interviewed, the growing media coverage of Afro Reggae and references to venues considered prestigious serve as evidence that AR has been going through a transformation, including a gradual expansion of its activities, since its foundation. Most businesspeople perceived these changes as positive, linked to the group's new international ties, through musical shows and tours abroad, as well as international partnerships and fund-raising. The businesswoman who had seen Banda Afro Reggae's shows in the 1990s praised the effects of international travel on it members: "I think it's very good because people have an opportunity that they have never had before, of getting to know the outside world, so to speak. Feeling they can achieve, dream, make things happen. They could never have dreamed of going to the United States to play for Americans. . . . I think that this international part is very good for them. Even for the publicity itself and for raising international funds."

In the other interviews, the image of AR reinforced by the media led the interviewees to associate Afro Reggae with other NGOs and institutions in Rio de Janeiro, particularly Viva Rio, a renowned social organization well publicized in the media and, like Afro Reggae, founded in 1993 as a response to the growing violence in Rio de Janeiro. The male project manager who mentioned and praised Viva Rio expressed his trust in Afro Reggae like this:

> I donate money to Criança Esperança, to Doctors Without Borders, to organizations whose consistency I trust . . . I have a very positive image of them. I have relatively little knowledge of them, but I have

an extremely positive image of them. So, for example, if I were asked to donate money to Afro Reggae, I would probably have a positive response . . . because my perception is that it is a worthy and positive work. [This positive image comes] from the media coverage, from the way it was shown . . . always in a positive way and praising their work, calling attention [to it].

Because businesspeople in Rio de Janeiro do not generally have any reason to visit poor communities tormented by waves of violence or controlled by paramilitary groups (militias), their information about Afro Reggae's activities comes primarily from mass media and the cultural industry. This leads them to define Afro Reggae's main activities as "social and cultural projects with children and youth in situations of risk." The risks mentioned included the involvement of young people in drug trafficking, drug use, violence, and socioeconomic exclusion. None of the interviewees could be more precise about which activities Afro Reggae actually develops or specify in which favelas AR develops its projects. Nor could they remember the context of the group's foundation as a nongovernmental organization. With one exception, none of the interviewees associated Afro Reggae with identity issues linked to ethnicity or to racism, which the organization itself presents as among its primary concerns.

Despite not having contact with Afro Reggae's projects and activities (beyond the shows) or with the daily realities of people who benefit from the projects, the businesspeople interviewed defined Afro Reggae's actions and activities in the terms that the group wants its audience to use. As a result of media coverage, which is carefully cultivated by Afro Reggae itself, businesspeople evaluate the group's work as efficient and tend to agree that Afro Reggae seeks and, in fact, succeeds in promoting better self-esteem and access to cultural resources that are crucial to a better exercise of citizenship. This perception was expressed through phrases such as "affirmation of values" and the construction of a "positive identity through culture." A partner in an industrial enterprise expressed himself in similar terms when he indirectly praised Afro Reggae this way: "The best path is to give a future . . . to give access to culture and education."

AFRO REGGAE IN A COMPLEX AND DANGEROUS TERRAIN

In contrast to the straightforward accounts of Afro Reggae's successes presented in the media, the group succeeds by performing delicate balancing acts in a complex terrain. Throughout the twenty-plus years of Afro Reggae's existence, Vigario Geral, the favela where the group originated, has experienced ongoing hostilities with the adjacent favela of Parada de Lucas, controlled by a rival drug gang. The conflicts among traffickers, including an intricate succession of partial truces and violent attacks, produced deep-seated hostilities between residents of the two favelas. The dynamics of trafficking, along with the construction of favela identities, are themselves the products of police and government complicity in the drug dealing enterprise and the provision of weapons to traffickers (Neate and Platt 2010).[2]

Many police in Rio's favelas are themselves poor, at times hiding their work identities from their neighbors and accepting bribes from traffickers. Others moonlight in unlicensed private security firms, "artificially creat[ing] fear and then sell[ing] security."[3] Such police violence is tolerated and even encouraged by public officials, themselves implicated in the system of payoffs as they attempt simultaneously to profit from and contain violence in the city's poor zones. On multiple occasions in Rio, police have killed alleged criminals as well as street kids as part of their jobs or for extra pay (Neate and Platt 2010, chapter 13). Indeed, "in the state of Rio de Janeiro, according to data of the Secretariat of Public Safety for the year 2005, the police were responsible for 14.2% of intentional violent deaths" (Ramos 2006, 420). In the everyday tasks of patrolling the city, police are pressed to carry out harassment, controlling people's movements by delaying or detaining them—routine actions that generate additional hostility and fear on the part of favela residents. At the same time, neighborhood associations, which have both formal and informal roles in local administration, routinely coexist with, include, and even protect drug traffickers. Together, the associations and the traffickers watch movement in and out of the favela, defining "friends" and "enemies." In this context, drug gangs are often the major provider of social services and crisis aid to residents, whose location in favelas cuts them off from routine services provided by government in "o asfalto"—the paved part of the city (Neate and Platt 2010, chapter 15).

To operate in this context and carve out a physical space and domain of action safe from violence and drug trafficking, Afro Reggae carries out intensive negotiations in multiple fields of power—an ongoing process that is not part of the group's public story. A leader of Afro Reggae who had himself been a trafficker explained the centrality of his trafficking experience to the organization: "To do my work for Afro Reggae, I need to have this side to me. In a way the work in itself is a curse and my knowledge is the instrument that I use to orient the whole institution. When everyone from Afro Reggae leaves the favela and goes home, I sit and talk to the traffickers because there are people there who trust me and tell me things that they wouldn't even tell the guy sitting next to them. I have to keep doing this, having conversations and swapping ideas" (Neate and Platt 2010, 42–43).

In working to diffuse explosive situations, Afro Reggae has acted as go-between with traffickers, at times using connections to the press, government officials, and international NGOs to mitigate conflicts, including arrests and gun battles. In one instance, Afro Reggae successfully pressed Amnesty International to issue a press release, which in turn brought about a police occupation that averted further escalation of violence. "The whole saga had exhausted us all and I felt it would be the last time we tried to mediate," José Junior recounted. "What amazes me is that, since then, we've carried on trying to mediate" (Neate and Platt 2010, 105). Mediation occurs not just through political connections but linguistically and culturally as well. In calling its first cultural center the Centro Afro Reggae Vigario Legal, a play on the name of the favela (Vigario Geral), Afro Reggae enacts a word play on the word "legal," which in Portuguese means both "legal" and "cool." As the group worked to create new forms of social interaction, safety, and citizenship from a base in this cultural center—an enduring reform that operates by a logic distinct from that of the world around it—AR "concentrates not only on resignifying the favela as 'lawful' to the outside, but also with presenting civil society as 'cool' within the favela . . . in that sense 'legal' brings together the double effort . . . that Afro Reggae must employ in Rio" (Arias and Collins 2010, 35).

In carrying out this "double effort," Afro Reggae navigates discursive and physical dangers simultaneously, as "movement leaders find themselves torn between obligations of substantially different scales" (Arias and Collins 2010, 8). In constructing its projects and presenting them publicly, Afro Reggae must act within the discursive framework provided by the state, foundations, and business. At the same time, by reworking these frameworks—as the group simultaneously reshapes borders around territory and the flow of arms to remap favelas on the ground—Afro Reggae creates and secures a new, alternative space with its own norms and rules. In the words of Desmond Arias and John Collins, groups like Afro Reggae "need to be able to maintain space between themselves and armed groups, while also building contacts with resourced state officials and civic organizations who would not want to have direct public contact with armed groups. Finally, civic groups also must maintain the support of their client population that are seeking patronage to survive and who have to deal directly with the various armed groups that operate in their community" (Arias and Collins 2010, 7). To carry out this balancing act, Afro Reggae manages "the plays of resignification and collusion that constitute political belonging" in

Brazil (Arias and Collins 2010, 6), where supposed equality of citizenship plays out amid legalized distinctions among citizens (Holston 2008, 6). Afro Reggae itself must work in areas that function at the intersection of the legal and the illegal (Arias and Collins 2010, 6). In so doing, AR leaders "are rights entrepreneurs—they are able to mobilize culture, identities, and contacts throughout the world to encourage a certain regime of rights" in the favela of Vigario (Arias and Collins 2010, 25).[4]

AFRO REGGAE EMBRACES A BUSINESS MODEL AND DRUG-TRAFFICKING STRUCTURE

AR fosters a new regime of rights both by adopting a business model and by mimicking the tight-knit structure and loyalty codes of drug-trafficking organizations. In Junior's words, "even though the traffic is criminal, a 'bad thing,' so to speak, it has some extremely positive aspects like loyalty, discipline and hierarchy" (Platt and Neate 2010, 30). In addition to borrowing from trafficking's internal practices, Afro Reggae borrows from trafficking's culture: "In a way, Afro-Reggae consciously mimics the organization of the traffic—our clothes, our structure, even our slang—because we want to mirror what attracts young people. But, of course, we try to show that you can make money and attain power through other means—through your creative abilities" (Platt and Neate 2010, 130).

Even more importantly in the evolution of Afro Reggae, and earlier than many social movements, AR adopted a business model in its language and practices.[5] Soon after the movement formed, Junior recounted, "I began to learn about what it meant to be an entrepreneur" (Platt and Neate 2010, 161). Junior speaks the language of foundations and business—he can pitch a proposal to the Ford Foundation, Petrobrás, or Vale do Rio Doce, the world's largest producer of iron ore. He is known for his frenetic energy and his ability to speak the language his interlocutors want to hear. He unabashedly accepts contributions from businesses in exchange for placing corporate logos on Afro Reggae swag and publicity and for use of AR's own logo on corporate products. In the words of Patrick Neate and Damian Platt (2010, 170), "The most important written representations for Afro Reggae's work are the numerous press articles they attract (in both local and international media) that allow them to develop a kind of 'cultural asset base' that, in partnership with all sorts of business, can be turned into money."

Junior told of a businessman who offered to "buy" the Afro Reggae Band for one year and pay AR three million *reais* for the publicity it would generate. Junior rejected the offer, but not because of an aversion to marketing the band as a product. Rather, he saw that the businessman wanted "to make something like seventeen million *reais*" from it, that he saw profit in the band (Platt and Neate 2010, 171). Afro Reggae's leaders also see that profit potential, and they have restructured the organization accordingly. In 2006, they made use of an innovative organizational form created by Brazilian legislation—an NGO that is able to generate profit and can bid to manage government-funded social programs.[6] Their new NGO, called Gas, not only manages the music production side of the organization but also sells services that Afro Reggae offers, such as workshops, lectures, and consultancies, to government agencies and private businesses (Platt and Neate 2010).

Junior observed that Ford Motors was a company that started a foundation and that Afro Reggae is a foundation that started a company. "Either we can work like any other NGO, depending on continued outside funding," he explained, "or we can create products of high artistic and cultural quality for commercial consumption and develop partnerships with companies, foundations, and government for mutual benefit" (Platt and Neate 2010, 172). As Neate and Platte (2010) put it, "They recognize that they have unusual products and skills on which they can capitalize in a commercial environment." Junior explained the arrangement by which Afro Reggae subgroups are going to be funded directly by Petrobrás and Vale do Rio Doce: "We're going to have a partnership with them that has never happened before. I can show you a graph of the visibility of AR in the media and then you'll understand the interest of such companies. We are going to use their company logo in our projects and we will get around nine hours of TV coverage this year. If they paid for this coverage commercially, it would cost them more than one hundred million *reais*. We give them what they want, but we make sure the last word in any decision making is ours" (Platt and Neate 2010).

Questioned about the risks of accepting, and becoming dependent upon, corporate sponsorship, Junior spoke of "the logic of quality and profit" (Platt and Neate 2010, 173). "I have to carry on in the real world," he explained. If he doesn't accept money from particular countries or businesses, "I'll just be stuck in my ghetto and I won't speak to anyone." As an actor in the market economy, Afro Reggae is a "social company," freely giving away the knowledge it has acquired "to other social projects in Brazil and around the world." In so doing, Junior said, "Afro Reggae will continue because we're on a road and there's no turning back. This is a capitalist world and we have to survive. Who knows? Maybe this is a quiet revolution, the revolution of the social capitalist movement." As a social company (*empresa social*), Afro Reggae can establish new forms of contact between the worlds of social movements and business. With a business-oriented staff, the group can experiment in synthesizing what one observer of the group characterized as "passion" and "management"—terms that when used together symbolize the transition from the realm of social movements to that of business, creating a "symbiosis without prejudices" (da Cunha 2008, 13) between the social movement and business worlds. With large resources from just a handful of businesses and banks, and with Afro Reggae's new staff, "all projects developed in the city, in the country, and abroad became entirely 'professional.' Furthermore, this know-how made it possible for the group to turn itself into a manager of other potential groups. In Rio, along with four other groups that were strongly inspired by Afro Reggae's social success, Afro Reggae forms 'F4,' a pool of four NGOs that rather than competing for the same resources, acts as a network in complementary projects with similar fund-raising strategies" (da Cunha 2008, 14).

AFRO REGGAE MIRRORS THE PATH OF LEFTIST ACTIVISTS IN RIO

Afro Reggae's business orientation complements and facilitates its complex balancing act in Vigario Geral and other favelas, where it constructs a terrain that is "legal" and "cool" among community residents, drug traffickers, and police. In embracing a business language and internal structure, accepting business funding, and forming partnerships with city governments, Afro Reggae rejects the confrontational stance that characterized the relationship between Brazilian social movements and the private sector from the 1970s through the 1990s. In establishing this pro-business and pro-partnership position, Afro Reggae has forged a path taken by many social movements and leftists activists in Brazil in the new millennium. Since the mid-1990s, these groups have migrated from forming autonomous and combative social movements—mobilizing in the streets and making demands on the state—to developing NGOs, projects, and partnerships that work within the system to secure resources and enact reform.

In Enduring Reform interviews, leftist activists in Rio, including Afro-Brazilians prominent in movements against racism, questioned but ultimately endorsed the within-the-system approaches, arguing that these approaches are the only game in town and that that they can be effective, even as they shape and limit social movement claims. João, who began his organizing during the period of military dictatorship, explained how the skills developed in fighting for the right to organize and in combatting racism as a structural problem became resources that would later be used for "advocacy" in dialogues with private businesses and government agencies. Thinking back on his own past of mobilizing against racism toward workers and for the rights of children, he now argues for the value of changing corporate cultures from within by offering symbolic awards for achievements in affirmative action.

Inês, who works for a monitoring and advocacy organization that does not accept private sector funds, underscored the agenda-shaping that occurs even when the private sector is not involved, in the way foundations and governments allocate resources. The institution in which she works, she said, "ends up restricted to a pre-established agenda, where certain questions have no place" (da Cunha 2008, 10). For Inês, particular terms and measures infiltrate the thinking of her coworkers as they implement innovative projects, "standardizing the language of politics in an increasingly professionalized universe" (da Cunha 2008, 11). Her clear-sightedness regarding the influence wielded by funders has led her to a position similar to that of João, one of openness rather than hesitation regarding support from business. "I am a super-revolutionary in this sense," Inês explained. "I think that you have to use private capital" (da Cunha 2008, 10).

Inês's colleague Paulo goes further. When he moved from an activist organization to the local office of a North American foundation, where he learned to write reports and grant proposals, Paulo explained, he "went over to the other side" (da Cunha 2008, 12), a stance he maintained when he returned to activism. As da Cunha (2008) puts it: "Contrary to Inês, Paulo does not resent the pragmatism of the agendas. He seems rather more critical of the radical projects of social transformation, which he learned about when he was a leftist militant. As he moved into the universe of NGOs and foundations, he learned to 'negotiate,' and this seemed to him to be the key element in the relationships between social movements and their counterparts. Beyond sharing resources, the relationships established between agencies and social movements produced an 'exchange' and mutual learning."

Mauro, who works for a cultural NGO, spoke in an even more positive fashion of the value of financial relationships with the private sector. Da Cunha (2008, 14) explains: "Based on actions like those developed by Afro Reggae and other groups, Mauro suggested, the difference between capital and social movements slowly diminishes. The professionalization of all of a group's members, direct and indirect beneficiaries of its social projects, allows the distribution of resources that were once concentrated in the hands of the leadership. People's lives in favelas, where the activities of many cultural NGO's occur, experience a transformation." As social movements develop these new relationships with business, foundations, and government, the movements encounter and internalize new languages and logics: of themes and criteria for funding; of prioritizing and assessment; and of dialogues, partnerships, and prizes. They grapple with and frequently adopt the language of "management." Those who see the downsides of this shift, like Inês, are nevertheless unashamed of its necessity. They know that some issues are more marketable than others, and they willingly move in those directions, producing what Inês called "the banalization of agendas and expectations" (da Cunha 2008, 11). As a result, "the change in strategy turns out to have been simultaneously a change in language. Social movements not only needed to survive with those resources, but also to work to secure them. Part of the work of militants has gradually become that of perfecting funding strategies and developing the capacity to access different 'agendas'" (da Cunha 2008, 18–19).

Businesspeople and other observers have noted this approach and wrestle with its implications for Afro Reggae. A high-level executive in a Brazilian company commented on the connection between AR shows and the group's earnings: "They have a whole publicity campaign, even [stating] that everything will be reinvested to allow the group to continue with the workshops, to generate more funds to carry on with the projects" (Ossowicki 2008, 10). Functioning like a business, she observed, does not mean operating by a commercial logic alone: "This is a band, but not a commercial band. It's a band with a purpose, with a specific project" (Ossowicki 2008, 10). Businesspeople praise Afro Reggae's growth and the transformation to a business model that occurred in the 2000s. Most businesspeople perceived these changes as positive, relating them to the group's new international relationships, which are linked to shows and tours abroad as well as to partnerships and fund-raising outside Brazil (Ossowicki 2008, 11–12).

In contrast, a high-level executive in a transnational company identified the downside of these relationships: "There's an intermixing between NGOs and corporations quite common nowadays, and the first thing that comes to my mind is questioning the authenticity and the real purpose of these institutions" (Ossowicki 2008, 14). This executive suggested that "the growing commercialization of Afro Reggae's practices was expressed both in a change in size and in the transformation of their actions: it diverted the attention previously given to the communities to profit-seeking. This could be seen in the commercialization of social projects in expensive theaters for rich audiences, so that social actions would in fact occur too far from the communities that should be the focus of the projects" (Ossowicki 2008, 15).

João, the activist who moved from militancy against the dictatorship to advocacy for affirmative action, does not see this commercialization in a negative light. Some of Afro Reggae's leaders, he explained, learned to negotiate with foundations and private institutions when they worked with the organization he had founded. After that, however, Afro Reggae and his own organization pursued different paths, in part because of the extent to which the private sector became interested in funding Afro Reggae (da Cunha 2008, 7). As da Cunha (2008, 14-15) has observed, "Politics and professionalism, in João and Paulo's accounts, and passion and management, in Mauro's words, seemed to produce a particular exchange of language and practices. Mauro is proud to see this kind of symbiosis without prejudice [between social movements and business]. . . . Young people engaged in projects, when not professionally involved, took home resources and new knowledge. The notion of exchange, in Mauro's interpretation, seems to be more directly linked to the transfer of resources."

SUCCESS AND THE LIMITS OF BROADER CHANGE

Afro Reggae's success in securing financial resources and running itself like a business enables its growth and brings approval from businesspeople and the media. Afro Reggae is an enduring reform because it establishes a new set of practices and values—based on rights and citizenship—at a nodal point of Brazil's "violent democracy" (Arias and Goldstein 2010). In the very favelas where the state and elected officials coproduce crime and insecurity with traffickers, local community leaders, and police, Afro Reggae produces kids who play music, look other people in the eye, know that they have rights, and reject the boundary between favela and outside. Afro Reggae also produces the outlines of a fresh relationship with the police, as AR has traveled to another state to run percussion workshops for police there. In those workshops, the participants discussed the experiences that young people in favelas have with the police and what it is like for the police to patrol inside the favelas (Ramos 2006, 426-27). After the percussion training, a group of policemen appeared with the Afro Reggae Band on television.

While producing these landmark innovations, Afro Reggae potentially circumscribes the deepening of reform through its business approach, along with the narrative it promotes in the media and the images it markets in its products. Scholarly and journalistic accounts alike have praised Afro Reggae's novel programs and suggest the possibility or even likelihood of ripple effects, but provide no empirical work on these links. In contrast, the Enduring Reform Project interviews show that by marketing itself through conventional images of favelas as poor and crime-ridden, with Afro Reggae providing an identity and a way out through culture, the group has obscured the more complex dynamics of favela life. The responses of businesspeople indicate that the learning process instigated by Afro Reggae's presence—by the talent and agency it makes visible and the recognition it elicits—does not translate into businesspeople's thinking politically or structurally about improving conditions of exclusion and deprivation in Rio.

The key media products of Afro Reggae's self-presentation suggest the dynamics by which this simultaneous opening and self-limiting may occur. For example, in the award-winning documentary *Favela Rising* (2005), produced with AR's support and assistance, Vigario Geral is presented as a bleak and gun-filled place. The grainy, saturated coloring of the film precludes any sense of ordinary people going about their lives. Vigario's physical geography is misrepresented, portrayed from the film's opening scene as a series of hillsides overflowing with shacks, in conformity with conventional picturesque images of Rio's favelas, while in reality Vigario is flat, one of a succession of level shantytowns far from the city center and out of sight. Afro Reggae's leadership is similarly misrepresented in the film, with José Junior's pivotal role—as outsider and cultural dynamo who speaks alternately the language of the street and of the traffickers, of foundations and entrepreneurs—written out and replaced with that of Anderson Sá, the earnest and thoughtful Vigario resident and survivor of the 1993 massacre. Similarly absent from *Favela Rising* is Marcia, the lone woman among Afro Reggae's original leadership, who in an interview spoke of nurturance at the core of AR's success and mission.

Favela Rising's portraits of Vigario, as a hillside zone of crisis where every child is a potential victim of the drug traffickers, suggest, like most media coverage, that the solution to favela violence is Afro Reggae, a hip group that can lure kids from trafficking and provide them with another path through and out of the favela. While subversive to a point, this view offers no vision or steps toward a broader reshaping of the relationships between favelas and the outside or re-creation of life within the favelas. The tough love excludes Marcia's nurturing, and Anderson's earnest solidity excludes Junior's multilingual trickster visions, which under his deft guidance have become part of a complex reality in Vigario Geral and other favelas where AR works. Afro Reggae's self-portrait does not admit into the mix yet other experiences of favela life, such as the economic expansion and dynamism occurring in some favelas, built on residents' rootedness in and commitment to their neighborhoods (Neuwirth 2004, chapter 1), or the intricate economic connections between favelas and the city's more prosperous regions (Perlman 2010), which if reconfigured could create an underpinning for economic security within favelas themselves.

What, for example, might economic and political solutions to the poverty and violence of Vigario look like, apart from the worthy bringing in of private sector and foundation funding and the construction of a culture of citizenship? What might citizens work to reconfigure? Afro Reggae's portrait of favela life writes out the politics that might sustain police reform (Leeds 2007), and it writes out the ability of coalitions of NGOs, government officials, and police to lower levels of violence. Such a coalition indeed lowered levels of violence in Vigario dramatically between 1996 and 2000 (Arias 2006, chapter 5).

In *Culture Is Our Weapon* (Neate and Platt 2010), a book rich in description and documentation, produced together with Afro Reggae, the need to seduce kids away from pervasive violence is highlighted, rather than the possibility of successful political coalitions to combat violence. The book provides a dramatic and insightful view into the lives of drug traffickers in Vigario and the adjacent Parada de Lucas favela through extensive interviews with traffickers who have joined Afro Reggae. However, those are the only interviews of participants the book provides. By focusing on traffickers who have switched sides, Neate and Platte have left out the story of the daily lives of favela residents who work two jobs, travel hours to get to and from their places of employment, expand their houses, and send their kids to school. These ordinary residents of favelas have made family and neighborhood life the center of their social activities (Wheeler 2002).

By fostering an individualist and market subjectivity in a zone of violence, Afro Reggae successfully performs a spectacular balancing act, bringing resources into favelas and giving kids a fresh view of themselves as well as a view out. "Nonetheless," as Arias and Collins (2010, 36) have observed, "the effort to be both 'lawful' and 'cool' in part ties Afro Reggae's hands." The group must work with state officials and does not advocate open confrontations. It cannot move explicitly against traffickers, since that would put members in danger and make the group "uncool" in the favela. "Thus Afro Reggae's forms of engagement can go far in helping young people who participate in their programs, but they are limited" (Arias and Collins 2010, 36).

BUSINESSPEOPLE WASH THEIR HANDS OF THE MATTER

These limits come full circle when businesspeople shift their view from the successes of Afro Reggae to the need for change in the entrenched patterns of poverty, exclusion, trafficking, and violence that characterize Rio de Janeiro. Businesspeople see Afro Reggae as acting nobly and effectively to improve the lives of a small number of young people—bringing citizenship through culture. However, AR's stylized portrait of favela reality, reproduced by the media and accepted by businesspeople, suggests no way of reconceptualizing the city's economy and politics or of mobilizing to bring about a reconceived urban space. Instead, businesspeople insist that the broad problems of poverty and violence in Rio de Janeiro are the responsibility of the state, but that the state is incapable of addressing them.

Businesspeople explain their own and the city's experiences with violence through a process of distinction-making and mapping. All of the businesspeople interviewed defined violence as Rio de Janeiro's main problem, although poverty, social inequalities, and the poor quality of public services were also mentioned, in vaguer terms and without concrete examples. They speak of Rio as a city plagued by violence and chaos, widespread political neglect, and lack of state action. This context was presented in starkly pessimistic terms as a "critical moment," a process of "social degradation," a situation of "social chaos," and a "war" that increasingly affects all sectors of the city's population. Businesspeople cited clashes between drug traffickers and police, as well as militia actions and massacres in the favelas and the city's outskirts, as recurrent and frightening phenomena, but at the same time as distant from their own daily lives—things they became aware of only through the media. Businesspeople emphasized the differences between the insecurity they themselves feel and the violence that occurs in parts of the city where they don't generally go or that they do not know personally. One project manager interviewed defined social exclusion as something that affects the whole society. However, he said that when he complains about the growing violence, he is complaining about middle-class violence and that this same middle class always has ways of protecting itself by hiring private security and other services. Other businesspeople explained that "these are not issues I can discuss" or "I have no contact [with this reality], I don't go to other parts of the city" or "it's not on my doorstep, it's very far from my reality."

Although they experience it differently from those who live in the favelas, businesspeople sense violence and its effects getting closer. They described this in terms of fear and insecurity, exemplified by the growing number of homeless people, the risk of robberies, burglaries, kidnappings, and street shootings, and the continual expansion of the favelas. Many interviewees described personal strategies to deal with the surrounding situation: avoiding exposure and calling attention in the streets, not venturing through neighborhoods and areas considered violent, changing one's routine, and so on. All the interviewees mentioned some personal experience of violence. These businesspeople placed the responsibility for increasing levels of violence on the deficiencies and inabilities of the state and the political system, and they offered pessimistic assessments of public policy. Despite the fact that the Brazilian economy has grown—something businesspeople attribute to the market economy—and the deepest poverty has diminished, they describe the country's overall situation as getting worse. Several of the interviewees said they had voted for the Workers' Party (Partido dos Trabalhadores, PT) in 2002 and 2008, believing that under President Lula's administration the country would improve in such areas of social inequality as poverty, violence, education, and public health. However, they expressed disappointment with the current political scenario and with the PT itself, suggesting that political parties no longer have visions or programs that reflect an idea of how society should be organized. Lack of competent management and corruption were also mentioned as factors that make it impossible to develop a more egalitarian and democratic society.

It was in this context of distrust (defined as "zero credibility in politicians" by one of the interviewees) in political solutions for social problems, particularly violence, that businesspeople evaluated NGOs in general and Afro Reggae's activities in particular. They underscored that the responsibility for effective social change lies with the state and politicians and that NGOs and socially responsible business projects served as potential collaborators. But these businesspeople believe that without long-term public policies—whose effectiveness would depend on reforms in the electoral system and in how government functions—nothing will change. One interviewee who took a positive view of Afro Reggae's activities, and hoped the group's activities would provoke some kind of local transformation, admitted nonetheless that he was "totally skeptical" regarding the possibility of broad social change. Another businessman explained that companies and NGOs he considers "serious" play their part as best they can, but that the real responsibility lies with the state. This conclusion was repeated in different ways by all interviewees.

Their own involvement—and sense of responsibility—ends with financial contributions to Afro Reggae and other NGOs, along with programs of corporate social responsibility. The project manager mentioned earlier defined the roles of the state and NGOs as a division of labor, where the first should take care of certain basic services and the second, with their more specific knowledge, would have other functions. Even so, he believed the state would have to be the "coordinator" of this division of labor, "the same way the central bank is the coordinator of the private credit sector." This division of labor was also described with regard to the role of companies. Several of the businesspeople agreed with the executive of a transnational company in prioritizing "in-house" corporate social responsibility initiatives. Like Afro Reggae, these initiatives would reflect business imagery and language: "There is great concern with how corporations and people could somehow get involved. But what one ends up trying is a more in-house solution, in the sense of taking advantage of the business image and the possibilities the business has of building something that can relate to what we, as a corporation, believe. . . . I think that businesses tend to contribute in a more personalized way . . . it will either be something that has to do with the workers . . . or something that has to do with the business."

In the context of Rio de Janeiro, businesspeople do not believe that Afro Reggae and other NGOs promote deep transformations and change society. This is a task, they said over and over again in our interviews, for which the state is responsible and that only the state can accomplish. Yet they insisted categorically that the Brazilian state is incapable of doing this. Businesspeople do believe that Afro Reggae could play a role with localized and immediate impact, just as they perceive themselves as fulfilling their own role as agents of the market economy, generating jobs and economic growth. While businesspeople accept and approve of Afro Reggae's activities, they do not think the group can improve social conditions generally, do not perceive themselves as having any responsibility beyond the level of the firm, and see no prospects for effective government action. Afro Reggae's own self-presentation in a business language, along with its representations of favelas as zones of desperation to be rescued by Afro Reggae, do little to disrupt this analysis.

NOTES

This chapter, conceptualized and largely written by Jeffrey W. Rubin, has a complex authorship that represents the strengths, drawbacks, and longtime horizons of collaborative research. The introductory sections on Afro Reggae were cowritten by Jeffrey Rubin and Emma Sokoloff-Rubin, and the quotations in this section are based on interviews conducted by Jeffrey Rubin in Vigario Geral and downtown Rio in 1997, 2001, and 2002. As part of the Enduring Reform Project, interviews with businesspeople were carried out by Martin Ossowicki (at the time a graduate student in social anthropology, Museu Nacional, Universidade Federal do Rio de Janeiro) and with leftist activists by Olivia da Cunha (professor, Museu

Nacional, Universidade Federal do Rio de Janeiro) in 2008. Both Ossowicki and da Cunha, for different reasons, left the project after writing their Enduring Reform research reports in 2008. The section of this chapter titled "Afro Reggae Mirrors the Path of Leftist Activists in Rio" draws on da Cunha's research report. All activists discussed in this section are referred to by pseudonyms in the text. Ossowicki's research report, which analyzed his interviews with businesspeople about Afro Reggae, provides the text for the sections on business, which have been translated from the original Portuguese by Clarissa Becker and edited only slightly in preparing this chapter.

1. The phrase "divided city" comes from Brazilian journalist Zuenir Ventura (1994), whose book *Cidade Partida* (The divided city) brought the explosive situation in Vigario Geral to public attention.

2. In the favelas of Vigario and Parada de Lucas, key gun battles took the course they did because of the presence or absence of police affiliated with one or the other of the favela gangs (Neate and Platt 2010, 142).

3. Neate and Platt 2010, 119–20, 125–26. On the relationship between instilling fear and selling security, see also Laura Roush's (2009) dissertation on neighborhood groups in Mexico City.

4. Arias and Collins (2010) are referring to the music group Bem Aventurados, in Rocinha in Salvador, but the point applies to Afro Reggae as well.

5. Ramos (2006, 423) has described the "market-oriented" stance of a range of projects in the favelas of Brazilian cities that are based on artistic and cultural activities. She describes their focus on individual careers and life histories, so that "the media, success, and fame are understood as ingredients of political militancy."

6. They had long had Afro Reggae Artistic Productions Limited, a company that managed the concerts and the work of the main band, but initially this sat beneath Afro Reggae, the NGO, which runs the social programs (Neate and Platt 2010, 171).

REFERENCES

Arias, E. 2006. *Drugs and Democracy in Rio: Trafficking, Social Networks, and Public Security*. Chapel Hill: University of North Carolina Press.

Arias, E., and J. Collins. 2010. "Searching for Security." Unpublished manuscript.

Arias, E., and D. Goldstein. 2010. "Violent Pluralism: Understanding the New Democracies of Latin America." In *Violent Democracies in Latin America,* edited by E. Arias and D. Goldstein. Durham: Duke University Press.

Carvalho Suarez, M., and L. Casotti. 2009. "Marketing Orientation in the Third Sector: The Art of Afro Reggae." *Latin American Business Review* 10: 217–36.

Gomes da Cunha, O. 1998. "Black Movements and the 'Politics of Identity' in Brazil." In *Culture of Politics, Politics of Cultures: Re-visioning Latin American Social Movements,* edited by A. Alvarez, E. Dagnino, and A. Escobar. Boulder: Westview Press.

Holston, J. 2008. *Insurgent Citizenship: Disjunctions of Democracy and Modernity in Brazil.* Princeton: Princeton University Press.

Junior, J. 2003. *Da Favela Para o Mundo*. Rio de Janeiro: Aeroplano Editora e Consultoria Ltda.

Leeds, E. 2007. "Serving States and Serving Citizens: Halting Steps towards Police Reform in Brazil and Implications for Donor Intervention." *Policing and Society* 17 (1): 21–37.

Neate, P., and D. Platt. 2010. *Culture Is Our Weapon: Making Music and Changing Lives in Rio de Janeiro*. New York: Penguin.

Neuwirth, R. 2004. *Shadow Cities: A Billion Squatters, a New Urban World*. New York: Routledge.

Ossowicki, M. 2008. "Research Report: Enduring Reform Project." Prepared for project conference in Porto Alegre. November 21–25.

Perlman, J. 2010. *Favela: Four Decades of Living on the Edge in Rio de Janeiro*. Oxford: Oxford University Press.

Ramos, S. 2006. "Brazilian Responses to Violence and New Forms of Mediation: The Case of the Grupo Cultural Afroreggae and the Experience of the Project 'Youth and the Police.'" *Ciência y Saúde Coletiva* 11 (2): 419–28.

Roush, L. 2009. "The Language of 'Crisis' and the Uses of Indefinition in Mexico City." PhD dissertation, New School for Social Research. Chapter 5, "'Diccionario Diabólico': Clandestine Intermediation and Mass Mediation."

Ventura, Z. 1994. *Cidade Partida*. São Paulo: Companhia das Letras.

Wheeler, J. 2002. "Emerging Democracies and Markets: Family and Community in Rio de Janeiro's Favelas." Unpublished manuscript.

Yudice, G. 2003. *The Expediency of Culture: Uses of Culture in the Global Era*. Durham: Duke University Press.

Zimbalist, J., and M. Mochary, directors and producers. 2005. *Favela Rising*. Sidetrack Films and VOY Pictures.

8

BUSINESS RESPONSES TO PROGRESSIVE ACTIVISM IN TWENTY-FIRST-CENTURY LATIN AMERICA

Vivienne Bennett and Jeffrey W. Rubin

SINCE THE 1980s, Latin America has undergone a political sea change, moving from authoritarian, dictatorial, and one-party systems to a politics of continuing and deepening democracy with differing trajectories in each country. Supporters of democracy before and during the transitions have envisioned not only credible electoral competition but processes of citizenship, policy making, and economic development that would ensure and deepen basic rights and grapple with persistent problems like violence, lack of services, economic and cultural exclusion, and inequality. During the same period, most Latin American economies moved from policies of protectionism and strong government regulation, embodied by a mid-twentieth-century emphasis on import substitution, to a neoliberal model based on trade liberalization, privatization, and increased foreign investment.

However, across the globe, where the neoliberal model has been implemented, it has generally failed to close the gap between rich and poor, and has fostered growth by protecting investors and leaving the majority vulnerable to cyclical economic downturns. Latin America is no exception and has remained the most unequal region into the twenty-first century (Kim 2013), such that the new normal is one of declining poverty accompanied by persistent inequality.

In 2009, in Brazil, Chile, and Mexico, which combined have nearly 70 percent of Latin America's population and GDP, the richest 10 percent of the population held an average of 42 percent of national income (Castañeda 2011). At the same time, levels of violence have skyrocketed, with unprecedented brutality related to gangs, drug trafficking, and violent crime, complemented by the absence of adequate state administrative and policing capacities (Arias and Goldstein 2010). Highly unequal in terms of distribution of wealth and resources, lacking basic security in daily life, but increasingly democratic in terms of electoral procedures and some civil liberties, Latin America is in a new phase of development.

Throughout the twentieth century, poor Latin Americans engaged in struggles to improve their daily lives. From rural land invasions by peasants to squatter settlements by the urban poor, from street blockades to mobilizations for water to the base communities of liberation theology, ordinary people in Latin America have organized to secure basic needs. Social movements and projects for progressive change have exhibited considerable range and creativity in the half-century following World War II, including efforts to forge unprecedented relationships among social movements, mobilized citizenries, and governments. During most of the twentieth century, however, those who organized for progressive change did so at great risk to themselves, exposed as they were to the responses of governments that did not hesitate to use violence and repression with impunity. Leaders of movements small and large were threatened, roughed up, jailed, tortured, disappeared, or killed. Businesspeople and business associations routinely supported this government repression of popular groups in the name of economic interest and what they argued was economic necessity. Even in those rare cases where businesspeople expressed initial openness to reform—for example, as part of midcentury "populist" coalitions—they reverted quickly to an underlying hostility to progressive change (Brennan 1998, Hamilton 1982, Sáenz 1992, and Schneider 2004).[1] The dynamics of the Cold War allowed them to take this position boldly and with impunity.[2]

However, as Ann Helwege has shown in her chapter for this book, although the decades from 1940 to 2000 saw substantial economic growth and development in many Latin American countries, the period was not a uniformly good one for business elites. In contrast to scholarly and popular assumptions that businesspeople secured their economic interests by supporting political repression, Helwege argues that the policies they got—during periods of import substitution industrialization, heterodox economic responses to crisis, and neoliberal restructuring alike—did not generally serve them economically in a consistent manner. Economic crisis recurred, and repression created costly instability. Helwege's chapter shows that since the transitions to democracy, businesspeople have begun to recognize this mixed record of the authoritarian past, as they discern some of the benefits of economic policies promoted by the region's democratic governments.

As electoral democracy proceeded, Latin American social movements changed, in terms of internal dynamics, goals, and strategies (Rubin 2011). As Wendy Wolford shows in chapter 2 of this volume, they shifted from promoting revolutionary demands for overthrow of the state and capitalism to mobilizing around alternative forms of property relations, development, and political voice within democratic systems, at the same time developing a more diverse and at times more democratic set of internal practices. Many activists have moved from the streets into the institutions, although others remain in the streets, mobilizing and protesting in old ways as well as in more egalitarian and horizontal new ones (Sitrin 2012 and Alvarez et al. forthcoming). Despite the ravages of neoliberalism for much of the population—and as democratic theory would predict—spaces have been forged where progressive reforms have occurred and endured, reforms that have improved poor people's economic status, political voice, and sense of dignity and citizenship.

Concerned with whether and in what ways these reforms will endure and perhaps expand to new and different spaces within existing states and markets, the Enduring Reform Project asks how businesspeople—who supported the repression of reformist projects in the past—have responded to working, successful progressive reforms today. By interviewing both activists and businesspeople, our research adds new material and novel dimensions to the existing literature on recuperated factories, participatory budgeting, indigenous self-reliance, the Afro Reggae Cultural Group, and three-for-one remittance programs. All five of these cases led to positive outcomes that were feasible within the parameters of the existing market system and the forms of democratic politics in their respective countries. None of these cases are revolutionary in nature or promote a take-over of the state. All represent combinations of ideas, people, and activism that grew out of varying alliances among social movements, civil society organizations, NGOs, and governments. All found ways to work within the system to make demonstrable improvements in poor people's lives, whether through a stronger sense of cultural identity and dignity, enhanced control over resources that are central to poor people's lives, or greater political voice and more effective citizenship.

In the preceding chapters, we hear businesspeople speak. One of the hallmarks of the Enduring Reform Project was the open-ended interviews in which businesspeople reflected on their knowledge and experience with respect to

the reform projects in their regions. In all five cases, businesspeople responded
to progressive reforms in more tolerant and less repressive ways than they
would likely have employed before the 1980s. In Zacatecas, local entrepreneurs,
multiple levels of government, and migrants now cooperate in one of Mexico's
most transparent and uncorrupt public programs, thanks to the work initiated
and controlled by the heretofore invisible migrants themselves. In the highlands of Chiapas, the city's ladino elite has shifted from a centuries-old position
of overt racism and hostility regarding the presence of Maya in the city to new
forms of cultural and economic accommodation.

In Buenos Aires, Argentina, businesspeople and bankers who overcame the
stigma of association with the working class to continue their business dealings
with the worker-owned factories have changed their views regarding the identity of workers. They have come to recognize workers' competence and accord
them dignity in ways that were unthinkable in the past.In a move that further
enabled these changing relations, the city government supported the worker-
owned factory initiative by creating the legal framework for the transformation from privately owned bankrupt firms to worker-owned cooperatives, thus
establishing an institutional commitment to innovative forms of ownership and
use of economic resources.

In Rio de Janeiro, the private sector funds monthly concerts in the city's
favelas and city parks, hosting Afro Reggae's bands together with national stars
while bringing the cultural group to the attention of city residents. Private
sector financial support and praise for Afro Reggae has raised the group's profile
and budget, as businesses affix the group's logo to corporate publicity. Meanwhile, in Porto Alegre, the private sector has struggled to accept the empowerment that participatory budgeting has brought to the city's poor residents and
seeks to replace it with a model based on corporate social responsibility.

This highly summative overview of business responses to the progressive
reforms in the five case studies suggests a remarkable change regarding the
extent of tolerance for such reforms in Latin America today. Factory workers
taking over bankrupt factories in Argentina in the past? Impossible to imagine.
Indigenous Maya outnumbering ladinos as residents of San Cristóbal de Las
Casas? Unthinkable for the Maya and nightmarish for the ladinos even thirty
years ago. Poor slum dwellers deciding on a portion of the municipal budget
in Porto Alegre anytime before 1989? Out of the question. In all of our case
locations, elite influence over resources, policy, and politics until the 1980s
was so pervasive that any project not perceived by political and economic
elites to be in their own interest would likely face state or private repression.
This does not mean that all oppositional activities were repressed, but rather
that repression was part of the standard arsenal of responses that could be

used by most Latin American governments in the twentieth century with the support of business elites. In striking contrast, today's democratic context in Latin America presses businesspeople to endure, accept, and at times promote progressive change in unprecedented ways, even as they may also seek to channel or outmaneuver it.

CONCLUSIONS OF OUR RESEARCH

Four Points

The cases examined in this book illustrate a range of progressive reform projects, from worker-run factories to participatory budgeting, and of business responses, which vary from deep recognition to hostile outmaneuvering. In addition to analyzing the histories and outcomes of these cases, our research suggests four conclusions regarding the interaction between business and progressive reform in Latin America's twenty-first-century democracies. First, the cases in this book demonstrate that business responses to progressive reform do not follow directly, or even primarily, from economic interests narrowly defined, but from a wider set of motivations and a more complex calculus of interests. How businesspeople interpret reform projects, understand their own interests, and respond to reform is shaped by the timing and process of reform efforts and the contexts in which they take place, as well as by cultural understandings of who is involved in these efforts and what is at stake. Factors that influence these cultural understandings on the part of businesspeople include whether and how a business language is used by the reform project, how the reform becomes visible to businesspeople and the direct experience they have with it (including whether and how they are "invited"), how the reform is characterized by the media, and whether there are elements of shock, surprise, and/or crisis associated with the reform.

Second, in addition to the centrality of culture and interpretation to shaping the course of business responses to progressive reform, we have found, counterintuitively, that stable and deepening democracy does not necessarily make positive responses more likely. Rather, our cases suggest that while democratic contexts are essential for the reforms we describe to take root, businesspeople may be more likely to respond positively over time to progressive reform initiatives that occur in situations of crisis. Third, the cases examined suggest that reform projects with redistributive economic goals may be more acceptable to businesspeople than reforms that empower excluded groups politically, even (and indeed especially) when such empowerment occurs through transparent democratic procedures.

Fourth, our research suggests that new bargains being forged today are characterized by an exchange of acceptance of market structures by activists for recognition of the citizenship and human dignity of marginalized people by businesspeople. Being party to such an exchange is contingent and risky on both sides, as activists and excluded groups risk buying into a system that impoverishes them and limits their political room for maneuver, while businesspeople risk empowering people whose long-term goals may include significant transformation of the economic and cultural status quo. This fragile exchange of market acceptance for recognition, we argue, is the next stage of democratic deepening in today's Latin America—a potential pathway to expanded citizenship and well-being.

UNDERSTANDING THESE FOUR POINTS

Our research shows that contrary to assumptions that private property is inviolate in the eyes of businesspeople, their responses to property seizures, like responses to other reformist actions, depend on interpretation. In Buenos Aires, the workers who seized private factories illegally and claimed control over factory production achieved the highest degree of recognition and legitimacy from local businesspeople among all of our cases. This is due to how these businesspeople understood the context in which the factory seizures occurred and how they interpreted their own experiences doing business with such factories. The key to understanding the possibilities for civil society–based projects in democracies thus lies not only with political institutions and the seemingly objective economic interests of businesspeople, but also in the local histories of cultural perceptions and experiences with regard to those interests and institutions and how they play out in the course of reform initiatives.

Several of the cases examined here identify the centrality of *moments of surprise or shock* in stimulating new ways of thinking and establishing different rules on the ground. The Zapatista uprising in Chiapas challenged elite perceptions of Indians and their capacities. The uprising also influenced elite responses to Maya self-help projects in San Cristóbal's *colonias* and Maya electoral strategies citywide. In Buenos Aires, when workers took over bankrupt factories, businesspeople were stunned. The shock provoked by the transformed human and infrastructural landscape then contributed to openness to novel production partnerships.

In Porto Alegre, Rio de Janeiro, and Zacatecas, reforms changed *the ways in which marginalized people became visible*, thereby prompting businesspeople to reconceptualize whom the people involved in reformist initiatives were and how they fit in the social landscape. In Zacatecas, poor migrants moved from invisibility, in terms of economic clout and identity, to recognition and even prominence as transnational citizens who contribute significant economic resources to their hometowns. In Porto Alegre, publicity about participatory budgeting meetings and investment decisions put poor *vilas* on the elite radar screen, while in Rio, the megashows organized by Afro Reggae once a month in different parts of the city brought the performers from the favelas and thus favelas themselves into the media spotlight. In each case, the presence of previously excluded groups in the public sphere made what were previously "open secrets" about the existence of poverty and deprivation into publicly acknowledged facts.

Even the "fact" of poverty is open to interpretation. *Media representations of reform* played a key role in the process of visibility and reconceptualization, vilifying participatory budgeting in Porto Alegre and garnering praise for the three-for-one remittance program in Zacatecas with equal effectiveness. In the former, the press asserted the incompetence of the poor and the manipulation of participatory budgeting by the Workers' Party as incontrovertible facts, with reckless disregard for considerable evidence to the contrary. In the case of three-for-one, in contrast, the migrants from Zacatecas, seen initially as worthless laborers who left impoverished towns of women, children, and the elderly in their wake, were reconfigured in newspapers as admirable transnational citizens, pooling their savings to contribute to the infrastructure and productive economies of their hometowns.

Businesspeople's subjective experiences of themselves being included or excluded from reform processes—of *whether and how they were "invited" to reform*—simultaneously reflected and shaped their positions toward progressive reform in their cities. Porto Alegre businesspeople's acute and emotion-laden claim that they hadn't been invited to participatory budgeting—which functioned through well-publicized and open meetings—played a central role in their opposition to the project. In contrast, in Zacatecas, businesspeople's identification with migrants as businesspeople and their sense of involvement in the process of resource allocation fortified their embrace of the three-for-one program and its expansion to include private sector contributions to new productive projects in a four-by-one arrangement.

The languages in which reform initiatives are described shape the acceptability of reform and, in turn, its prospects for enduring and deepening. The presence or absence of "business language" is particularly key in this regard. In

Zacatecas, the casting of three-for-one in a business language made it acceptable and intelligible to nonmigrant businesspeople. Afro Reggae's use of a business- and NGO-inflected language made it acceptable to Rio's elite business community but also functioned to shape and limit the program's capacity to ameliorate economic deprivation and political exclusion in the favelas. Meanwhile, in Porto Alegre, framing participatory budgeting in a political language of democratic procedure and grassroots empowerment engendered private sector hostility.

Our findings of the centrality of surprise, visibility, media representation, experiences of invitation and inclusion, and contestation over language in shaping the course of progressive reform demonstrate the centrality of culture and representation in explaining constraints and opportunities for within-the-system progressive reform. The case studies demonstrate that businesspeople neither adopt a unified stance as a group nor hold internally coherent positions; instead, they maintain fragmented and inconsistent worldviews that provide room for maneuver for reform initiatives. This room for maneuver reflects the current democratic context and the counterintuitive possibilities it offers. In democracies, as Albert Hirschman suggested in his path-breaking *Journeys toward Progress* (1968) a half-century ago (during another period of increasing political democracy), crisis and threat may foster dialogue and innovation rather than subvert it. This is what happens, to small but discernible degrees, in the Enduring Reform cases. The relative security provided by enduring democracy with regard to basic economic and political arrangements can prevent crisis from escalating to polarization, enabling key actors to consider more productive, negotiated alternatives.

Economic disaster in Argentina, for example, enables some businesspeople to understand their relationship to workers differently. Indigenous rebellion in the San Cristóbal region presses elites to reconsider their past racist practices and, in the process, their beliefs about Indians and citizenship. In these cases, crisis forecloses the possibility of some conventional, repressive responses to reform and at the same time opens the door to unconventional thinking. Conversely, the absence of threat or crisis for the private sectors of Porto Alegre and Rio appears to facilitate the perpetuation of long-held prejudices and assumptions on the part of elites there, as businesspeople ignore the agency and competence of shantytown residents (in Porto Alegre) and declare the state's responsibility for grappling with problems of poverty and violence while also proclaiming the state's inability to do so (in Rio).

Brazil's relatively stable and successful trajectory in recent years, in which economic growth and deepening political democracy have been mutually rein-forcing, contrasts with business responses to reform in Porto Alegre and Rio, which are the most negative and among the most mixed, respectively, among the cases examined in this book. Conversely, greater unevenness in democratic practices at the national level and a far greater sense of uncertainty or instability, as is the case in Mexico and Argentina, have not precluded notable local progressive reform successes. This seemingly paradoxical conclusion may result from a degree of complacency that accompanies the functioning of democratic institutions at the national level. In Porto Alegre and Rio during the period we study, businesspeople assumed that the national government would take care of social welfare issues and/or is the only appropriate location for such concerns to be addressed. This enabled them to ignore critical local issues of poverty and exclusion or to wash their hands of them, whether or not they believed the national government is capable of dealing with the problem or was attempting to do so.

Systemic crisis and economic threat have not historically prompted elites to countenance progressive reform in Latin America, and expanding democracy at the national level might be expected to increase business openness to reform regionally. Our paradoxical conclusion—that relatively stable democracy may inhibit business openness to reform and crisis promote it—reflects the disjuncture between national and regional systems of power, in which hegemony is constructed and contested on multiple geographic levels and social and cultural arenas, as work on Mexico has notably shown (Joseph and Nugent 1994, Rubin 1997, and Gillingham and Smith 2014). In order to understand the bargains and power relations on which national political arrangements rest, we must focus on subnational dynamics of reform.

In Latin America today, as businesspeople and governments navigate complex global economic relations, economic issues have proven to be disaggregable and negotiable, at least in contexts where goals of "socialism" are off the table. That is what occurred as businesspeople negotiated with worker-run factories in Buenos Aires and as businesspeople in Zacatecas accommodated to new sources of funding for public works projects and innovative forms of administration of those projects. In contrast, proposals that democratize political relations continue to raise the specter of a complete reversal of power relations. As businesspeople in Porto Alegre stated candidly, they can be outvoted in participatory budgeting meetings. This realization and the fear that elites construct around it account for businesspeople's uniform hostility to participatory budgeting and their tenacious and successful efforts to overturn it. At the local level, indications that democracy is growing, as in San Cristóbal, or that it is robust and empowering, as in Porto Alegre, promote elites in these cities to try to outmaneuver or limit empowering and democratic political reforms.

It is in this context that the exchange of acceptance of market structures by activists for recognition of the citizenship and human dignity of marginalized people by businesspeople provides a pathway forward for enduring reform. This fragile exchange of market acceptance for recognition permits experimental arrangements to persist and, potentially, expand, despite unease among businesspeople about democratic empowerment. In Buenos Aires, the fact that workers in recuperated factories sought to function within market norms, rather than change them, created the context in which some businesspeople could accord recognition to workers. This in turn facilitated the creation of institutional and legal norms on the one hand and on-the-ground practices at the level of both the worker-owned factories and the companies that did business with them on the other, which deepened workers' dignity and the nonhierarchical workplace relations they had forged. In Zacatecas, the use of a business language coupled with goals of municipal improvement on the part of migrant activists facilitated recognition of these migrants' human worth and citizenship rights on the part of businesspeople and political leaders, which in turn led to expanded investment programs and new political rights for migrants. Of course, as the Brazilian and Chiapas cases show, acceptance of democratic political procedures and support for private sector growth on the part of activists may bring recognition without change (Rio de Janeiro), limited and contested recognition (San Cristóbal de Las Casas), or no recognition at all (Porto Alegre). The cases in this book suggest that the next stage of democratic deepening in Latin America may depend on how the exchange of market acceptance for recognition—fraught with uncertainty and risk for all groups involved and conditioned by the factors of culture, interpretation, and politics outlined above—proceeds in the coming decades.

HOW ENDURING REFORM PLAYS OUT: OUR FIVE CASES REVISITED

We revisit the five cases to illuminate how each of the factors just discussed has played out on the ground. Business responses to reform are shaped by factors of culture and representation such as surprise, visibility, media representation, experiences of invitation and inclusion, and language. Businesspeople's conceptions of their interests, of the protagonists and beneficiaries of reform, and of democratic politics are formed through these experiences and lenses. Contestation over reform plays out through processes of according or denying degrees of recognition, of articulating and implementing counterproposals, and of transforming the mechanisms of mainstream politics. While the impact of these factors depends on context, our five cases suggest that businesspeople are more likely to respond positively to reform in situations of crisis and when reform projects seek to change economic relations rather than empower people through democratic mechanisms.

As social scientists, we agree with Albert Hirschman and John Womack that the truth—and the principal lessons—of important events, be they the Mexican revolution in Morelos or battles for reform in Latin American cities today, can be found "in the feeling of it" (Hirschman 1970, 330 and 343, quoting Womack 1970, x). In the accounts that follow, we seek to convey "the feeling of it," by weaving together the texture, spirit, and significance of individual reform projects with the factors that shape business responses and make room for maneuver for reform projects in democracies today.

Recognition and the Experience of New Economic Relations

In Buenos Aires, *recognition deepens reform*. Businesspeople who engaged in commercial relations with the worker-owned factories (*fábricas recuperadas*) and negotiated business deals with the workers themselves changed their minds and began to use a language of recognition toward the workers regarding both their capacities and their rights. Their business practices then fell into line with their new beliefs, and they extended their business dealings with the worker-owned factories with confidence. When the workers took over the shuttered factories, they had no experience with the business side of the operations. To do business with their factory's former suppliers and customers, they had to learn management skills. This included acquiring ease with the business language that was used up and down the production chain but that had not been part of their world before the bankruptcy of their factory. The workers' abilities to master this new language made communication feasible with their business partners. At the same time, a nonbusiness language of workers' rights to ownership and preference for nonhierarchical authority relations in the workplace coexisted with the use of business language regarding production in the capitalist marketplace. The importance of this linguistic and conceptual balancing act, combined with businesspeople's use of a language of recognition, is a significant factor in the success of the worker-run factories. Businesspeople and workers changed their understandings and actions through an iterative process, within the parameters of the capitalist market system.

The factory bankruptcies that started off the worker-run factory movement took place during Argentina's severe economic crisis of the early 2000s. There was extensive media hostility to the factory takeovers as well as widespread outcry among businesspeople across Buenos Aires who saw the takeovers as an assault on private property (no matter that it was their peers who had left their factories in bankruptcy to begin with). At the same time, businesspeople themselves were experiencing unprecedented economic vulnerability. It was in the context of crisis and instability that businesspeople were invited by workers to renew their business dealings with the reopened worker-run factories. The businesspeople who engaged with the workers running the recuperated factories (though not businesspeople who rejected such relationships) succeeded in overcoming deep class and cultural prejudices against workers, media hostility, the opposition of their peers, and economic threat.

As these businesspeople worked closely with the workers in the very circumscribed realm of production and sales, they lived truly extraordinary experiences, developing along the way new recognition of the competency and humanity of the workers themselves. The relationship between the workers and businesspeople relied on the capacity of both groups to innovate and to communicate at a time of economic vulnerability for each of them. Businesspeople who were used to cutting deals with each other at the country club or over cocktails had to find new spaces where they could negotiate with the workers; workers who were used to working on the line had to evaluate suggestions from their business customers regarding how to improve production. That businesspeople were able to change their beliefs about the capacity of workers in a time of crisis, breaking with the majority of their peers and successfully engaging in business with the worker-run factories, is a counterintuitive outcome.

Counterproposals and the Reassertion of Political Control

In contrast, in Porto Alegre, the hostility of businesspeople to participatory budgeting led them to develop counterproposals for city budgeting that took some of the progressive reform's goals and accomplishments into account but failed to offer deep recognition to poor people as autonomous and competent subjects with rights. Despite evidence of robust and effective citizenship on the part of poor people, and despite the experience (for a small minority of businesspeople) of joining participatory budgeting and forming effective alliances with the residents of poor neighborhoods, businesspeople in Porto Alegre did not change their negative views of poor people as lazy and inferior. Businesspeople's relative well-being, including the successes of Brazil's democracy and economy at the national level, appears to have contributed to their unwillingness to see what was occurring in front of their eyes and to their refusal to accept the legitimacy of participatory budgeting.

Participatory budgeting was a transformative municipal project carried out by the leftist city government of Porto Alegre during a long period of transition to democracy and economic growth in Brazil. For two decades, participatory budgeting had been widely visible in Porto Alegre, not least through political ads and in electoral campaigns. Despite this, the local media did not report on its activities accurately or in depth. The media's portrayals and analyses of participatory budgeting created an ongoing negative discourse that coincided with the perceptions that businesspeople held about the program. As a result, businesspeople were very aware of participatory budgeting in their city—and uniformly opposed to it. Not only were they averse to attending meetings in poor neighborhoods, but those who did attend were disturbed by the condition of meeting halls, the crowds they encountered, and the need to interact in a participatory process with the poor.

Businesspeople also wanted to be directly invited to participate; they were unable to view a deeply participatory process as including them by its very nature, since they were accustomed to processes in which they chose whom to include or were specifically invited themselves. The minority of interviewees who did attend participatory budgeting meetings had their requests approved, and the infrastructure work they wanted was completed by the city. They reported that participatory budgeting facilitators from city hall, who routinely attended local meetings, took steps to include them in the discussions and that they themselves forged successful alliances with participants from poor neighborhoods in order to secure the necessary votes for their own projects. Despite these successful outcomes, and despite their support for democratization generally, the businesspeople who joined in participatory budgeting and successfully secured infrastructural improvements for their neighborhoods still did not view the process as positive. The language of participatory budgeting was one of empowerment for those who historically had been shut out from any participation in city governance. However, that same language was not empowering for those who had historically been networked into city governance; to the contrary, the inclusive language of the program was anathema to them, despite—or indeed because of—its genuinely democratic content. Participatory budgeting meetings were run by a strict arrangement of parliamentary procedures culminating in voting, and not one businessperson interviewed suggested at any point that this process was not strictly adhered to. As a result, businesspeople could easily be outvoted if they did not work to make cross-class alliances, and they knew this. Businesspeople who never attended participatory budgeting meetings, along with those who had attended the meetings and obtained positive results, never came to see the poor as competent people with dignity, as worthy of any recognition at all. Despite the thematic plenaries and multiyear plans for the city, among other innovative processes implemented by the participatory budgeting program, businesspeople neither "saw" nor understood the actions through which marginalized people had become engaged citizens through the program; they rejected the idea that poor people should exercise political power through direct participation.

In 2004, the leftist Workers' Party was voted out of power and replaced by a centrist mayor more allied with the city's elites. The new city government limited the reach of participatory budgeting and added a new program called Governança Local, which developed a model of private-public-NGO partnerships without open meetings. In this program, which government officials argued was more democratic because it invited businesspeople and other civic elites explicitly, voting was not encouraged, and neighborhood activists and NGOs together constituted only a third of the participating groups. Businesspeople were *invited* to participate in Governança Local, which they willingly did. At the same time, businesspeople developed their own philanthropic programs within the parameters of corporate social responsibility to try to sustain and re-exert control over regional social welfare programs and decision making.

Ultimately they achieved this by supporting the centrist mayoral candidate, whose platform put forth a version of their anti–participatory budgeting position. In the case of participatory budgeting, then, businesspeople developed *counterproposals to outmaneuver reform* by making use of the electoral process, allying with opposition political parties, putting forward platforms, and winning elections. In this configuration of business response to reform, a progressive reform came into view through political and media publicity, spoke a language of democratic political empowerment rather than business and markets, did not occur in a time of crisis but rather one of well-being and growth, and was actively opposed and misrepresented by the media. With such factors in play, businesspeople did not see participatory budgeting as a valuable form of citizenship for all sectors of the city, but rather evaluated it by applying old formulae about the inferiority of the poor. In this case, experience to the contrary did not affect their initial view.

Crisis and Competing Proposals

In San Cristóbal, ladino residents could not escape noticing the enormous changes in their city as it went from a purely ladino town of twenty-five thousand in the 1970s to a city of about two hundred thousand in 2010; 40 percent of the city's population is now indigenous Maya. The indigenous presence is everywhere: in the streets, in the markets and shops, in the state and federal legislatures. As much as ladinos tried over the past four decades to preserve their strict class and ethnic superiority, to continue their complete exclusion of indigenous people from any but the most menial and subordinate roles, and to retain their view of indigenous Maya as subhuman, forces beyond their control took over. Jan Rus and Gaspar Morquecho Escamilla detail in their chapter the factors that caused massive migration from the highland indigenous region to the city of San Cristóbal, the spread of indigenous colonias around the city's ladino core, and the expansion of indigenous Maya urban residents into many of the city's economic sectors. Until 1994, the ladinos viewed these processes with increasing alarm, intent on preserving as much of the status quo as possible.

The Zapatista Rebellion in 1994 was an experience of complete shock and crisis for the ladinos. Never had they imagined that indigenous people could organize themselves and fight back against centuries of fierce oppression and degradation. The rebellion served as a catalyst that forced the city's ladino residents to think and act differently toward the Maya. In the interviews conducted by Rus and Morquecho, ladino interviewees signal 1994 and the Zapatista Rebellion as the moment when things began to change, even though the changes to the city had been happening for more than fifteen years by that time. Once the rebellion began, securing stability took priority over reestablishing the old status quo. Over time, ladino elites modified their explicit and deeply ingrained racism of past centuries to coexist economically and politically with an increasingly self-conscious, self-reliant, and militant Maya majority in the city. As in Buenos Aires, this change in perceptions and actions occurred through an iterative process, as elites and Maya encountered and responded to each other in the new context. In this case, shock and crisis are a clear causal variable in explaining shifts in ladino perceptions of the indigenous city residents.

The shift in ladino responses to the indigenous Maya is visible starting in the late 1980s, as ladino businesses expanded during a period of economic growth and the owners came to appreciate the steady supply of labor from the indigenous city residents, as well as their value as customers. Simultaneously, some city politicians realized that they could exchange services for votes in the indigenous neighborhoods. While strictly utilitarian from the ladino perspective, these shifts also ruptured the exclusionary status quo of the prior centuries, making the Maya even more visible and ubiquitous, and slowly contributing to shifts in the perceptions of some ladinos from viewing the Maya as subhuman to seeing them as at least minimally competent in new roles. Faced with exclusionary and racist behaviors from the ladinos, the indigenous Maya were forced to organize among themselves, which they did with innovation and success. In one example, when ladino police did not provide security for indigenous neighborhoods, the Maya developed the innovative practice of "taxi policing," in which hundreds of indigenous taxicab drivers, all connected via CB radio, functioned as an ad hoc policing system solely for the benefit of the indigenous city residents.

In this context, to try to retain and exert some control over the indigenous neighborhoods around the city, ladino elites spoke insistently and for the first time of the need for urban planning in the Maya colonias. For example, the raising of public health issues reflected simultaneously a degree of concern for basic aspects of Mayan health, fears about health problems that would transcend poor colonias and affect elites as well, and, consequently, the interdependence of Maya and ladino in an increasingly complex urban environment. Elite reliance on planning as a response to changing demographic and political realities functioned as a means of registering this changing perception of Maya residents of the city, while keeping decision making in their own hands (because urban planning occurred within the municipal governance structures that ladinos still controlled). At the same time, the city's increasingly educated Maya, many of whom have now lived and worked in the United States as migrants, envision expanding their own marketing, transportation, and policing networks, competing in conventional economic and political arenas, and eventually governing the city.

In the face of such rapid, profound, and ongoing change, the indigenous Maya in San Cristóbal have succeeded in forcing a degree of recognition. While some ladinos cling to their overt racism, others combine partial recognition of the Maya with ongoing racist assumptions. This is an evolving process, pushed forward by a sense of crisis and threat in a context where outright repression is less feasible than in the past. The spectacular 1994 rebellion through which the Maya came into view for ladinos, and the subsequent period of fear that ladinos experienced, promoted a partial reconsideration of their racism and antidemocratic views. New commercial opportunities for the ladinos in the wake of the rebellion also contributed to this process. Thus in San Cristóbal, *competing visions mediate reform*; the city is the terrain for an active struggle over race, humanity, and rights. Ladino and Maya visions constitute competing alternatives for the future of the city that play out in the urban spaces that the two groups occupy in overlapping ways.

Business Language and the Limits of Progressive Social Policy

In Rio de Janeiro, there was widespread acceptance by the corporate business sector of Afro Reggae's projects. Indeed, corporations eagerly supported Afro Reggae's work because of the positive publicity they gained from being associated with a hip music group. The media in Rio de Janeiro covered Afro Reggae's events and showed them in a very favorable light. Afro Reggae gained visibility across the city from the combination of spectacular shows, business sponsorship, and media coverage—all of which contributed directly to Afro Reggae's ability to do its groundbreaking work in favelas. However, over time, as a result of its partnerships with the business sector, Afro Reggae significantly modified its own language and goals in accordance with a business model of organization and marketing. Their use of a "business language" made their projects more acceptable to business but contributed to limiting the scope and outcomes of the Afro Reggae program itself. Its original goals of broad social change for the favelas became much less visible, even as specific programs expanded inside favelas and the group gained significant reach internationally. While businesspeople praised the effectiveness of Afro Reggae's initiatives, their own narrow conceptualization of the problem of favela poverty and their inability to envision broad solutions—reinforced by Afro Reggae's marketing of itself in shows and media—created barriers to deeper social change.

Prior to their involvement with Afro Reggae, the businesspeople interviewed for Rubin's chapter tended to view favela residents the way many of the residents of the *asfalto* (paved parts of the city) did—as ignorant, untalented, incapable, useless, and dark-skinned. Through their work with the group, businesspeople revised their views, coming to recognize and value the talent and potential of favela residents, qualities that were immediately evident to them in Afro Reggae's leaders and performers. The way Afro Reggae came into view—through high-profile shows to which businesspeople were invited and where they were served hors d'oeuvres back stage—instantly transmitted a favorable view of the group and their access to it. Businesspeople found the business approach of Afro Reggae appealing, including the group's management techniques, its language of marketing and profit, and its ability to match its programs to the philanthropic concerns of businesses and foundations.

However, businesspeople saw Afro Reggae's work in the individual, market-oriented way in which the group presented it. Afro Reggae could be effective one child and one neighborhood at a time, but businesspeople believed that would scarcely make a dent in Rio's long-standing problems of inequality and exclusion, which they insisted were the state's role to address. At the same time, businesspeople viewed the state as incapable of undertaking such a task, and yet they did not see it as their own role to try to address such issues. They would contribute financially to Afro Reggae but not address the structural factors contributing to violence and poverty. Thus, while their partnerships with Afro Reggae brought about a big shift in how businesspeople viewed favela dwellers, it did not bring about any shift in how they viewed their potential roles and responsibilities in addressing the social issues that had been Afro Reggae's initial priorities.

In the case of Afro Reggae there is more acceptance by businesspeople than in the previous cases, but that acceptance is self-limiting. The business sector in Rio could grasp the city's social problems but did not want to be involved with them. Business support for Afro Reggae's ventures, which was integral to the group's successes, brought awareness of the talent and dignity of favela youth but did not extend to social policies that might lessen violence in the favelas and improve education, housing, and access to jobs. With Afro Reggae, *business language limits reform*. Afro Reggae's adoption of a business language and approach, which they did to gain corporate sponsors, pressed the group to present the problems of favelas in apolitical terms, limiting the scope of their objectives. In turn, this gave businesspeople a program they could endorse: innocent favela youth face the power and lure of the drug traffickers, and only Afro Reggae can save them.

Business Language and the Expansion of Progressive Social Policy

Lastly, in Zacatecas, *transnational interactions from the bottom up facilitate reform*. The success of the three-for-one migrant remittance program has transformed the old worldview that cast migrants as invisible and corruption in Mexico as inevitable. Before the migrants started their hometown associations in the United States in the 1990s, they were the invisible poor who had to leave their own country and live in poverty in another, working jobs at the lowest rung of the ladder to save small amounts of money to send home. Even though it had been known for years (starting with Lozano Ascencio 1993) that the sum total of migrant remittances constituted one of the largest sources of foreign income for Mexico (today it is the largest source after oil, industrial production, and financial services), the individual migrants who sent money home remained invisible and unrecognized. Thanks to the success of the migrant-driven three-for-one program, not only have the migrants become visible, they are accorded recognition as successful Mexican citizens with rights.

In the case of three-for-one, the use of a business language in describing and enacting the program promoted rather than circumscribed its expansion, with businesspeople finding the language of three-for-one compatible with their own (changing) worldview. This synergy resulted from the transnational position of Mexican migrants, who became visible in new ways because of their dual identities and their growing economic clout, which was derived by applying their pooled savings to specific projects back home that they controlled. The migrants' innovative insistence on transparency and accountability was heeded because they provided the initial remittances that were the foundation of the program, at the same time as the program itself supported the business sector across Zacatecas by creating new business opportunities. These factors together—the use of a business language, the transformed identity of migrants, and the economic clout that resulted from their pooling of resources—led to broader and more audacious programs than those initially envisioned by three-for-one activists and policy makers.

From the start, three-for-one was a partnership between migrants in the United States, businesses in Zacatecas that bid for contracts to carry out the work projects funded by the program, and the government (initially the state government with two-for-one and then also the federal government with three-for-one). The three-for-one program was transformative in many ways. It transformed the social position of the migrants from invisible to visible and from irrelevant to significant in the economic sphere of Zacatecas (and later in other states as well)—and this paralleled the change in how businesspeople viewed migrants. It transformed the long-standing corrupt dealings between the state and business enterprises into transparent and accountable partnerships—at least for the work that was carried out under the auspices of three-for-one. Thus businesses that had operated via personal connections and bribes were forced to operate in new ways. It was transformative for the landscape of Zacatecas, where new roads, water and sewerage systems, public lighting, and other infrastructure projects made lives better. Indeed, the program was so favorably viewed, including by the local media, that gubernatorial candidates made commitments to it in their campaigns and expanded it once in office.

BUSINESS RESPONSES TO PROGRESSIVE REFORM

Since the 1990s, the combination of democracy, shifting social movement strategies, and new business worldviews has created openings for local and regional projects of progressive reform. The initiatives described in this book encounter degrees of openness and tolerance on the part of businesspeople that would have been unthinkable during the overlapping periods of import substitution industrialization, populist political coalitions, early efforts to achieve democracy or socialism, and military dictatorship that characterized Latin America during much of the twentieth century. How businesspeople respond to reform projects today is shaped by cultural understandings of who is involved in them and what is being contested, rather than by conventional definitions of economic interest. Our research suggests that situations of crisis make business openness to reform more likely, as do goals that privilege economic betterment over political empowerment, and that the dynamics of reform projects play out in part through exchanges of market acceptance (on the part of activists) for recognition (by businesspeople).

While these cases indicate surprising openness to reform on the part of businesspeople today, they also make clear the limited reach of several of the reform projects and the severe obstacles they face. Despite international renown, participatory budgeting was effectively outmaneuvered by a coalition of businesspeople and conservative politicians because of its democratic commitments. Worker-run factories gained adherents among businesspeople, but only when direct commercial experience led to shifts away from class hostility, which occurred among a small minority of the private sector. In the face of startling indigenous rebellion and effective Mayan self-help networks, elites in San Cristóbal recognized the humanity and equality of indigenous people only in small and equivocal steps. At the same time, each of these reforms endures, establishing alternative forms of power relations, material distribution, and cultural recognition within existing structures of politics and markets.

At stake in Latin America today is the very possibility of producing substantial gains for those majorities who have been excluded from the benefits of development and democracy in the past. As businesspeople grapple with enduring reforms that demonstrably improve the lives of poor people, the capacity of Latin America's nascent democracies to follow through on long-delayed promises of citizenship and well-being is put to the test.

NOTES

1. B. Weinstein (1996) has presented an important case of elite business commitment to social welfare training and education programs in São Paulo.
2. See Joseph and Spenser 2008, Grandin and Joseph 2010, and a host of studies of Cold War–era repression and the establishment of military governments throughout Latin America.

REFERENCES

Alvarez, S., G. Baiocchi, A. Lao, J. Rubin, and M. Thayer, eds. Forthcoming. "Interrogating the Civil Society Agenda, Reassessing 'Un-Civic' Contention: An Introduction." In *Beyond Civil Society: Social Movements, Civic Participation, and Democratic Contestation*. Durham: Duke University Press.

Arias E., and D. Goldstein. 2010. "Violent Pluralism: Understanding the New Democracies of Latin America." In *Violent Democracies in Latin America*, edited by E. Arias and D. Goldstein, 1–34. Durham: Duke University Press.

Brennan, J. 1998. "Industrialists and *Bolicheros*: Business and the Peronist Populist Alliance, 1943–1976." In *Peronism and Argentina*, edited by J. Brennan, 79–124. Wilmington: Scholarly Resources Books.

Castañeda, J. 2011. "What Latin America Can Teach Us." *New York Times*. December 10.

Gillingham, P., and B. T. Smith. 2014. *Dictablanda: Politics, Work, and Culture in Mexico, 1938–1968*. Durham: Duke University Press.

Grandin, G., and G. Joseph. 2010. *A Century of Revolution: Insurgent and Counterinsurgent Violence during Latin America's Long Cold War*. Durham: Duke University Press.

Hamilton, N. 1982. *The Limits of State Autonomy*. Princeton: Princeton University Press.

Hirschman, A. 1968. *Journeys toward Progress: Studies of Economic Policy-Making in Latin America*. Westport: Greenwood Press.

Hirschman, A. 1970. "The Search for Paradigms as a Hindrance to Understanding." *World Politics* 22 (April): 329–43.

Joseph, G., and D. Nugent. 1994. *Everyday Forms of State Formation: Revolution and the Negotiation of Rule in Modern Mexico*. Durham: Duke University Press.

Joseph, G., and D. Spenser. 2008. *In from the Cold: Latin America's New Encounter with the Cold War*. Durham: Duke University Press.

Kim, Jim Yong. 2013. "Latin America's Next Challenges." *Los Angeles Times*. July 1. Online at http://articles.latimes.com/2013/jun/30/opinion/la-oe-kim-latin-america-20130701. Accessed July 1, 2013.

Lozano Ascencio, Fernando. 1993. *Bringing It Back Home: Remittances to Mexico from Migrant Workers in the United States*. Monograph series no. 37. La Jolla: Center for U.S.–Mexican Studies, University of California–San Diego.

Rubin, J. 2011. "From Che Guevara to Subcomandante Marcos: How Radical Priests, Indians, Feminists, and Workers Transformed the Latin American Left in the 1970s." Paper presented at the conference "The Global 1970s Project: The Radical Decade in Global Perspective." Boston University. November.

Rubin, J. W. 1997. *Decentering the Regime: Ethnicity, Radicalism, and Democracy in Juchitán, Mexico*. Durham: Duke University Press.

Sáenz, E. 1992. *La Ofensiva Empresarial: Industriales, políticos y violencia en los años 40 en Colombia*. Bogotá: Tercer Mundo Editores.

Schneider, B. 2004. *Business Politics and the State in Twentieth-Century Latin America*. Cambridge: Cambridge University Press.

Sitrin, M. 2012. *Everyday Revolutions: Horizontalism and Autonomy in Argentina*. London: Zed Books.
Weinstein, B. 1996. *For Social Peace in Brazil: Industrialists and the Remaking of the Working Class in São Paulo, 1920-1964*. Chapel Hill: University of North Carolina Press.
Womack, John, Jr. 1970. *Zapata and the Mexican Revolution*. New York: Vintage, 1970.

APPENDIX
ENDURING REFORM PROJECT, INTERVIEW TEMPLATE

THIS INTERVIEW TEMPLATE was translated into Spanish and Portuguese and provided in all three languages to the *Enduring Reform* researchers. The interviews were open-ended, with the template providing an outline for how the researchers might proceed. Interviews were conducted with both business-people and leftist activists in each case location. The sections in italics suggested opening questions; the sections without italics offered follow-up questions.

PART I OF THE INTERVIEW:
Exploration of the Subject's Knowledge about the Reform Case and His or Her Relationship with It

What we want to explore with you, basically, is this: your thoughts, experiences, and actions toward (name of reform case goes here) since it got started. (Interviewer may choose to say something more specific about the beginning of the reform case, such as "since factories were first taken over by workers during the crisis.")

We know this may be a really big question and that it has different facets. But we've learned that the best way to learn what people think about (name of reform case goes here) is just to ask the question and let you describe your experiences.

(Note to researchers: This is a "Grand Tour" question, in which there are three subtopics: the interviewee's *thoughts*, *experiences*, and *actions* regarding the reform case. Please prompt the subject to address all three topics).[1]

Time permitting, the following questions also should be explored if they are not brought up by the interviewee:

- What do you know about the reform case?
- How has your knowledge changed over time?
- What contributed to changes in your knowledge about this reform case?

- What do you think about the reform case?
- How have your opinions and position changed over time?
- How do you explain the changes in your opinions and position?

- How have you *acted* toward the reform case?
- How have your *actions* changed over time?
- How do you explain changes in your *actions* over time?

Definition of "Action": How the interviewee has *acted* toward the reform case is a key part of the ER research, and possibly difficult to access. As we see it, there are three components of "action." As Part I of the interview progresses, researchers can use the questions below to elicit further information about the subject's actions regarding the reform case.

1. Have you had any contact with any person, program, event, or activity *directly connected to the reform case*? Can you describe them? What have been the most important contacts and interactions? Were there watershed moments?

2. Have you had contact with people *outside the reform case* about the *reform case*? (Where has it been discussed or where have responses been formulated?) What was the content of those contacts and what kinds of effects or impacts did they have on the functioning of the *reform case*?

3. Have you been involved in any *discussions or activities related to the kinds of things the reform case does*? (Interviewer might say what the reform case does—for example, "related to indigenous education" or "related to the provision of basic services for poor neighborhoods?") Have new projects or initiatives been undertaken to address these issues?

Strategies for eliciting further information in Part I of the interview:

- *Example questions* ("Can you give me an example of a time . . .")
- *Structural questions* ("We've talked about . . . Now I want to ask you a slightly different kind of question. I'm interested in getting a list of all the different . . ."
- *Presuming questions* ("How did you . . . How much did you . . . When did you . . ." Rather than asking simply *whether or not* the person did . . .) These should be used judiciously as the interview progresses.
- *What-was-left-out questions* ("Is there anything you would like to tell me about that I haven't thought to ask you?")

PART II OF THE INTERVIEW:

Subject's Worldview: What Are the Principles and Opinions That Shape Her or His Responses to the Reform Case?

The purpose of this section is to learn about how the interviewee thinks the world works. We want to understand the set of beliefs, principles, and opinions (about what is possible/impossible, good/bad, appealing/frightening, etc.) that the interviewee uses to perceive, interpret, and engage with the reform project as well as with issues of reform generally.

The beliefs we are after might concern poverty, democracy, the workings of the economic system, reform, the interests of business/leftist activism, human nature, culture, etc. While we speak of a "set" of beliefs, we realize that an interviewee's beliefs might be internally contradictory and that an interviewee's actions might or might not reflect her or his beliefs.

We think that the best way to explore the subject's "worldview" is through a focus on specific issues or problems, rather than to ask the interviewee what she or he thinks of big issues like democracy or the economic system or race (and better than just asking the interviewee what her or his worldview is!). That is why we decided to start with the following question, "What do you think are the three most serious problems most people in your city face?" Each interviewer will need to adapt this question and the ones that follow it to particular interviewees and contexts.

In this part of the interview, we'd like to know your views about the context in which this reform case is happening, about how things work and what you think should happen.

So we're going to ask you some general questions about (city/state) *and* (country).

What do you think are the three most serious problems most people who live in (the case city) *face?*

The interviewer should follow up the question about "the three most serious problems," with further questions like the following, as appropriate:

- *Do you think it is important to address some of these problems (or one in particular)?*
- *Why?*
- *Do you think it is possible (to address these problems)?*
- *How can these problems be addressed?*

In the course of asking interviewees about serious problems and how they might be addressed, the researcher should explore and observe the "worldview" of the interviewee with respect to government, politics, the economic system, etc., to the extent that you can with the time available. Here are some questions that you might use to get at this "worldview" (you can ask these questions directly or use them to guide your note taking):

- What is the role of the government/the state in addressing social problems?
- What is the role of democracy in addressing social problems?
- What is the role of politics and political parties in addressing social problems?
- Whose responsibility is it to deal with these problems?
- How have other societies dealt with these problems?
- How do the workings of the economic system affect social problems and potential solutions to them?
- Can the "rules of the game" of the economy be modified to address social problems?
- Is reform valuable for social stability?
- Are reform and social stability valuable for business/leftist activism?
- What does poverty/exclusion/unemployment/lack of education/ violence/crime mean to the interviewee? How much can the interviewee say about these things? How close can the interviewee get to the experience?
- Does the interviewee speak in gendered or racialized terms, explicitly or implicitly? How are gender and racial categories evoked or referenced?

PART III OF THE INTERVIEW:

Wrap-up Discussion on the Reform Case

1. *Is there anything about* (the reform case) *that you didn't think of earlier that you'd like to add?*
2. *Earlier you mentioned* _____.

[Use this prompt as a bridge to ask further questions about the reform case that were not covered earlier or that came up in the context of Part II of the interview regarding the interviewee's worldview.]

3. *Is there anything you would like to tell me about that I haven't thought to ask you?*

NOTES

1. Our terminology for different types of questions is drawn from Beth L. Leech, "Asking Questions: Techniques for Semistructured Interviews," as well as from other articles in the section titled "Interview Methods in Political Science: Symposium," in *PS: Political Science and Politics* 35, no. 4 (December 2002).

CONTRIBUTORS

COEDITORS

Jeffrey W. Rubin is associate professor of history and research associate at the Institute on Culture, Religion, and World Affairs (CURA) at Boston University. He received his PhD in political science from Harvard University. Rubin was the principal investigator for the Enduring Reform Project and one of the researchers for the case studies on participatory budgeting and the Afro Reggae Cultural Group. He is the author of *Decentering the Regime: Ethnicity, Radicalism, and Democracy in Juchitán, Mexico* (Duke University Press, 1997), the coauthor of *Sustaining Activism: A Brazilian Women's Movement and a Father-Daughter Collaboration* (Duke University Press, 2013), and coeditor of a 2015 special issue of the *Latin American Research Review,* titled *Lived Religion and Lived Citizenship in Latin America's Zones of Crisis.* He is also co–principal investigator of the University of Massachusetts–based project "Social Movements and Twenty-First-Century Cultural-Political Transformations" and coeditor of its forthcoming publication *Beyond Civil Society: Social Movements, Civic Participation, and Democratic Contestation* (Duke University Press). Rubin received a MacArthur Foundation Research and Writing Grant and a Fulbright Fellowship for his work on democracy and grassroots innovation in Brazil and a Sabbatical Fellowship from the American Philosophical Society for his work on *Sustaining Activism* and *Enduring Reform.* He has also received grants from the Open Society Foundations, the Ford Foundation, and the Mellon–Latin American Studies Association program. Rubin has been awarded fellowships at the David Rockefeller Center for Latin American Studies at Harvard, the Institute for Advanced Study in Princeton, the Center for the Critical Analysis of Contemporary Culture at Rutgers, and the Center for U.S.–Mexican Studies at the University of California–San Diego.

Vivienne Bennett is professor of border studies in the Liberal Studies Department at California State University–San Marcos (CSUSM). She received her PhD in Latin American Studies at the University of Texas–Austin. At CSUSM, Bennett was chair of her department for ten years, and she served as the director of the Center for Border and Regional Affairs. She was the co–principal investigator for the Enduring Reform Project. She is the author of *The Politics of Water: Urban Protest, Gender, and Power in Monterrey, Mexico* (University of Pittsburgh Press, 1995), the coeditor of *Opposing Currents: The Politics of Water and Gender in Latin America* (University of Pittsburgh Press, 2005), and the author of numerous journal articles and book chapters on the politics of water and on social movements in Mexico. Bennett has twice been a visiting research fellow at the Center for U.S.–Mexican Studies (at the University of California–San Diego). She also served on the center's International Advisory Council and was a member of the center's Fellowship Selection Committee. She has been a Fulbright Fellow in Mexico as well as a Scholar in Residence for the Social Science Research Council's Pre-Dissertation Fellowship Program. Bennett was a plenary speaker at the Stockholm Water Symposium and has been invited to give talks at universities nationally and internationally.

CONTRIBUTORS

Sergio Gregorio Baierle is a political scientist with expertise in public policy and social movements. After studying history, urban sociology, literature, and theater, he completed a master's degree in political science at the State University of Campinas (UNICAMP). In 1990, he joined the NGO Centro de Assessoria e Estudos Urbanos (CIDADE), where he worked until 2012. The main objective of CIDADE is to carry out research and advise civic organizations to promote an equal dialogue with municipal authorities, so as to open public spaces for participation and rights at the community level. Baierle has also worked as a researcher on the Municipal Innovations Project in the UK and Latin America (2006–8), coordinated by Professor Jenny Pearce (of the Department of Peace Studies at Bradford University), as well as on the Brazilian Growth Acceleration Program (2008), organized by Action Aid Brazil. Concomitantly, he has worked for the Central Bank of Brazil as an analyst in the areas of foreign capital, public debt, and payment systems. He has extensive experience as a consultant on participatory budgeting and civil society issues.

Carlos A. Forment is associate professor in the Departments of Sociology and Politics at the New School for Social Research, Graduate Faculty. He is author of *Democracy in Latin America, 1760–1900: Civic Selfhood and Public Life* (University of Chicago Press, 2003); *Public Centers of Sociability and Everyday Forms of Nationhood in Nineteenth-Century Latin America* (University of Chicago Press, in press); and *Shifting Frontiers of Citizenship: The Latin American Experience* (coedited with Luis Roniger and Mario Sznajder, Brill, 2012). Forment is currently working on a book manuscript titled "Citizenship and Its Fragment: Democratic Life in Argentina in the Wake of Neoliberalism."

Ann Helwege is a senior research fellow at the Global Development and Environment Institute (GDAE) at Tufts University and a research fellow at the Global Economic Governance Institute (GEGI) at Boston University. She was recently a visiting associate professor of international relations at Boston University, where she taught classes that focused on social equity, the environment, and economic policy in Latin America. She holds a PhD in economics from the State University of New York at Buffalo. She was previously an associate professor of urban and environmental policy and planning at Tufts University, where she also taught classes on Latin American economies in the Fletcher School of Law and Diplomacy. She is the coauthor of *Latin America's Economy* as well as coeditor of *Latin America's Economic Future* and *Modernization and Stagnation: Latin American Agriculture*. Her recent work focuses on how the boom in commodity prices affects the lives of Latin America's poor, both in terms of income and exposure to environmental injustice.

Gaspar Morquecho Escamilla is a political activist and organizer who as adviser to the Comité de Defensa and then CRIACH (Consejo de Representantes Indígenas de los Altos de Chiapas) participated in the founding of San Cristóbal's urban indigenous movement in the early 1980s. A journalist, he writes regularly for the national newspaper *La jornada* as well as for television and radio stations in Chiapas and the regional newspapers *Tiempo* and *Expreso Chiapas.* He is the founder and former owner of the Mono de Papel bookstore and Ediciones Pirata, which makes available at moderate prices works of political, economic, and social analysis of Chiapas. He is a professor of history at the Universidad Autónoma de Chiapas. Among his works are *Un proceso de organización indígena en los Altos de Chiapas* (Universidad Autónoma de Chiapas, 1992), *La otra mejilla . . . pero armada*, with Dolores Aramoni (*Anuario* CESMECA, 1996), *Mujeres de Chiapas a tres años de la matanza Acteal* (Ediciones Pirata, 2000), and *Bajo la bandera del*

Islam (Ediciones Pirata, 2004). For access to the previous two years of his news-paper columns, go to http://alainet.org/active/show_author.phtml?autor_apel lido=Morquecho&autor_nombre=Gaspar.

Fernando Robledo Martínez is professor of economics at the Universidad Autónoma de Zacatecas. For many years he headed the Instituto Estatal de Migración for the state government of Zacatecas, Mexico. He has also chaired a working group of state immigration offices nationwide. Robledo Martínez received his master's in economics from the Universidad Autónoma de Zacatecas. He was the founder, in 1989, and director of the first nonprofit center for the study of immigration, the Centro de Información y Estudios Migratorios de Zacatecas. Robledo Martínez is the author of numerous working papers and publications on migration. He is coauthor of *En torno a los Derechos Humanos* (Universidad Autónoma de Zacatecas and Comisión Estatal de Derechos Humanos del Estado, 2001) and *Hacia una política migratoria del Estado Mexicano* (Instituto Nacional de Migración, Secretaría de Gobernación, Mexico, 2006).

Jan Rus is a research professor at the Centro de Estudios Superiores de México y Centroamérica (CESMECA) in San Cristóbal de Las Casas. An anthropologist and historian, he has worked in the highlands of Chiapas since the early 1970s. His current projects focus on labor migrations and the urbanization of Chiapas's Maya. From 1985 to 2007 he and his wife, Diane, were coordinators of the Taller Tzotzil, a Maya-language publishing project in San Cristóbal, and from 2003 to the present, Rus has been associate managing editor of *Latin American Perspectives*. His books include *Mayan Lives, Mayan Utopias: The Indigenous People of Chiapas and the Zapatista Movement*, coedited with Aída Hernández and Shannan Mattiace (Rowman and Littlefield, 2003); *El ocaso de las fincas y la transformación de la sociedad indígena de los Altos de Chiapas, 1974-2010* (Universidad de Ciencias y Artes de Chiapas, Consejo Nacional de Ciencia y Tecnología, 2012); and *Jech li balamile / Así es el mundo: Historia viva de los mayas tsotsiles,* with Salvador Guzmán Bakbolom and Diane Rus (Universidad de Ciencias y Artes de Chiapas, forthcoming).

Heather Williams is associate professor and department chair of the Politics Department at Pomona College. She received her PhD in political science from Yale University. She is the author of numerous books, articles, and working papers on Mexico, the U.S.–Mexico border, migration, and the environment. These include *Social Movements and Economic Transition: Markets and Distributive Protest in Mexico* (Cambridge University Press 2001, 2007); *Planting Trouble: The*

Barzon Debtors' Movement in Mexico (Center for U.S.–Mexican Studies, UCSD, 1996); "Fighting Corporate Swine," (*Politics and Society*); "Mobile Capital and Transborder Labor Rights Mobilization" (*Politics and Society*); and "Both Sides Now: Migrants, Democracy, and the Struggle for Accountability in Zacatecas, Mexico" (in *Politics from Afar*, edited by Terrence Lyons and Peter Mandaville). With the help of a Mellon Foundation New Directions Grant, she is currently expanding her work to the study of the politics of water and watersheds in Latin America and the U.S.–Mexico borderlands.

Wendy Wolford is Polson Professor of Development Sociology at Cornell University. She received her PhD in geography from the University of California–Berkeley. Wolford is the coauthor of *To Inherit the Earth: The Landless Movement and the Struggle for a New Brazil* (Food First, 2003) and the author of *This Land Is Ours Now: Social Mobilization and Sugarcane in the Brazilian Northeast* (Duke University Press, 2010). Wolford has published on social movements, the politics of ethnography, and the dynamics of the struggle for land in Brazil. She was a postdoctoral fellow with the Yale Agrarian Studies Program in 2004–5, an associate professor of geography at the University of North Carolina–Chapel Hill, and a fellow at the Institute for Arts and Humanities at UNC. Her ongoing work is located primarily in Brazil, Ecuador, and the United States and is supported by grants from the National Science Foundation and the Andrew W. Mellon Foundation.

INDEX

Note: Page references in *italics* refer to figures and tables.